D1087306

The Battle of
Bosworth

The Battle of
Bosworth

Michael Bennett

ST. MARTIN'S PRESS   New York

Copyright © Michael Bennett 1985

First published in the United States of America in 1985

All rights reserved. For information, write:
St. Martin's Press, Inc.
175 Fifth Avenue
New York, NY 10010

Printed in Great Britain

Library of Congress Cataloging in Publication Data

Bennett, Michael J. (Michael John), 1949–
    The Battle of Bosworth.

    Bibliography: p.
    Includes index.
    1. Bosworth Field, Battle of, 1485.   1. Title.
DA260.B46   1985   942.05   85-14292

ISBN 0-312-06972-3

PREFACE

Anniversaries are a mixed blessing for historians. On the one hand, they invest their subjects with a spurious topicality. On the other hand, by concentrating public attention on old landmarks they provide an incentive for scholars to sharpen the focus of their research, and to share their findings with that wider community which also seeks pleasure and meaning from the past. It was not my idea to write on Bosworth Field and 1485, but I took on the project with enthusiasm. I knew that others had made the task easier for me. For a start most of the major sources for the reign of Richard III have been published, a great boon for an English historian based in Australia. On this point it is fitting to pay tribute to the Richard III Society and Alan Sutton Publishing for harnessing lay enthusiasm and business acumen in support of fifteenth-century scholarship. I would like to record my gratitude to the late Professor A.R. Myers, who first introduced me to the study of Richard III, Dr Colin Richmond, who gave me early encouragement, Mr J.R. Tinsley, who welcomed me to the Battlefield Centre during the winter recess, Peter and Carolyn Hammond for not only selecting the pictures but also sharing their expertise on Ricardian matters, Airlie Alam for her work on the maps, and my mother, who assisted with the index. Finally I dedicate this book to my wife Fatimah, who has supported this work since its conception, and to my daughter Masni, whose birth by deflecting me from other projects made possible this one.

M.B.

Hobart, Tasmania
May, 1985

CONTENTS

LIST OF ILLUSTRATIONS

MAPS

Photographs and illustrations were supplied by, or are reproduced by kind permission of the following: Aerofilms Limited (11, 23); Society of Antiquaries of London (8, 12, 48); Ashmolean Museum, Oxford (14); British Library (15, 18, 38, 41); Trustees of the Chatsworth Settlement (64); University of Ghent (9, 10); Peter Hammond (16, 17, 19, 21, 24, 34, 40, 44, 49, 57); Oliver Harris (54); Trustees of Lambeth Palace Library (13); Leicestershire County Council Department of Property (50, 53, 58); Leicestershire Libraries and Information Service (43, 46); Leicestershire Museums, Art Galleries and Records Service (65, 66, 67); National Portrait Gallery, London (26, 61); Castle Museum, Nottingham (37); Julian Rowe (51, 52); Stowe School (1); Board of Trustees of the Armouries, H.M. Tower of London, crown copyright (3, 4); Victoria and Albert Museum, London (27); Trustees of the Wallace Collection, London (6, 7, 55, 56, 70, 71, 72, 73, 74, 75); Geoffrey Wheeler (1, 5, 20, 25, 28, 33, 35, 36, 39, 42, 45, 47, 59, 60, 62, 68); York City Archives (2).

Picture research by Carolyn and Peter Hammond.

Jacket: detail from the mural painting of the Battle of Bosworth, The Three Tuns, Atherstone; border incorporating symbolic representation of Henry's Welsh dragon triumphing over Richard's boar, from an engraving by George Vertue. Photograph and jacket concept: Geoffrey Wheeler. Design: Martin Latham.

The Battle of
Bosworth

1 News from the Field

It was harvest time. Before the full heat of the late summer day the battle was over. King Richard III was slain, and the mightiest army assembled in England within memory was shattered. Many lay dead, their bodies mangled in the press, but many more had thrown down their arms without a fight, and either taken to their heels or fallen in with the rebels. Whole battalions had held aloof on the side-lines, and their commanders now set out to ingratiate themselves with the victors. The obscure adventurer Henry Tudor, flushed with a remarkable triumph in his first military engagement, moved with his captains to a hill south of the battlefield which might serve as a vantage-point from which to direct the mopping up operations. It was on this elevation, later called Crown hill by the local populace, that the jubilant soldiers acclaimed their young leader as king, and one of the captains placed on his brow a coronet found among the debris in the field.

It was probably still afternoon on 22 August 1485 that Henry VII led his triumphant cavalcade, bringing in tow many noble captives from the royal army and the naked corpse of his rival, through the gates of Leicester. The townsmen would already have received reports of the upset, and would have prepared an appropriate reception. Already reports of the battle would have spread to other neighbouring towns, as men fleeing from the field and messengers specially deputed for the task relayed the intelligence. Before nightfall the city of Coventry buzzed with the tidings, and in the course of the following day the news could have reached most of the major population centres of England. On the vigil of St Bartholomew, the evening of the day after the battle, the mayor and aldermen of York assembled in the council chamber in considerable agitation to hear 'that King Richard late mercifully reigning upon us was through great treason . . . piteously slain and murdered to the great heaviness of this city'.[1] This intelligence was owed to John Sponer, whom they had sent to Leicester for this purpose, but who in all likelihood had gained his information actually on the road. Presumably the city fathers of London were as well organised, and also had reports of the defeat of Richard III by 23 August.

Hard on the heels of the first messages, winged by fear or self-interest, there would have come to London and all the county towns of the kingdom what amounted to an official communique from Henry VII. In addition to ordering firm measures for the cessation of fighting and feuding, it informed the general

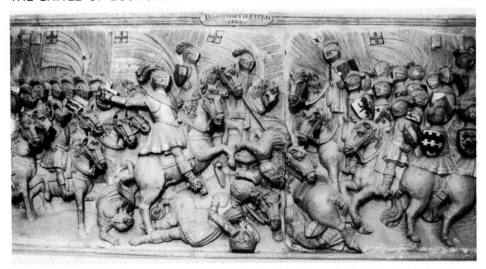

Wood carving now at Stowe School, depicting the Battle of Bosworth. Probably dating from the middle of the sixteenth century, and possibly commissioned by an Earl of Oxford.

public that Richard III and his more prominent noble supporters, the duke of Norfolk, the earls of Lincoln and Surrey, Viscount Lovell, and Lords Ferrers and Zouche, had been slain. Apart from the later act of attainder which named two dozen more of the men who had fought against him, the new king was to provide no more information about the battle. In view of the widely held assumption that the first Tudor actively promoted the rewriting of history for propagandist purposes, the reticence in official circles as to what happened in the battle needs to be stressed, and indeed is one of the many mysteries of this time. Even as late as 1500 Bernard André, poet laureate and official biographer of the king, had no coherent account to give of the battle, leaving a blank space for the episode which for some reason he was unable to fill.[2]

As rumour and report spread outwards from the epicentre at Bosworth in ever widening circles, and as the thousands of men from the various armies returned to their homes, there can have been no shortage of accounts of the battle. Unfortunately even participants might have found difficulty in making sense of the manœuvres, and there can have been precious few observations which were not garbled, partial and partisan. Judging from the few extant accounts, it is painfully apparent that from its very source the flow of news was broken and muddied on the banks of ignorance and fear, and deflected by streams of self-interest and propaganda. The official communiqué, for a start, either wilfully or unwittingly misled the public. At least three of the nobles whom it claimed to be dead were in fact alive. Similarly the report which reached York contained the bizarre information that the duke of Norfolk, who in fact had laid down his life in the Ricardian cause, had betrayed the king.

It is small wonder that even the basic items of report, that King Richard was slain and that Henry Tudor had taken the crown, were for some time in doubt in many quarters of the realm. Quite deliberately the late king's corpse was kept on

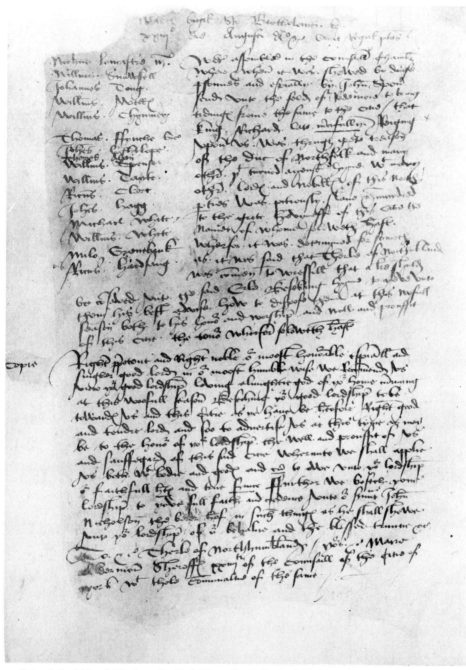

Epitaph for Richard III, from the York House Books (Books 2/4, folio 169), recording the 'grete hevynesse of this cite' at his death.

public view, and it is perhaps significant that, contrary to the pattern in such affairs, no one ever claimed that he survived. Presumably the slow progress of the new king to London and his triumphal entry into the capital served to bring home the reality of the new regime to individuals and communities across southern England. On the other hand, despite the regular flow of news across the Channel, doubts persisted for quite a long time on the continent. According to a letter written from Rome by Cardinal Sforza on 30 September, the English ambassador had received news that evening that King Richard had been 'cut in pieces' by his people. Yet as late as 20 October the bishop of Imola could write to the pope from Mayence that 'according to common report which I heard on my way here, the king of England has been killed in battle. Here, some people tell me he is alive, but others deny it'. Meanwhile, on 5 November in writing to the king of England about a piracy problem Ferdinand and Isabella of Spain wisely left a blank for the king's name, presumably to be hurriedly filled in by the emissary on arrival in England.[3]

In a relatively short while, however, the rulers of Christendom had access to better information. It is a remarkable fact that three of the earliest and fullest accounts of the battle, and indeed the only account which names an eye-witness informant, come from the continent. The most curious is the memorandum on English affairs prepared for the Spanish monarchs by Diego de Valera early in 1486. While there are some obvious errors, it contains much independently verifiable information on events from 1483 to the time of writing, and it includes an account of the battle of Bosworth derived from Juan de Salazar, a Spanish soldier-of-fortune who had actually fought on the side of Richard III.[4] The actors and actions described have presented problems for historians: it refers to the 'grand chamberlain' who commanded the king's vanguard, and to a mysterious 'Lord Tamerlant' who with the king's left wing wheeled round to join the rebels in their attack on the royal host. For the most part historians have dismissed this testimony as irremediably muddled. Yet Salazar was a seasoned soldier who actually participated in the battle, and the information provided in this account, when read right, is far less idiosyncratic than has been supposed.

Two other European men of letters who wrote up an account of the battle in the following years were Philippe de Commines and Jean Molinet.[5] Though both men were engaged in works which were not to be completed for another decade or so, there is every reason to suppose that their accounts of the defeat of Richard III were written before 1490. Neither can be dismissed as partisan. Based at the French court, Commines had met Henry Tudor, and was interested in following through the success of what was after all a French backed expedition. Yet he was no one's fool, and firmly expressed his scepticism of the pretender's claims. Molinet, a historian in the service of the duke of Burgundy, is even less vulnerable to the charge of anti-Ricardian prejudice. Both men were shrewd political analysts. Commines provides valuable information on the mounting of the expedition and stresses the importance of the support provided by Lord Stanley. Sadly he has next to nothing to say on the fighting itself. It is in the military arena that Molinet, an undeservedly neglected source, comes into his own, dedicating several hundred words to the battlefield manœuvres. His description of Richard III's battle formation, with its vanguard and rearguard,

Composite Gothic field armour, of the type made in Northern Italy for export to Western Europe, about 1480. The right gauntlet, the tassets and the besagues are modern restorations.

and his discussion of Henry Tudor's tactics, deserve to be taken at least as seriously as the later accounts of Polydore Vergil and his English translators. He also provides much interesting circumstantial detail, including the most authentic report on the death of King Richard. Despite some confusions, he was clearly well-informed. He is the earliest source for many items of information which subsequently appear in oral traditions as well as in the standard histories.

For all their problems, the continental sources compare most favourably with what has survived from English pens from before around 1490. There is the eccentric antiquarian John Rous of Warwick, whose writings, which span the change of dynasty, reveal first flattery of and then a vitriolic attack on Richard III.[6] Though scatter-brained and malicious, he does include a few useful snippets of information about the battle, noting that the king bravely went down fighting and crying out against the treason of his subjects. More sober but scarcely more informative are a number of town chronicles, which though preserved in later copies, might well have been composed on a year to year basis.[7] The recently discovered London annals in a College of Arms manuscript include a notice of the battle at 'Redesmore', which might well have been written in November 1485, at the end of the mayoral year. For the most part such entries are terse statements of fact, often merely summarising the official report. In most towns Henry Tudor's proclamation would have been entered into the mayor's book, and at York its factual errors were corrected by a conscientious clerk. Some annalists had access to a wider range of sources, and tried to provide a more expansive narrative. Robert Fabian is the best known of a group of London citizens, who were concerned to draw together the annals of their city into a fuller national history, and whose compositions included the so-called *Great Chronicle of London* as well as *Fabian's Chronicle*.[8] Both works locate the battle at Bosworth, and provide some valuable insights on the motives of the combatants. Their knowledge of what went on in the company of Sir Robert Brackenbury, keeper of the Tower of London, presumably derived from citizens who had been in his service. Unfortunately such works only assumed final form in the early sixteenth century. The most that can be claimed for the information on Richard III and Bosworth is that it had the authority of respectable citizens who were alive at the time and who were able to draw on eye-witnesses for at least some of their matter.

The only English writer to rival in time and style the writings of Valera, Commines and Molinet is the so-called 'second continuator' of the Crowland abbey chronicle. Curiously tacked on to a 'first continuation' of 'Ingulph's' chronicle, and then reworked by a third party with exclusively local interests, his composition is a remarkable political history of the civil wars from 1459 to 1485. From internal evidence it was written within a year of the death of Richard III, and though the composition of a churchman it reveals a shrewd understanding of human nature and a personal experience of affairs of state. Perhaps the author was no less a person than John Russell, bishop of Lincoln, and for a time chancellor of England. Certainly he was a man with similar qualities and experience. Not unnaturally his account of many key episodes of the Yorkist age commands wide respect, and indeed his comments on the general political scene in 1485 are most instructive. Its report of disaffection among the king's northern affinity, and its detailing the predicament of the Stanleys, provide vital clues as to the behaviour of key participants at Bosworth. On the other hand, the author is neither well-informed about, nor particularly interested in what actually happened in the battle. An unfortunate error in Fulman's original edition, repeated in Riley's translation, has even given the impression that he was unreliable on the basic facts of the battle, but a line missed from the manuscript clearly reveals that he knew who was slain and who had fled.[9]

For over a generation, indeed, there seems to have been no reasonably full and coherent account of the battle of Bosworth committed to writing, still less a version with any pretensions to literary quality. It might in part have been the virtual impossibility of composing a narrative which would preserve the honour of all the participants, particularly those still alive or whose families were still powerful, and a deep reluctance to open up old wounds by probing too deeply into their motives and manœuvres. Bernard André almost certainly felt this sort of constraint, and preferred to say nothing about the battle at all, except that it was fought on a Saturday, on which point he was in any case in error. At the same time the lack of any adequate history of the events around 1485 was of a piece with the generally lamentable state of historical scholarship in England. In his *History of Richard III*, Thomas More set new literary standards for his fellow countrymen, but his enterprise was more to produce a Renaissance morality play than to write accurate and balanced history. For the present purposes, however, it is still disappointing that More concluded his account with the usurpation, and his English translator only carried it forward to the end of 1483.[10]

It was left to an Italian, a native of Urbino who first came to England in 1502, to provide his adopted countrymen with a well-written, thoughtful and coherent version of their recent past. In his *Historia Anglica* Polydore Vergil offered his readers a narrative of the battle of Bosworth, which almost by default has become the standard account for subsequent historians. A fluent and elegant Latinist, and steeped in classical learning, he was a careful historian by the standards of time, and he was not afraid to challenge many of the cherished myths of early British history. Like all good historians, however, he was the victim of his sources, and for most of the fifteenth century he had precious little to go on besides vernacular continuations of *Polychronicon* and *The Brut*, and the better London chronicles. For more recent events, he turned to what might now be termed 'oral history', and it must be assumed that most of his information about Bosworth was provided by his patrons at the Tudor court, some of whom were eye-witnesses. For want of any better information, most historians have taken his words on trust, and used them as the starting point for attempted reconstructions of the encounter. His words on the general lie of the land and the siting of the camps, the disposition of the armies and their division into battalions, the tactics of the commanders, and the progress of the battle have been plagiarised and fleshed out countless times over the centuries. Unfortunately he has been more often read in a late Tudor translation than in the original Latin, and in one vital respect this practice might have led to misconstruction: what Vergil referred to as 'battle-lines' the first translator and all subsequent historians have transformed into 'vanguards'.[11]

Polydore Vergil is the last historian who can usefully be regarded as a primary source for the events of 1485. For all their indignation at the Italian's debunking of aspects of their national history, Edward Hall and a new generation of British historians slavishly followed his narrative of the Bosworth campaign, as for most of the fifteenth century. Their few interpolations are of dubious value. The anecdote that the duke of Norfolk was warned of the treachery that was to take place in the battle might reflect a well-founded tradition. At least it does not seem to have been an authorial invention. The long set-speeches that Hall attributed to the two chief protagonists are another matter. There are authentic touches to them, but the most that can be said is that there was a strong oral tradition which guided his imagination and kept it within bounds. At times Hall's freewheeling translation and imaginative amplification of Vergil have proved curiously influential. In his speech to the troops Henry Tudor is presented as

Equipment of the type worn by a common soldier during the Wars of the Roses, consisting of a barbute, a form of sallet, a brigandine, a pair of sleeves of mail, and a standard or collar of mail. Italian, about 1480.

referring to the enemy ahead and uncertain allies on each side, which statement seems to be the basis for the popular assumption that the Stanleys had armies both to the north and south of the field. Then at the point when the rebels are described by Vergil as having the sun at their backs, Hall amplifies the description by adding that their enemies had it on their faces. If based on evidence other than Vergil, both statements provide important clues as to troop dispositions. Yet if the former is nothing more than a glib turn of phrase and the latter a mindless elaboration then obviously there is nothing to commend them.[12]

In the course of the second half of the sixteenth century the account of the battle of Bosworth first offered by Vergil, then translated and amplified by Hall, became the standard version. It was the basic source for almost all Elizabethan and Jacobean writers, and through the influence of the histories of Holinshed, the drama of Shakespeare, and the verse of Beaumont, it gained even wider currency.[13] Of course it must be stressed that Vergil was the sole source of this tradition. Apart from his own authority as a historian, the most that can be said is that this vision made sense to Englishmen who might well have remembered hearing eye-witness accounts or had access to local reports. The problem is that this version, to which repetition, amplification and the power of print lent a spurious authority, might well have driven other accounts from the field. The chance survival of the Crowland chronicle must give pause for thought on what might not have withstood the ravages of time. Certainly valuable information contained in foreign sources was either overlooked or ignored, as is well illustrated by the Scots writers. In his Latin history of Scotland John Major provided new details on Bosworth, and in his later vernacular history Robert Lindsay of Pittscottie added a great deal more material. Both record the presence in Henry Tudor's army of a Scots contingent under such captains as Alexander Bruce.[14] It is perhaps easy to understand why English writers chose not to register such information in Tudor times, and why equally it reappeared in the English literary tradition under James I. On the other hand there are other elements in Lindsay's account which cannot be so readily inserted into the standard version. In addition to some decidedly apocryphal material, he offered an account of troop deployments and battlefield manœuvres that is reminiscent of De Valera's report, which he could scarcely have seen.

The establishment of an 'authoritative' version of the battle of Bosworth might also have driven from the field traditions which had been preserved by word of mouth or in song. For several generations at least there must have been a whole body of miscellaneous information about the events of 1485 available to the oral historian, and indeed public knowledge of what had happened at Bosworth must have depended for a long time on the tales of eye-witnesses, raconteurs and balladeers. Bernard André gave the impression that there were many, not entirely consistent stories in circulation around 1500, while Vergil admitted his dependence on the testimony of old men at the Tudor court. Many recollections died with the chief participants, and there can have been precious few still alive to proof-read Vergil's history. Yet some memories were passed on and eventually committed to writing. In the reign of Queen Mary Lord Parker recorded the tale frequently told in the household of Lady Margaret Beaufort by a man called Bigod who had been with Richard III on the morning of the battle. In far more detail than the Crowland chronicle, he recalled the scene of confusion when wine and chalice could not be found for the performance of the mass.[15] At around the same time Robert Lindsay of Pittscottie was writing up traditions which had been preserved in his neighbourhood by the descendants of Alexander Bruce. Snippets of local lore were soaked up in other writings. John Leland recorded the names of some Rutlandshire men who fought for Henry Tudor. According to Cornish legend, Sir Henry Bodrugan, a local knight of some notoriety, was in the field with Richard III. John Beaumont related the story of two Leicestershire friends who found themselves on opposite sides of the fray. In 1620 the Leicestershire antiquarian William Burton claimed that only forty years previously there had been villagers alive around Market Bosworth who remembered the battle.[16]

It is certainly the case that the historian needs to be wary of what is reported as popular tradition. A great many of the stories passed down though the ages sound apocryphal. The Scots chronicler Lindsay included a splendid, but scarcely credible tale about a highlander named MacGregor who stole Richard III's crown shortly before the battle. A servant of the bishop of Dunkeld, ambassador from James III, he admitted the theft, explaining that since it had been prophesied that he would hang as a thief he was determined not to shame his family with petty larceny. The king enjoyed the story so much that he was set free.[17] While being no less preposterous, few other legends are as engaging. There is the predictable story about the bed in which Richard III slept at Leicester. The king's treasure was found hidden in the mattress, but it brought its discoverer ill fortune.[18] At the same time it often turns out that a so-called folk tradition, far from being orally transmitted through the centuries, has originated from bookish sources, and then suitably embroidered with romantic frills has begun to masquerade as the voice of the people. Though Leicestershire born and with a knowledge of local traditions, Beaumont drew most of his information from the standard sources, while Sir George Buck, who prided himself on being the great-grandson of a prominent Ricardian killed at Bosworth, had to turn to chronicles and records to learn about the battle.[19] J. Nichols, the eighteenth-century Leicestershire historian, recorded the story of a woman in the neighbourhood of Bosworth who had in her possession old writings about the battle, which were destroyed by a thoughtless cook in need of kindling for her fire. The likelihood is that they were antiquarian jottings from printed materials, though none of the points said to have been made in them seem to be derived from the standard works. What is especially curious is that they included information on the death of Richard III which corresponds strikingly to the report received by Jean Molinet on the continent some three hundred years previously.[20]

Orally transmitted material could transcend mere anecdotage. In ballad form, in particular, whole narratives of the battle of Bosworth could be passed down through the generations, often doubtless committed to written notes, some of which perhaps finished their days by fuelling a kitchen fire. There can be no doubt that from as early as 1485 itself numerous songs and ballads were composed to meet the demands of a predominantly illiterate population to hear the news and relish the drama of the historic encounter. Unfortunately there are only three ballads extant which relate to Bosworth, all of which seem to emanate from north-west England, where the house of Stanley held sway. The most valuable for historical purposes is *The Ballad of Bosworth Field*, which also survives in a prose version, but *The Rose of England* and *Lady Bessy*, though rather more romanticised, are not without their interest.[21] The problem is what reliance can be placed on them. No matter how soon after the battle they were first composed, they were not committed to writing for a century and more. There are some anachronisms, not least the fact that one version ends with prayers for James I. There is a concern for a strong story line and a pandering to popular taste in their simplifications and romanticisations. At the same time there are clear signs of deterioration over time: events that have been missed out, places that have been garbled, names that have been muddled. Yet it is possible to make some quite positive points. Most obviously the garbling itself suggests a long period of oral transmission. It is particularly pleasing to find that there is an Elizabethan prose summary of *Bosworth Field* which can be put alongside the Jacobean version: the texts are sufficiently close to tell that they are versions of the same work, but sufficiently different to suggest that their common source was several generations removed. At the same time there is much internal evidence which suggests an early date of original composition, not least perhaps the manner in which parts of the action are described as if by an eye-witness.

Ultimately the value of the ballad tradition must be judged in terms of the quality of the information it provides. Though blatantly fanciful in parts, and partisan in spirit, *Bosworth Field, Rose of England* and *Lady Bessy* do present information about 1485 which cannot be dismissed out of hand. Leaving aside for the moment the insights which they might provide regarding the politicking and plotting of Richard III's reign, they offer significant details about the battle which are not mentioned in the standard histories, but which find support in other evidence to which the balladeer cannot be supposed to have access. Thus *Rose of England* maintained that the rebels decided to attack the flank of the royal army, a point also made by the Burgundian chronicler, Jean Molinet. *Bosworth Field* testified to the use of cannons in the battle: a point again made by Molinet, and seemingly confirmed by archaeological evidence.[22]

The most striking addition made by the ballad tradition to the body of evidence relating to the battle of Bosworth is a list of over a hundred lords and knights who were with Richard III. Hitherto scholars have been troubled by the inclusion of noblemen for whose presence there is no other evidence, the garbled nature of many of the names, and the impossibility of identifying some of them at all. Yet the more it is studied the more authentic the body of information appears. First of all it offers the most comprehensive list of men whose presence in the royal army is recorded elsewhere, including not only all the eight peers who are mentioned in the chronicles, but also the majority of the knights whose participation in the battle was later documented in the act of attainder. In addition there are the names of dozens of lords and knights, whose attendance on the king seems not improbable given their close attachment to the Ricardian cause: privy councillors like Lords Audley, Grey of Codnor and Maltravers, northern friends like Lords Fitzhugh, Scrope of Bolton, Scrope of Masham, no less than seventeen of Richard III's 'knights of body', and a large number of other northern knights, some of whom were retainers of the king and others of the earl of Northumberland. Indeed around two-thirds of the names are readily identifiable as individuals active in politics at the time, and most of the others bear recognisable surnames. Since there are two slightly different texts, it is possible to unscramble some of the more garbled names. The men named variously in the ballad and prose summary as Sir Robert 'Utridge' or 'Owlrege', Sir Henry 'Bowdrye' or 'Landringham', and Sir Alexander 'Fawne' or 'Haymor' might well have been Sir Robert Ughtred of Yorkshire, Sir Henry Bodrugan alias Bodringham of Cornwall, and Sir Alexander Baynham of Gloucestershire. All could have been at Bosworth, but none of their names would have meant anything to north-western audiences. An oral tradition which preserved so

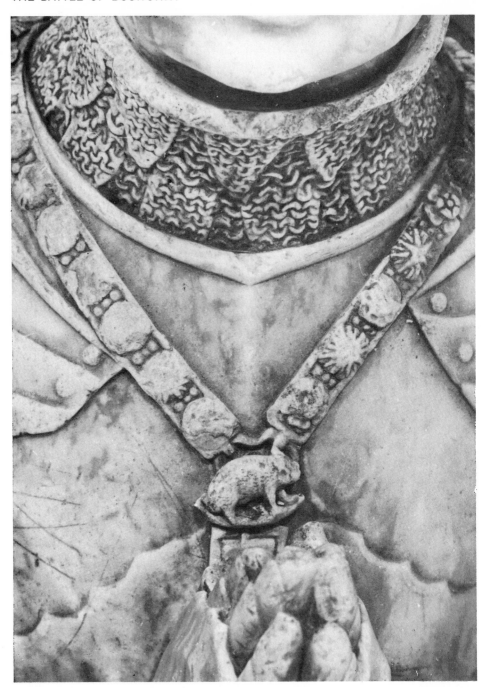

Effigy of Ralph Fitzherbert (died 1483) from Norbury, Derbyshire, showing the Yorkist livery collar and the pendant boar badge of Richard III.

remarkably faithfully the names of so many Ricardian stalwarts for over a century must have originated in firm intelligence derived from the field by a Stanleyan herald or spy. The only alternative is to claim that the ballads were the product of a later antiquarian, who was equipped with an extraordinary knowledge of fifteenth-century politics and possessed of a sufficiently devious intelligence to throw in a few wild spellings.

Acceptance of the ballad testimony on the composition of Richard III's army has a more general significance than simply adding to the cast in the drama of Bosworth. Most basically it reinforces and fleshes out the statements in other sources that the royal host was both large and distinguished, and challenges the assumption made by almost all historians that the king was attended only by a narrow circle of nobles. Of course, it also presents its difficulties, compounding, for example, the problem of explaining the defeat of the king and the behaviour of his leading subjects. Yet there is good chronicle evidence to support the proposition that large numbers of notables in the royal army declined to fight, and it is beyond dispute that the overwhelming majority of the men who bore arms against Henry Tudor escaped attainder or other recorded punishment. At the same time the pattern of events implied by the ballad tradition might well be capable of furnishing new insights into the nature of the Tudor settlement and of helping to explain the strange reticence in so many quarters as to what actually happened at Bosworth.

*   *   *

The sources available for the study of the battle of Bosworth are meagre, frequently muddled, inconsistent, often distant in time from the events described, and subject to partisan distortion. Even the most basic points of historical fact are difficult to establish. Though there are many problems of chronology, the dating of the battle does seem incontestable. Most accounts correctly refer to the 22nd August 1485, or in the case of John Rous the eighth day of the Assumption. Of course, Henry VII confused matters by dating his own reign from 21 August, while to add to the confusion Lord Stanley later recalled meeting Henry Tudor for the first time on 24 August, which seems most unlikely. Bernard André thought the battle took place on a Saturday; the Chronicle of Calais confidently ascribed it to St Bartholomew's eve; Polydore Vergil gave the date as 11th kalends of September 1486.[23] At the same time the battle went under a variety of names, reflecting in some degree the perspectives of the various informants. The first reports said that Richard had been killed at 'Sandeford', while other early notices referred to 'Redesmore' and 'Brownheath'. In the years that followed men talked of a battle on the Warwickshire border, near Coventry or at Merevale. Only gradually did the name of Bosworth, the largest settlement adjoining the battlesite, sweep all its rivals from the field.[24]

The historian might be forgiven for throwing up his hands in despair when confronted with testimony of this sort, or clutching at one particular account to the exclusion of others. The 'truth' about the battle of Bosworth, is certainly an unattainable ideal, but there are at least strategies of questioning, analysis and interpretation which help to clarify the score. As regards the dating and general site of the battle, for example, it is possible to evaluate the evidence, rather than accept simply one testimony as true and another as false. Thus the chronology of 22 August 1485 can be established beyond doubt not just because it is recorded in several independent sources and alone fits the time-frames implied in them, but also because some of the inconsistent evidence can be satisfactorily explained. Bernard André thought the victory was won on a Saturday because by the end of his reign Henry VII had won two other battles on that day; Lord Stanley simply associated the event with the nearest 'red letter day', the feast of St Bartholomew; Polydore Vergil, in true Renaissance style, provided the correct Roman version of the date, but fell into gross error with the year, perhaps by over-correcting the London chronicle tradition which followed mayoral years rather than calendar years. Similarly the apparent contradictions with regard to the name of the battle can be satisfactorily resolved. 'Sandeford', 'Redesmore' and 'Brownheath' were improvisations drawn from the terrain itself, and meant nothing to people from outside the immediate locality. Others slotted the battle into their own mental maps. John Rous, the Warwickshire man, noted that the battle took place 'on the border of the counties of Warwick and Leicester'. Juan de Salazar, who perhaps made his escape southwards, or the Spanish merchants, who knew English commercial centres, located the action in the neighbourhood of Coventry. The Crowland chronicler, true to his cloth, pinpointed the battle by reference to Merevale abbey. The triumph of Bosworth was only assured by its adoption by Vergil and Hall, though the name might also have been independently promoted by the court and popular tradition.

The sources thus need to be examined and cross-examined, and the historian, like the successful barrister, has his own cards up his sleeve. He might well have visited the site of the battle and thus know more about the lie of land than many of his witnesses. Unfortunately the landscape around Bosworth provides precious few new clues, despite attention from many amateur archeologists and antiquarians. A major problem was that the land was drained and enclosed in the sixteenth century. When Raphael Holinshed inspected the site in Elizabethan times he had difficulty in reconstructing the scene described by Vergil, most particularly the boggy land around which the rebel army skirted. In the early seventeenth century William Burton recalled that at the enclosure of the manor of Stoke quantities of armour and a great number of large arrow-heads had been dug up. Eighteenth century antiquarians also sought to make sense of the site. From time to time more skeletons, weapons and cannon shot were excavated, but unfortunately precious little was properly documented or dated. To confuse matters further, there had been a skirmish on the battlesite between the Royalists and Parliamentarians in the Civil War.[25]

To reconstruct what happened on 22 August 1485 it is also possible to draw on a mass of evidence regarding the men of the hour. As full a knowledge as possible of their personalities and backgrounds, their ambitions and anxieties, their records in the past and their behaviour after the event, must assist the process of elucidation and explanation, or at the very least will provide the best available guide in linking apparent motive to hypothetical action, or known action to likely motive. It will be pertinent to draw on knowledge of the age in which the chief protagonists lived so as to make evident the institutions, values

German mail shirt of the second quarter of the fifteenth century, worn under field armour.

and technologies which shaped their political options and military strategies. Indeed it will be necessary to go back some distance in time from the battle of Bosworth. Most basically it is hoped to establish some sense of its meaning for the participants. At the same time a presentation of facets of the fifteenth-century background will certainly be indispensable in any attempted assessment of the place of 1485 in English and British history.

2 Civil War and Common Weal

The chain of events leading to the battle of Bosworth is composed of innumerable strands, many of which can be traced back through several generations. Few commentators at the time failed to connect the events of 1485 in some wise with the dynastic strife and civil wars of the previous thirty years, which in turn were often presented as stemming from the consequences of the deposition of Richard II in 1399. In the hands of Tudor historians this perspective was moulded into a powerful myth, which not only served to legitimize the new regime but also chimed in with new political and moral attitudes. It was this vision which William Shakespeare stamped indelibly in the consciousness of later generations, a vision of the fifteenth century as a drama whose first act sees the deposition of Richard II, whose subsequent acts chronicle the rise and fall, and the bloody feuding of the houses of Lancaster and York, whose crisis is the battle of Bosworth, and whose blessed resolution is the establishment of peace and harmony under the Tudors. Even in recent times it made sense for at least one eminent historian, A.L. Rowse, to adopt the Shakespearian perspective on the background to the battle of Bosworth.[1]

It is a compelling tale, an artfully crafted image of the past. For all its propagandist value and its elements of wilful distortion, it was not a grossly cynical fabrication. For the most part the Tudor vision was a genuine attempt on the part of sixteenth-century writers to make sense of their national experience. Of course, most modern historians find it unsatisfactory and spend much time exorcising it from the public mind. Yet, even if its general plot and moralising refrain are to be jettisoned, its chronology might well be worth retaining. Obviously the drama culminating in the battle of Bosworth was set against a back-cloth of institutions and ideas which stretched back over several generations, if not centuries. In the forging of this landscape events of the late fourteenth century have an especial importance: the Black Death, the French wars, the Peasants' Revolt, Lollardy, the Chaucerian achievement, and so on. Above all, even if it can no longer be claimed that the Wars of the Roses began with the deposition of Richard II by Henry IV in 1399, there are many senses in which the events and experiences of the time shaped the course of English politics until long after a third Richard had been supplanted by a seventh Henry.

* * *

For Shakespeare the dramatic cycle which would end at Bosworth field began in the last years of Richard II's reign. For the historian it is a matter of tracing the build up of tension between the monarch and his leading subjects over the previous twenty years of his reign. In large measure the problems were inherited from his grandfather Edward III. The old king's long and glorious reign, which had seen English armies triumphant in France and the nation united behind the war-effort, ended in defeat, disillusionment and discord. Edward himself slipped into an unmanly dotage, his court was rife with amours and intrigue, and his government grew corrupt and rapacious. To add to the troubles of the time, Edward, prince of Wales, the Black Prince, died of cholera, leaving his unpopular brother, John of Gaunt, duke of Lancaster, at the centre of the political stage. In a remarkable demonstration of their outrage the commons in parliament openly defied the government in 1376, and successfully impeached the king's chief ministers. When the old king died in 1377, the succession passed to his grandson, the Black Prince's son. With the accession of the ten-year old Richard II, the nation hoped for new beginnings, but more wisely prepared for the worst.

Traditionally the fate of kingdoms without adult rulers was pitiable. During the minority of Richard II there were considerable difficulties. English military fortunes continued to decline, and resentment at government taxation continued to mount. In the so-called Peasants' Revolt of 1381 the commons rose in rebellion, ominously blending political demands with larger social and ideological concerns. Yet the broadly-based minority council served the realm surprisingly well, and the major political problems of the reign emerged only as the king began to shake off his tutelage. Young Richard seems to have been brought up with too exalted a notion of his regality, naturally nourished both by sincere counsellors seeking to dignify the monarchy and by avaricious courtiers on the make. Successful government depended less on high absolutist theory and the affirmation of will, however, than on the king's ability to secure the active co-operation of the great men of the realm, and it was here that the king's political apprenticeship was woefully deficient. Hamstrung at the outset by his immaturity and inexperience, he was also unlucky with the personalities with whom he had to deal. The leading magnates were older men, comrades-in-arms of Edward III, too proud and prickly to tolerate an untried and petulant youth. Royal uncles were rarely an asset, and Edward III had been too prolific for the comfort of the realm. After Edward, the Black Prince, there had been Lionel, also dead, but with a daughter whose blood line would pass through the Mortimers to enrich the blood royal of the house of York. The next brother was John of Gaunt, the greatest magnate in the realm. Angered and hurt by his exclusion from power by men suspicious of his ambitions, he made no positive contribution to national politics until the 1390s, when the king's childlessness perhaps raised the prospect of a Lancastrian succession. Then there was Edmund of Langley, duke of York, who remained, rather surprisingly given the ambitions of his descendants, very much the political lightweight. It was the youngest brother, Thomas of Woodstock, duke of Gloucester, who lacking the prospects to match his own sense of worth was to prove the most troublesome to the king. When the young king showed himself determined to be his own master, it was this uncle who led the aristocratic opposition which humiliated

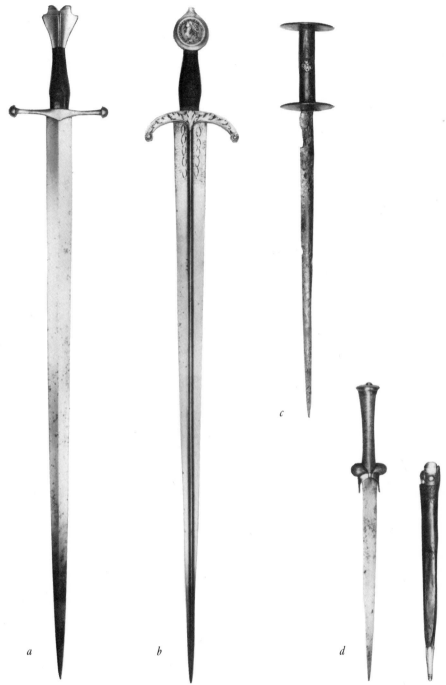

a   b   c   d

Swords of the fifteenth century: (a) Italian, about 1460, weight just over 2 lbs, length nearly 35 inches; (b) Italian, about 1490, hilt probably later.
Daggers: (c) French roundel dagger, a very common type, about 1440–50; (d) Flemish ballock dagger and sheath (also known as a kidney dagger), very common in England and the Low Countries, about 1450–60.

him and struck down his ministers and cronies, first in 1386 and then more brutally in 1388.

Richard II was a mercurial character, and the constraints imposed on his rule during his long minority add to the impression of improvisation and inconsistency. In so far as a mature style of government can be fitfully discerned, it tended towards what would later be termed absolutism. He was concerned to build up the majesty, power and resources of the monarchy, maintaining a splendid court, developing the royal household as the mainspring of government, and using the crown lands and other territorial acquisitions as the power-bases for a strong national monarchy. His foreign policy, though pacific with regard to France, was far from supine. His dealings with the papacy and empire, in particular, seem to imply the sorts of conceptions of sovereignty which were not to find full expression until the reign of Henry VIII. Indeed many of his vigorous policies, from exacting good behaviour bonds from potentially troublesome subjects to maintaining a royal bodyguard, anticipate the strategies of the Tudor monarchy. What historians have hailed as far-sighted when implemented by the first Tudors, however, earned Richard II nothing but opprobrium. Like his later namesake, Richard II found that his regime was too narrowly based: he had a small circle of courtier friends, but most of the magnates were disaffected; he was greatly cherished in his 'principality' of Chester, but was roundly hated in London and many other parts of the realm. Henry of Bolingbroke, his exiled cousin, returning to claim his inheritance as duke of Lancaster, led a successful rebellion against his 'tyranny'. Richard was forced to abdicate, and Henry claimed the throne in his place.

Henry IV seems not to have enjoyed his ill-won crown. The blithe and popular Henry of Bolingbroke rapidly became the lonely, guilt-ridden and embattled king depicted by Shakespeare. In large measure his problems were the perennial ones of English kingship, but they were greatly compounded by the nature of the usurpation. To a degree he was a victim of the constitutionalist rhetoric and the partisan following which brought him to power, and the old dilemma of building up a broad base of support among the nobility and gentry without totally bankrupting the crown presented itself in a peculiarly acute form. Of course, to the Elizabethan mind the deposition and probable murder of Richard II, for all his personal failings an anointed king, and the setting aside of the prior claims of the house of Mortimer, was the source of all the troubles of the Lancastrian line. It is probable that this opinion had some currency even in the reign of Henry IV. The new prince of Wales was to make the old Ricardian connection his own, and to honour the memory of the dead king during his own reign. There were powerful currents in the fifteenth century tending towards the exaltation of monarchy, and Englishmen were feeling increasingly edgy about their reputation as regicides. Perhaps the significance of the usurpation of 1399 lay not so much in establishing alternative dynastic claims and precedents for deposition, as in making the political nation more aware of the dangers of pushing constitutional liberties to the point of destroying the monarchical system.

The Lancastrian regime remained insecure until Henry V succeeded his father in 1413. Although the new king had to face a serious conspiracy early on, he was able to vindicate the legitimacy of the Lancastrian regime by his triumphs in France. In the traditional view Henry V is the model hero-king, a blessing accorded the English people at a dark hour as a token of divine favour. To the modern mind he appears cold, callous and sanctimonious, but to many contemporaries he was just, brave and pious, the qualities par excellence of the ideal ruler. Certainly his statesmanship, his military leadership and his concern for the church won him wide respect in Christendom, and provided the means by which his subjects found new pride in their national monarchy. Tragically, at the height of his triumph, within months of succeeding by treaty to the crown of France, Henry V died, leaving a babe in arms to succeed to both kingdoms. The Lancastrian regime on both sides of the Channel was to show surprising resilience during the long minority of Henry VI. Nevertheless writers in Tudor times had no doubt that it was during the reign of this unhappy, befuddled monarch that the cancer introduced into the body politic in 1399 worked its lethal course though the whole system, carrying off the house of Lancaster and sapping the life-blood of the whole nation.

It is certainly true that the dynastic issue re-emerged with a vengeance during the reign of Henry VI, though not in quite the manner that has been traditionally assumed.[2] The circumstances of the minority inevitably presented a severe threat to political stability, but as was seen in the reign of Richard II the English polity was mature enough to take minorities in its stride. Loyal to the memory of Henry V, a broadly based regency council was able to rule quite successfully during the 1420s and early 1430s, and significantly its main problems arose from within rather than from outside the house of Lancaster. More problematic was a king whose assumption of power coincided with, and accelerated the deterioration of English fortunes in France, and whose exercise of authority was fitful, feckless and partisan. Never far below the surface, aristocratic factionalism and popular unrest were kindled by favouritism at court, corruption in government, violations of justice, ruinously high taxation, and humiliation on the continent. From the 1440s the champion of the disaffected was Richard, duke of York. He lent his weight to the bitter indictment of the Lancastrian regime in parliament in 1450 and might well have encouraged the popular uprisings in Kent and elsewhere. Yet to say that the Yorkist challenge was not dynastic does not mean that dynastic considerations were important. With the king childless until 1453 and the succession uncertain, the high favour he showed his Beaufort, Holland and Stafford kinsmen seemed ominous. The duke of York, the next male Plantagenet, had good cause to feel slighted, while his smouldering resentment could only stiffen the resolve of the court clique to resist his claims. In the event it was Henry VI's debility rather than his death which gave York the public recognition which he desired, and in 1453 he was accepted as protector of the realm.

The Wars of the Roses was not primarily a struggle between rival claims to the throne. The Yorkist challenge was in the time-honoured tradition of aristocratic opposition to an unpopular government. In some quarters at least it might have been felt that the house of York, through their descent from Lionel, second surviving son of Edward III, had better title to the throne than the house of Lancaster, descended from the third son. The appeal to the name of Mortimer

Edward IV (1442–83), painted about 1518 from a lost original.

in the rising of 1450 certainly points in this direction. Yet this claim remained muted until the late 1450s. The brutal battle of St Albans was fought in 1455 with both sides professing their loyalty to Henry VI, and in the difficult years that followed all deference was shown to the befuddled king. On the whole it seems to have been the determination of Queen Margaret and the Lancastrian lords to secure their positions, and to avenge themselves on the Yorkists, which made the latter increase the stakes. In 1460 Richard duke of York made formal claim to the throne, but even then his allies showed themselves unwilling to countenance a deposition. Only in the weeks after the slaughter of the senior Yorkist lords at Wakefield did the remainder of the rebel coalition, headed by the earl of Warwick, acclaim York's son as Edward IV.

The accession of Edward IV took place at the darkest hour in the civil war. Through the 1450s England managed to pull back from the brink of war on a number of occasions. York's first military challenge in 1452 had been defused without loss of life, and even the slaughter at St Albans in 1455 did not lead immediately to a general conflict. Though there were alarms and excursions as lords built up their retinues and engaged in localised feuding, there was no open civil war until 1459. Even then the armies were reluctant to engage each other, and a show of the royal standard could disperse a rebel army. The formal attainder of York, the Neville earls and their supporters in the Coventry parliament inevitably hardened attitudes. In its turn, the Yorkist resolve first to secure the succession and then to displace Henry VI was calculated to divide the nation. By the end of 1460 there could be no compromise between the main protagonists, and there were few lords not embroiled in the blood-feuds already generated by the conflict. In fact in the first weeks of his reign Edward IV added to the count considerably. His crown meant little without a kingdom, and his first task was to defeat the large northern army assembled in the name of Henry VI. On the snow covered field of Towton, in the largest and most brutal battle of the war, the Lancastrian forces were shattered. Even then the stability of the new regime was tenuous: it took some time to broaden its power-base significantly, and to root out Lancastrian garrisons in the north and in Wales. As after the usurpation of Henry IV, it was former allies who eventually proved the greatest threat. The earl of Warwick, conspiring first with the king's brother and then with the Lancastrian court in exile, succeeded in driving Edward IV from the realm in 1470-1, and securing the 'readeption' of Henry VI. Only two stunning victories by King Edward in 1471 seemed to resolve the matter conclusively: at Barnet the Kingmaker was slain and his powerful affinity broken, and at Tewkesbury Edward prince of Wales, the last of the Lancastrian line, along with a number of other Lancastrian lords, was butchered.

At this point another powerful image of fifteenth-century politics intrudes: the overmighty subject. Like the view of the civil wars as contests between rival branches of the ruling house of Plantagenet, between the Red Rose and the White, the view of the wars as involving the recrudescence of aristocratic power and feuding had its origins in the fifteenth century, acquired hypnotic power through Shakespeare, and has remained influential even among professional historians. In a sense the views are complementary, alike placing weight on the ambitions of individuals, lineage politics, and the disastrous consequences of

Battle of Barnet, April 1471, from the fifteenth century French version of the Historie of the Arrivall of Edward IV *(Ghent MS 236).*

monarchical weakness. Indeed there can be no doubt as to the crucial importance of personal antagonisms and family rivalries in the civil strife which afflicted England from the reign of Richard II onwards, and there is much to be said for an approach which, as in Shakespeare's imaginative reconstructions, recognises the play of pride, honour and anger in what after all were often face-to-face encounters. The characters of individual kings always merit attention, but the personalities of the great men of the realm were almost as significant, as can be seen, perhaps from a comparison of the three dukes of Gloucester: Thomas of Woodstock, 'good duke' Humphrey and the future Richard III. All three were royal uncles angling to take charge of the ship of state, but their actions seem to be informed by different personal styles. In the small world of English politics it is easy to see how a weak or feckless king could become a prey to the sycophantic courtier and the forceful magnate, and recent work on the reign of Henry VI has shown the disruptive consequences of governmental partisanship and spinelessness in the countryside. Hatreds and jealousies at court fed into lineage rivalries in the country, as magnates excluded from royal patronage and denied justice sought to mobilise their local followings. At the same time the quarrels of the country gentry, endemic in landed society but usually contained by governmental and aristocratic adjudication and pressure, escalated fiercely, as rivals bound themselves in to nation-wide networks of patronage and protection. It was in this turbulent world that the more able magnates could dramatically extend their regional power, often supplanting the crown as the effective fount of patronage and justice in their country, bestowing on their supporters fees, offices and liveries, securing their advancement at court or in local government and maintaining their cases through pressure on the law courts. In some cases powerful aristocratic affinities, like that headed by York in the 1450s, or Warwick in the 1460s, could come close to winning control of the realm, either through the manipulation of pliant monarchs or ruthless exercises in king-making. To many historians the resurgence of aristocratic power was both a cause and consequence of royal weakness, and as 'bastard feudalism' it threatened to undo the constitutional and political achievements of several centuries of state-building.[3]

The high drama of personal ambition, dynastic aggrandisement and sheer warlordism has dazzled many observers of the fifteenth-century scene. Chroniclers of the time studded their accounts with the posturing of kings and magnates, and certainly assumed that their ambitions and anxieties, their feuds and friendships were crucial factors in politics. It was Sir John Fortescue, a chief justice under Henry VI, who first coined the term 'overmighty subject'. Yet the picture is misleading in a number of respects. It would be hard to demonstrate that politics were other than self-interested, but it can be readily shown that the process itself was nowhere nearly as simple and crude as is often implied. Most obviously the political nation, the men who had a stake and a say in the affairs of the realm, was far broader than the relatively exclusive circle of peers. In fact a far greater proportion of the lay wealth of the kingdom was in the hands of commoners, ranging from knights and squires whose incomes rivalled those of lesser lords, through merchants and lawyers whose liquid assets far exceeded many noble fortunes, to thousands of more modest gentry whose consequence in their own counties could still be considerable. However self-seeking in his bid for power, a magnate had first to win support from among such classes, and however wealthy in his own right, he would have found it beyond his means to retain with fees more than a fraction of his following. Of course 'good lordship' could take many forms, ranging from educational provision and the arrangement of marriages to arbitration of disputes and 'string-pulling' with the authorities, and the castle or 'great house' of the region acted as a magnet for the aspirations of the local gentry. Obviously a magnate's own status in the realm was vital in maintaining his affinity, and this factor further served to intensify competition at court. In comparison with their European counterparts the English nobles were unusually dependent on the monarchy for the maintenance of their port and dignity. Though a number of lords could hope to profit in a time of monarchical weakness, for the vast majority of nobles the collapse of royal government spelt disaster.[4]

It would certainly be unwise to underestimate the maturity of the English polity. At the accession of Richard II the English monarchy was already half a millenium old, and was arguably the most highly evolved polity in Christendom. A line of ambitious and determined rulers had succeeded in making the crown the cornerstone of national life, in breaking the forces of provincial particularism, offering law and justice to free- born Englishmen, and building up a remarkable bureaucratic machine. Most significant perhaps was the participation in this process of an increasingly self-conscious and politically articulate community of the realm. Spearheaded by the great feudatories, whose rebellions doubtless owed more to personal ambition than to the grand principles they affirmed, and developed and consolidated in council chambers and parliamentary assemblies, considerable constitutional progress had been made between 1215, when King John was obliged by his barons to accept legal restraints on his rule, to 1376, when the chief ministers of Edward III could be formally impeached by the parliamentary commons. In between times the government of Henry III was put into commission, the puissant Edward I was forced to accept further limitations on his rule, and the ill-starred Edward II had been deposed, for treason against the crown. By the late fourteenth century the political nation had entrenched the principle that parliamentary consent was necessary for general taxation, had gained some experience in restraining executive power, and could distinguish between the king as a person and the crown as the embodiment of the nation. Herein lay the paradox of the English polity often noted by continental observers: the monarchy was strong, but the kings were often humiliated by their subjects.

Beneath the glamour and gore of royal and aristocratic power-play, therefore, it is not surprising to find continuous appeals being made to grand constitutional principles and to a broadly conceived public opinion. While it is hard to see the selfish grandees who humiliated Richard II and Henry VI as champions of English liberties, there can be no doubt as to the importance of issues of principle in generating support for their enterprise. Quite a number of noblemen were well educated, and their political actions could be reflective as well as reflexive. Humphrey duke of Gloucester, whose book collection became the core of the Bodleian Library, and John Tiptoft, earl of Worcester, are only

Battle of Tewkesbury, May 1471, from the fifteenth century French version of the Historie of the Arrivall of Edward IV *(Ghent MS 236).*

the most notable of the peers whose learning shaped their political views. What might be termed ideological considerations more obviously carried weight among the clergy, the civil servants, the lawyers, and a whole constellation of career-minded gentry and educated merchants. Such men did not have clear-cut interests which attachment to a lineage might bring to the backwoods gentry. The patronage networks within which they moved were complex and fibrous, and inclined them to articulate their concerns in more abstract terms. It was the need to win over this body of opinion that led the Yorkist lords to generalise their grievances in petitions and manifestos, to talk of the 'common good' which ought to be promoted by governments, and to contrast it with the private advantages which court favourites were seeking. Despite the tendency of the Lancastrian regime to make its stand on its own legitimacy, Warwick and his new-found Lancastrian allies used it to great effect against Edward IV in 1470, appealing to the commons of England to acknowledge their record of concern for 'the welfare of the crown and the advancement of the common weal' and justifying their invasion by reference to their intended 'reformation' of the realm.[5] Of course, such rhetoric was double-edged. Whatever the sincerity of the propagandists, such notions became common currency in the Yorkist era. In this respect, as in so many others, the Tudor age would be the legatee of the fifteenth century.

The existence of a strong and vigorous civil society determined in many respects the character and course of the Wars of the Roses. For some time it has been recognised that the conflict was neither as sustained nor as socially disruptive as was traditionally imagined.[6] Campaigns were short-lived, with no more than twelve months' campaigning in the whole era, land was not systematically fought over or despoiled, and towns were almost wholly spared from pillage. It is possible that revisionism has gone a little too far, minimising the sacrifices and losses sustained by individuals and communities from time to time, but on the whole there can be no doubt that by continental standards the war involved little suffering for the population at large. To a degree the limited nature of the conflict had to do with military tactics, the need for swift movements across the country and to bring field armies to an early encounter. Yet military practice in the Wars of the Roses reflected the facts of English political and social life. For the most part the country was de-militarised. The lowlands to the south and east of a line from York to Bristol, in which the overwhelming majority of the population and wealth of the country was concentrated, presented few obstacles to the movement of armies. There were castles, but few which could have withstood a determined siege. In the 1470s Lord Hastings began building a 'castle' at Kirby Muxloe, not far from Bosworth, but it was more a crenellated mansion than a fortress. A number of cities and towns had walls, but their function was to collect tolls and keep out robbers. Above all, perhaps to a degree not often appreciated, what were termed 'strenuous' knights and squires, that is landed gentry who were active soldiers, were extremely thin on the ground in many southern counties. To a frightening degree military power was concentrated in the hands of the great lords of the Welsh marches and the north, with their large affinities of poor, but battle-hardened gentry. At crucial moments in the civil wars the decisions of such

Fotheringhay, Northamptonshire, birthplace of Richard of Gloucester in 1452.

magnates, notably the Nevilles, Percys and Stanleys, could be decisive. Even then there were important constraints operating, most notably that the English polity was so well integrated that there were few lords without allies and material interests in several parts of the realm. In a sense the horror felt for the ravages of war in fifteenth-century England testifies to the civilian nature of the society.

In other respects as well historians have sought to modify the traditionally dark picture of fifteenth-century English life. Just as lamentations against the ravages of war need to be taken in the context of several centuries of peace, so complaints about lawlessness and injustice must be related to expectations of law and justice. It is certainly the case that government corruption and aristocratic rivalries in the middle decades of the fifteenth century were disruptive of good order in the provinces. The letters of the Pastons of Norfolk illustrate many of the excesses of this time, when 'self-help' and strong-arm tactics, appeals to patrons and bribing juries became vital elements in the protection of legal rights. The civil wars both fed on and then further nourished local feuding. The lawlessness and fighting in north Lancashire in the second half of Edward IV's reign is a case in point.[7] In origin a property dispute between the Stanleys and Harringtons, it escalated into what became known as 'the king's great matters touching the good rule and good governance of Lancashire'. With Lord Stanley generally having government backing and the Harringtons gaining support from the earl of Warwick and, later, Richard of Gloucester, the struggle over Hornby castle and other lordships became enmeshed in northern power-politics for over two decades, not least at times of dynastic upheaval as in 1470–1 and 1485–7. Yet there is a real problem of balance in such matters. It certainly can be argued that the stamping-grounds of the Pastons and the Harringtons, were not representative of England as a whole. The Oxfordshire of the Stonor letters seems remarkably tranquil, while even the Yorkshire of the Plumpton correspondence seems to have been litigious rather than lawless, bracing rather than belligerent. Furthermore it is important to stress that chancery petitions and collections of private letters present the historian with a new kind of evidence, at once more informal, anxious and revealing than most government records. The reputation of the fifteenth century has suffered because for the first time the seamy side of the judicial system is graphically recorded.

There are obvious ways in which the reputation of fifteenth-century England has suffered by comparison with what is often referred to as the 'high middle ages'. One of the merits of starting with the reign of Richard II is to see how processes set in train in the late fourteenth century took a downward turn in the fifteenth century. In economic terms the Black Death is the great benchmark, establishing the general climate of demographic decline and economic stagnation. Interestingly enough there was a brief rally in the last decades of the fourteenth century, but the steady haemorrhaging from the body of the nation continued throughout the first three-quarters of the fifteenth century. There was a rural depression, as land values and food prices fell, and as wool exports declined precipitously. It is possible that the textile industry held its ground, with enormous potential for the future, but cloth exports did not begin their dramatic rise until the 1470s. It is also possible to talk about cultural decline. The great cathedral building programmes petered out, and aristocratic artistic patronage

Richard III (1452-85), painted about 1518 from a lost original.

diminished in the early Lancastrian period. Even more striking, the literary triumphs of the age of Chaucer, which had given England a vernacular literature worthy of serious contemplation, were scarcely followed through. Later Chaucerians were as dwarves on the shoulders of giants. Yet there are positive signs to be seen as well. The key is perhaps to count *per capita* rather than gross levels of economic production and cultural achievement. The effect of the Black Death seems to have been to produce a downward shift in the balance of economic power, bringing new wealth to the middling and lower ranks of society, and presenting difficulties for the large institutional landlords. This can be seen in cultural terms as well. It was a time when 'high culture' suffered but there was a massive extension of 'middle brow culture': the beautification of parish churches rather than the building of cathedrals, functional literacy rather than rhetorical embellishment, the printing press rather than the monastic scriptorium.

In the last decade of the reign of Edward IV it is thus possible to see English life in a precarious balance. For the first time in a generation there seemed a real promise of political stability. After 1471 the king's affinity grew in size as well as maturity to form a broadly based and experienced political establishment. The tempo of economic life was beginning to increase again: the king himself worked actively to promote English commerce, which was also stimulated by increased overseas demand. After decades of national humiliation England was again being drawn back into the mainstream of European life at a time when there were new and fresh currents of thought in the air. In all fields of life Englishmen were gaining confidence in their ability to plan for the future. Ambitious families were investing in the education of their sons: John Colet, the son of a London merchant, was destined to embark on a distinguished scholarly career at Oxford in 1483. Philanthropic churchmen and laymen joined together in the endowment of educational institutions to meet the rising levels of demand. Archbishop Rotherham and Bishop Stillington, two Yorkshiremen who founded schools in their native villages in the 1470s, were both sufficiently down-to-earth to include in their curricula subjects relevant to business and administration.[8] Perhaps the best symbol of the new spirit of optimism is the sign of the Red Pale at Westminster, where William Caxton opened his printing press in 1476. There was a spirit of idealism in the project: he shared the concern of many contemporaries for self-improvement, the advancement of the 'common weal' and moral reform. At the same time it was a hard-headed business venture, drawing on the technology and business experience of the Low Countries, and seeing in the increasing number of affluent and literate Englishmen and women a potential demand for vernacular works. The age of Caxton was a time when England looked back on the civil strife of preceding decades, and hoped that it was all behind them. The shrewd publisher even had an edition of Sir Thomas Malory's *Le Morte d'Arthur* in the pipe-line to enable his countrymen to see their recent experiences in the mirror of the past, and to help to inspire a national resurgence under a strong and glorious monarchy.[9]

3 The Year of Three Kings

At the beginning of 1483 Englishmen looked to the future with a confidence and optimism wholly unthinkable a generation earlier. Among their chief blessings they would have certainly counted their sovereign, Edward IV, and his promising heir, Edward, prince of Wales. From the callow youth who was raised to the throne in the awful winter of 1460–1, when the blood of so many noblemen had stained the frozen soil, the king had grown with his people, and for the most part won their hearts. It had taken ten hard years to establish his rule, all of which might have seemed in vain when he was driven into exile in 1470, but from his recovery of the throne in 1471 Edward IV had ruled with a majestic flair and a personal warmth wholly lacking in his Lancastrian predecessors. While his more serious-minded subjects were critical of his easy-going style and the moral laxity of his court, none could question that his rule had provided a framework within which the arts of peace could be cultivated and their fruits enjoyed. To some extent he was the fortunate legatee of the civil strife. Many of the old warhorses of the civil wars had been destroyed in the carnage of Barnet and Tewkesbury. The extinction in the male line of the house of Lancaster, the Beauforts and Hollands, and the emasculation of the Nevilles and other prominent lineages, left no credible focus for an opposition. Significantly it was left to one of the king's brothers, George, duke of Clarence, to toy with this role, but his desultory mischief-making came to an end in 1478. Around the crown there gathered an impressive group of courtiers and regional power-brokers to lend stablility to the regime: the dapper Earl Rivers, the queen's brother; the trusty and resourceful Lord Hastings; the powerful Lords Howard and Stanley. The king's second brother, Richard duke of Gloucester, was a model of loyalty in the north. A new generation of lords and squires were winning their spurs in foreign wars not civil strife. The French expedition of 1475 and the Scottish wars of 1481–2 saw the nation again united in arms and making solid, if not glorious gains at the expense of their traditional enemies. Encouraged by court pageantry and propaganda, Englishmen took pride in a national resurgence which sought inspiration from the Arthurian past and looked to a new age of achievement.[1]

Yet there were ominous signs, and the wary and superstitious saw them all too clearly. It was reckoned that the year would be a bad one for kings and princes. More alarmingly specific was the prophecy that England would see three kings in one year.[2] For all its institutional strength, men knew that the stability of the

Anthony, Earl Rivers, presenting a book to Edward IV; next to Edward are Elizabeth Woodville and their son Edward, later Edward V (Lambeth Palace MS 265, folio VI).

realm still depended on the fragile thread of the royal succession, and on the gossamer-like web of honour and interest which bound together the great magnates behind the throne. Edward IV was still in the prime of life, apparently physically robust if a little corpulent, but his sudden death would throw in jeopardy the achievements of the last decade. For all the hope placed in him, the prince of Wales was only twelve years old, and his premature succession could not fail to disrupt the precarious equilibrium which his bluff but firm father had maintained among the ambitious and jealous courtiers and power-brokers who supported the crown. There were dangers on a number of fronts. The record of royal uncles provided little comfort for a realm confronted with the prospect of another minority, but it was not the possible threat from Richard of Gloucester, the king's loyal lieutenant, which troubled men most at this stage. A cause for far wider consternation was the avarice, arrogance and ambition of the queen's kinsmen: not so much Rivers himself, but her other brothers, and most particularly her son by her first marriage, Thomas Grey, marquis of Dorset. Their inflated share of royal patronage had already provoked considerable resentment. Their clean sweep in the marriage market had enraged Warwick in the 1460s, and did not endear them to proud young aristocrats like the duke of Buckingham who had been forced into disparaging matches. As the prince of Wales was established in an independent household it was natural for his maternal kinsmen to predominate within it, and in the late 1470s through their position on his council they were able to build up a formidable power-base in parts of Wales and the Welsh marches. In the event of a minority, they would be bound to attempt to maintain their influence with the young king, if not in the hope of further aggrandisement at least out of fear of losing that they had won.[3] In their turn, their opponents at court and in the country, like Hastings and Buckingham could be expected to strain every nerve to resist the triumph of the queen's faction. Such men would inevitably look to Richard of Gloucester, whose position would also be necessarily compromised by a Woodville ascendancy. Historical precedent suggested that in the event of a minority he should step in to act as protector of the realm, though perhaps not as full regent. In other times the consequences of a take-over power by Gloucester, who was by temperament a soldier and by background a northerner, might have given the career politicians considerable cause for anxiety. In many respects, not least in his leadership of the old Neville affinity, he represented the forces whose intervention in metropolitan politics had blighted the 1450s and 1460s. If the courtiers, politicians and bureaucrats thought that they could use the king's brother for their own purposes, they were to be sorely disabused.

*　　*　　*

Around Easter 1483 Edward IV fell ill, and then apparently suffered a stroke, sending ripples of consternation through the realm. His condition was critical for two weeks, allowing would-be power-brokers at court and in the country time to take stock of the situation. The king summoned his counsellors to his bedside, enjoining them to make peace with each other, and to co-operate in the execution of his will, to which was now added a codicil that Gloucester should

Elizabeth Woodville, wife of Edward IV (c. 1437–92).

have the protectorate. His strong constitution held out until 9 April, but soon after his death a fierce power struggle began. Queen Elizabeth was well-placed to take the initiative. For all her misfortunes she has found few champions. The widow of the Lancastrian Sir John Grey, she was the 'older woman' who had stolen the heart of England's dashing young prince. Greedy and ambitious at the peak of her fortunes, she won little sympathy in her bereavement, as she and her kinsmen worked with unseemly haste and brazen determination to entrench their interests. She quickly secured the old king's treasure, her son Dorset summoned his retainers and stock-piled arms, while her brother Sir Edward Woodville equipped the fleet as a potential power-base. With the young king and his brother under their tutelage and some support among the churchmen on the royal council, they seemed to hold all the cards. It seemed that not even the wiles of Lord Hastings, the late king's chief counsellor and their chief rival, could stop them pressing for an early coronation, which would then obviate the need for more than a 'care-taker' protectorate.

Unfortunately a number of the key figures on whom this settlement would depend were absent from the capital at this critical time. The young king remained at Ludlow castle. Earl Rivers and Sir Richard Grey, his maternal uncle and half-brother, were with him. Richard of Gloucester was in the north, probably at Middleham castle. There were other prominent lords who instead of coming to Edward IV's funeral waited on events in the provinces. The duke of Buckingham, for example, remained on his estates in south Wales. From the first reports of the king's death such men must have found it hard to obtain reliable information about the manœuvres at Westminster, and were prey to scare-mongering. At this distance in time it is hard to apportion blame, but the factions around Westminster must bear considerable responsibility for the tragic events that unfolded. While the queen's party tightened its grip on government at Westminster, Hastings worked hard to sabotage its plans, notably by seeking to press the protector's claims and working on his suspicions of Woodville intentions.[4] In a stormy meeting at council, Hastings won acceptance for his proposal that the king's retinue in his progress to London should be limited to two thousand, while at the same time urging Gloucester to come well supported. As the two factions vied for tactical advantage, there were ugly confrontations between their retinues in the city. The realm teetered again on the brink of civil war.

Premature news of the king's death had arrived in York at the beginning of April, and Richard of Gloucester was thus given extra time to consider his position. Even when proper intelligence arrived, he moved with extreme circumspection. Unfortunately it is hard to fathom his mind at this stage, and all assessments of his personality and actions derive somewhat from hindsight. For Dominic Mancini and other near contemporary sources it is assumed that from the outset the 'wicked' uncle set his sights on his nephew's crown. Some modern historians have gone to the other extreme, depicting a man forced for his own safety to take the ultimate step of usurpation.[5] Presumably the truth lies somewhere in between, and it is vital to see Richard's character unfolding with events. There are no grounds for assuming that Richard was driven by the sort of singleminded ambition that Shakespeare attributed to him. He had been

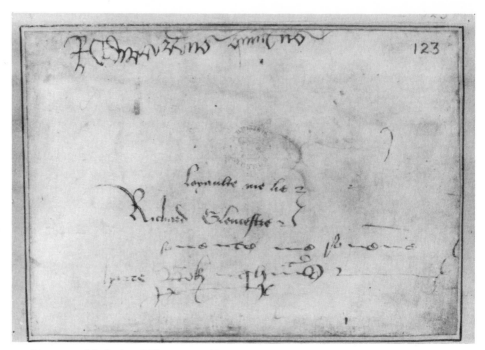

Signatures of the Dukes of Gloucester and Buckingham, with their respective mottoes: 'Loyaulte me Lie' and 'Souvente me Souvene', and above them the signature of the young king 'Edwardus Quintus' (BL Cotton Vespasian F XIII, folio 123).

conspicuously loyal to Edward IV, and there is little basis for the later legend that he had taken every opportunity to clear his path to the crown. In so far as a reputation before 1483 can be inferred it was for the bluff soldierly virtues rather than for political guile. What is known of his first actions at this time fit this picture. At York he led the lords and gentlemen of the region in an oath of obedience to the new king, and wrote personally to the council, protesting his loyalty to the king and his good will to the queen, but firmly asserting his claims to a full protectorate. For two months at least his behaviour was more or less consistent with the view that this position was the extent of his ambitions. On the other hand, there are a number of acts which, set alongside evidence of his later behaviour, make untenable claims of total disingenuousness.

It was on the last day of April that Richard of Gloucester seized control of events. As he led his retinue southwards into the midlands, he must have been alarmed by reports from the capital of the Woodvilles' political successes, perhaps even of their conspiring against him. It had been agreed that the royal progress to London should be routed to allow a juncture between the young king, Earl Rivers and their party for a stately procession into the capital. On arrival at Northampton Richard was angered to learn that the royal entourage had already pressed on to Stony Stratford, and cannot have been consoled by the lame excuses proffered by Rivers, who had remained behind to greet him.[6]

Obviously the Woodvilles were anxious that the king should arrive in the capital before the protector, but it is unlikely that any really sinister plot was afoot. The courtly and pious Rivers at least seems miscast in the role of arch-conspirator. His actions at this time display a basic innocence, perhaps spiced with a naive confidence in his ability to charm and perhaps even win over the protector. Unfortunately the wary Richard was listening to other sirens. With a keen eye for the main chance, the duke of Buckingham had been in early communication with Gloucester, and proffering his firm friendship he had also joined the protector at Northampton. Charming and articulate as well as vain and ambitious, he seems to have rapidly attained considerable personal influence with the protector. Talking late into the night after the departure of Rivers, there can be no doubt that he deliberately fed the protector's fears and sense of injured pride. Early in the morning of 30 April a pre-emptive strike against the Woodvilles was set in motion. Gloucester and Buckingham arrived in force at Stony Stratford. After paying their respects to Edward V, they laid charges of treason against his uncle Rivers and other prominent members of his household, and immediately dispatched them under guard to safe castles in the north.

The news was a major set-back for the queen and her friends in Westminster. There was a brief attempt to organise resistance, but with their enemies in the capital given new heart, with a considerable force advancing on London, and with the fleet under Sir Edward Woodville already at sea, there were no prospects of success. Hurriedly the queen took her younger son and daughters into sanctuary at Westminster, where they were joined by Dorset, the bishop of Salisbury and others. When the new king and the protector rode together into the city on Sunday 4 May, the day originally planned for the coronation, the Londoners gave them a rapturous welcome. As wagons full of weapons emblazoned with Woodville badges were displayed as evidence of a heinous plot against the protectorate, Gloucester was able to sweep to power on a tide of popular sympathy. Normally speaking his reputation as a successful soldier and a dour northern power-broker would have worked against him in metropolitan England, and indeed there doubtless were reservations in many quarters. Yet in the circumstances of the early summer of 1483, such qualities might have endeared him to the Londoners. To a people somewhat disgusted by the licentiousness of Edward IV's court, the greed of the queen and her relatives, and the cynical intrigues of recent times, the valiant and austere northerner might have appeared like a fresh and bracing wind.

For some time there was optimism that the ship of state could be restored to an even keel. Of course, while the king was still a twelve year old child, there could be few grounds for complacency, but during May and early June the prospect of political stability was more than a mirage. The protector took the helm, but otherwise the key-note of his regime was continuity. As befitted the late king's most trusted friend and counsellor, Lord Hastings found himself back at the heart of government. He continued as lord chamberlain, and was confirmed in the governorship of Calais and the mastership of the mint, valuable sources respectively of men-at-arms and money. With the conspicuous exception of the queen's kinsmen, the magnates who had held office under Edward IV were encouraged to put their weight behind the protectorate, which in fact

Garter stall plate of Henry Stafford, Duke of Buckingham, from St George's Chapel, Windsor.

reflected better than most governments the balance of power in the country at large. Even the clerical counsellors who had rather supinely followed the Woodville line were retained. Archbishop Rotherham was relieved of the chancellorship, but he and Bishop Morton of Ely remained on the council, while his replacement was the experienced and widely respected Bishop Russell. All in all, the regime was both broadly based and impressive in membership, and its preparations for a parliament and a coronation to be held in late June inspired further confidence.

In the second week of June the mood changed dramatically. The atmosphere in London became tense with intrigue, suspicion and fear. There are no surviving grants under Edward V's name after 8 June, and it might well be around this time that Richard finally determined to take the crown himself. Certainly there was a legion of unresolved problems and disquieting trends which could only be brought to a head and countered by decisive action. He was

on the horns of a dilemma. His term as protector was severely limited, and after
the coronation his position could deteriorate overnight. He had little enough
time even to establish himself sufficiently to secure a line of retreat. The queen
and her kinsmen remained thorns in his side. They refused to release the king's
young brother from sanctuary, and retained the late king's treasure and the fleet.
Rivers and others were in custody, but the council declined to accede to the
protector's demand that they be arraigned of treason. The unwillingness of
many of the councillors to back him to the hilt is understandable. In all
likelihood suspicions were already entertained of his real intentions. For the few
who might still have believed him the political innocent, there were even
stronger reasons for not offending the young king's maternal kinsmen, who
would have appeared the men of the future. By 10 June at least Richard and
Buckingham, his closest ally, had found their position intolerable, and
determined on a series of pre-emptive strikes against the men who they alleged
were conspiring against them. Urgent letters were sent north requesting military
assistance against the queen and her party who were plotting to destroy them,
along with other lords of the 'old royal blood' and notables from the north and
elsewhere.[7] Their targets now included Hastings, Morton and other members of
the council who had taken to conferring together privately, and through the
agency of Elizabeth ('Jane') Shore, a former royal mistress whose favours
embraced both the lord chamberlain and Dorset, had begun negotiations with
the Woodvilles.

It was time for a showdown, and again Richard surprised his adversaries with
the speed and ruthlessness of his actions. On Friday 13 June he summoned
Hastings and other suspect members of the council to the Tower of London for
a meeting.[8] Here he accused them of treason, and on a pre-arranged signal
men-at-arms arrested them. Hastings was dragged outside and immediately
executed. Rotherham and Morton were taken into custody, as was Lord Stanley,
who had been wounded in the scuffle. The news was spread around that a major
conspiracy had been discovered, and there followed a round-up of real or
potential enemies of the regime. It was probably at this stage that Sir John Fogge
took sanctuary at Westminster. Another associate of the Woodvilles, John
Forster, was seized at his Hertfordshire home, taken to the Tower, kept without
food or drink for several days, and then forced to compound for an immense
fine. What truth there was in the charge of conspiracy is hard to know. Thomas
More's view was that Hastings was destroyed because, having been sounded out
on the matter by William Catesby, he was determined to oppose any move to
dislodge Edward V.[9] Certainly by this stage the protector cared little for legal
niceties in his drive to take power, and the remaining councillors were not
inclined to defy him. It was agreed that a determined effort should be made to
have the duke of York released from sanctuary, on the grounds that he should be
at his brother's side at the coronation. On Monday the queen bowed to the
inevitable and handed over her second son to a delegation headed by the
archbishop of Canterbury, who then lodged him in the Tower with Edward V,
but within days the council had been persuaded by the protector to defer the
coronation until 9 November. It must have been at this time as well that orders
were sent to Sheriff Hutton to proceed with the execution of Rivers, Grey and

Baynard's Castle, London, home of Richard's mother, the Duchess of York, where Richard accepted the crown in 1483.

Sir Thomas Vaughan. In a few short days Richard and Buckingham had eliminated most of their chief opponents without any real opposition, but the alarming reports that they had 20,000 men converging on the capital were doubtless very persuasive to the churchmen, career-bureaucrats and citizens if not to most of the armigerous classes around London.

The stage was being set for the *coup d'etat*. After the commotion following the arrest and execution of Hastings, Richard worked hard to win the confidence of informed opinion of the city, and to woo the populace. Setting aside his mourning clothes in favour of a suitably regal purple attire, he entertained the mayor and aldermen in grand style, and cut a fine figure in the streets. The first straw in the wind was a sermon preached by Dr Ralph Shaw at St Paul's cross on Sunday 22 June. It took as its theme that bastard slips should not take root, and alleged that Edward's IV's marriage with Elizabeth Woodville was invalid, and thus the present king and his brother were illegitimate. Though manifestly politically motivated, the charge itself was not apparently Richard's concoction. It was Robert Stillington, bishop of Bath, a respected churchman, who informed the protector of the old king's pre-contract with another woman which should have prevented his alliance with Elizabeth Woodville. Richard and his friends now began to show their hand. On 24 June or thereabouts Buckingham eloquently addressed gatherings of lords and leading citizens on the latest disclosure, pointing out not only the illegitimacy of Edward V and his brother, but also the ineligibility to succeed, on the grounds of his father's treason, of Edward the son of the duke of Clarence. There is no doubt as to the identity of the man on whom the mantle of office would thus fall, and Buckingham organised a petition detailing the bastardy of the princes and the virtues and title of their uncle, and requesting the latter to assume the crown. On 26 June Richard formally received the petition at his lodgings in Baynard's Castle, and was immediately led in a stately procession to Westminster Hall, where he installed himself on the marble seat and was acclaimed as Richard III. Nothing had been left to chance. Many nobles and commoners, who had assembled for the now cancelled parliament, were in attendance. The new king delivered a well prepared speech about the maintenance of justice. Sir John Fogge, an associate of the Woodvilles, was coaxed out of sanctuary in the abbey, and as a gesture of reconciliation was ceremoniously received into royal favour. The coronation was set for 6 July.

The usurpation had been planned and executed with precision and flair. In the realm at large Richard seems to have achieved a remarkable feat, a near monopoly of effective military power. The great political machines headed by the queen and her party and by Lord Hastings had been immobilised, and in any case it might be that their capacity to raise armies was markedly inferior to the other great power-brokers. In his own right Gloucester controlled a formidable military following: in addition to the choice retinue he brought with him there had been a general mobilisation of the north in his name. Buckingham likewise drew a substantial force from his vast estates. The only other magnates able to commit troops on such a scale were the earl of Northumberland, and Lords Howard and Stanley. Richard worked on all three of them in the early summer. He already had some pact with Northumberland, who doubtless anticipated a freer hand in the north with his colleague's translation to the national stage. He soon had some sort of understanding with Lord Howard, who was granted the dukedom of Norfolk along with his share of the Mowbray inheritance which Edward IV had improperly allowed his second son Richard to retain. Stanley was a tougher proposition, no friend of Richard but too powerful militarily to attack directly. The only option was to seek to bind him to the regime with a combination of fear and favour, and for a few months at least this strategy worked.

With the military balance heavily in his favour, London fell into his hands like an over-ripe fruit. If on the national stage Richard and Buckingham had proved consummate soldier and strategist, in the city they were brilliant actor and impresario. Looking back it is hard to understand the smoothness of their take-over of power, especially since there were numerous lords and gentlemen present in the capital. Many notables must have acquiesced through fear: the execution of Hastings left them stunned and leaderless, if not running for cover. Others presumably thought to gain from the new regime, whether lords and knights previously excluded from power, or merchants like Sir Edmund Shaw, mayor of London, who hoped for lucrative royal commissions. Yet there is much that is hard to explain. The queen's surrender of her second son was critical to the plan, as also was the co-operation of prominent churchmen on the council. The motives of Robert Stillington, bishop of Bath, and Dr Ralph Shaw and Dr John Penketh, both influential theologians, in publicising the bastardy of the princes are hard to fathom. The bishop was a Yorkshire man, and the two preachers, also northerners, had connections with the mayor and possibly with

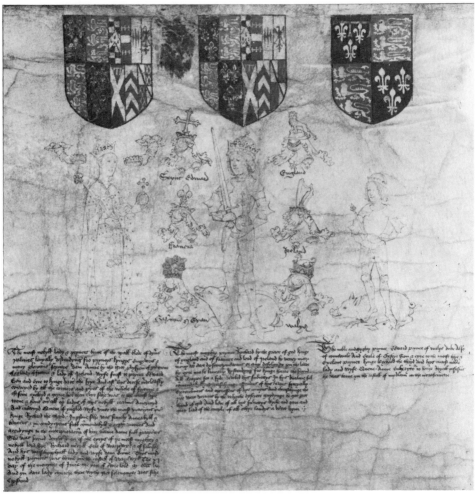

Richard III, Anne Neville and Edward of Middleham; contemporary drawings from the Rous Roll (BL Additional MS 48976).

Edmund Chadderton, treasurer of Richard's household, but there is no evidence of mercenary motives.[10] Since in later life all three seem to have regretted their involvement, it might well be that they were initially impressed by the protector's stand on moral issues. In the first flush of summer there were many others who came under his spell, who would subsequently seek to distance themselves from his regime. Perhaps what needs to be stressed is the mood of tension and anxiety which had built up in London, and individuals and groups feared not only for their own fortunes but also dreaded the renewal of civil strife. Relieved beyond measure to witness the peaceful transfer of power, men willed themselves to believe the propaganda and promises of the new king. Appeasement breeds its own illusions.

For a brief summer Richard III might have found contentment. His coronation was a triumph of pageantry and splendour. Preparations had after all been in train for some time. The ceremony was surprisingly well attended. The dukes of Buckingham and Norfolk played particularly distinguished roles, as also did the earls of Northumberland, Kent and Lincoln, and Lord Stanley. Queen Anne was resplendent, and the great ladies of the realm followed her train, not least Margaret countess of Richmond, Stanley's wife and the mother of Henry Tudor. The new king was doubtless heartened by this remarkable show of solidarity. In the weeks before and after the coronation he had the pleasant task of bestowing honours on old friends like Viscount Lovell and Lords Fitzhugh and Scrope, distributing largesse to his northern retainers and faithful servitors, and making a show of generosity to former enemies. He had reason to suppose that he had won acceptance from the leaders of the community of the realm, and as the business of government slackened for the summer he set out on a stately perambulation of his realm, to reassure and win the hearts of the populace at large though his majesty and munificence.

There can have been few who witnessed the coronation or joined in the festive atmosphere, however, who did not at some stage reflect on the plight of the young boy for whom the ceremony was first planned, and for his brother, who also now languished in the Tower. No matter how much people wished to overlook it, the orderly transfer of power had not been achieved without some bloodshed. Hastings was a respected elder statesman, Rivers was the best of the Woodvilles, highly regarded for his chivalrous honour and pious sensibility: it was hard to justify the execution of either man on grounds other than the harsh dictates of *raison d'état*. In this brutal age the prospects for the princes would have seemed bleak indeed: the security of the regime demanded their elimination. Young Edward himself seems to have recognised political realities, as also did many ordinary Londoners. Dominic Mancini reported that the young king prepared himself for death, while men in the street discussing the fate of the princes could not forebear from shedding tears. As the new king would discover, political necessity does not make the murder of innocent children any less palatable. The complicity of the political nation, however indirect, in the act might also explain the bitterness of the subsequent recriminations against him.

Of course, the fate of the princes in the Tower will remain a mystery, and there can be no conclusive proof that Richard was directly responsible.[11] What is clear is that over the course of the summer the populace of London, many of whom after all must have worked in or supplied the Tower, came to believe that they were no longer alive. Dominic Mancini reported that this was the current belief when he left London early in July, and as the summer progressed other reports of their murder circulated in southern England and the continent. There are hints which suggest that the king might not have actually ordered their murder. Assuming the princes were alive when he left the capital for the tour of the provinces, a letter from Minster Lovell on 29 July might just possibly allude to over-zealous servants taking upon themselves this crime. Referring to the arrest of men who 'of late had taken upon them the fact of an enterprise, as we doubt not you have heard', he instructed the chancellor 'to proceed to the due execution of our laws in that behalf'. It is not impossible that Sir James Tyrell,

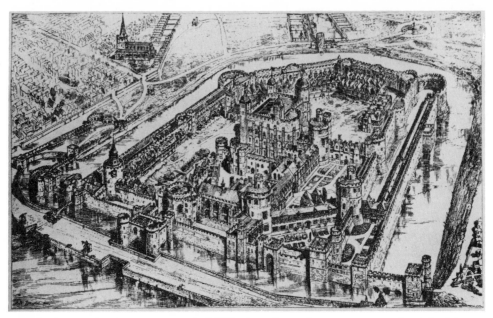

The Tower of London as it was in the Middle Ages; the royal apartments are to the south of the White Tower (drawing by H.W. Brewer).

who was later to 'confess' to the crime was implicated, but a recently discovered London chronicle, probably the earliest extant English record of the princes' fate, points the finger at Buckingham. There are interesting circumstantial details to support the charge. After the king's departure Buckingham was in effective command in the capital, and it is known that when the two men met a month later there was an unholy row between them. Of course, it might well be that Buckingham, not least after his rebellion, was used as the scapegoat. On the other hand the surprised and poignant outcry against Buckingham at the time of his revolt, as he 'who had most cause to be true', seems to allude to a far deeper bond between them than merely the great royal favour shown to the duke.[12]

For the moment the king had cause to be pleased with his progress. From Windsor castle he had ambled to Oxford, where the university community fêted and flattered, eager to seduce him perhaps from his known preference for Cambridge. At Minster Lovell, some miles further along the road, he was able to enjoy the hospitality of his close friend, Viscount Lovell, and inspect his recently completed castle. He pressed on to Gloucester, a town with special associations for him, and in an extravagant moment raised the small urban community to full civic status. His progress took him through Worcester, Warwick and Leicester, whence he sent letters to a large number of knights and gentlemen from the north-west to join his retinue.[13] He pressed on to Nottingham, whose castle he would refurbish and at which he would reside on many subsequent occasions, but the most exhilarating moments must have come after he had crossed the Trent to his old stamping grounds in northern England. The reception accorded him at York was particularly spectacular, and the formal investiture of his son as prince of Wales a few days later must have been the highlight of the tour and one of the few unalloyed joys of his reign. Indeed his honeymoon as king of England was cut cruelly short, appropriately enough within days of recrossing the Trent on his journey southwards. At Lincoln on 11 September he heard the distressing news that there were risings in various southern counties and, more distressingly, that Buckingham had become one of the chief leaders.

Fascinated by the flamboyant personalities and the 'over-mighty subjects' of the Yorkist age, scholars have shown more interest in discussing the motives of Buckingham than in making a proper assessment of the general movement to which he precipitately committed himself. At this distance in time the search for individual motivation, for all its fascination, bears little fruit. Like king-makers before and since, it might be that Buckingham had not been satisfied with the prizes he obtained. Perhaps there were, as early commentators report, some hitches in the promised restoration of the Bohun inheritance, or perhaps there were other expectations of the king that had been disappointed. Then there is the whole matter of the princes in the Tower. Given his key role in the usurpation, Buckingham had no cause to be squeamish about their fate, and indeed joining in the chorus of calumny against the king might well have been a means of disguising his own responsibility for the crime. What is often obscured through too close attention to Buckingham, however, is the degree to which the rebellion had a momentum wholly independent of the duke's machinations. Over the summer right across southern England there were meetings of lords, knights and gentlemen aiming first to restore the sons of Edward IV to the throne, and as rumours spread of their death, to retrieve his daughters from sanctuary. The marquis of Dorset and the Woodvilles obviously promoted the scheme, and some old Lancastrians were also involved, like Sir Edward Courtenay, claimant to the earldom of Devon, but the rebels were no mere creatures of aristocratic faction. Three main theatres of revolt have been identified – Kent and the south-east, south-central England and the West Country – and in each the chief conspirators were leaders of their respective county communities, with distinguished records of service to the crown both in local government and in the royal household itself.[14] Sir John Fogge, a rebel despite the king's offer of an olive branch, was a former treasurer and privy counsellor for Edward IV. Sir George Brown, Sir Thomas Bourchier, Sir William Norris, Sir Giles Daubeney, Sir William Berkeley of Beverstone, Sir William Stonor, Sir Walter Hungerford, Sir Thomas St Leger and John Cheney had all been numbered among the select band of 'knights and squires of the body' to the late king, and between them they had served as sheriff of almost every county from the Thames estuary to Land's End. Reports of the princes' deaths probably first shook the movement but then stiffened its resolve. Through the mediation of Margaret Beaufort a marriage was projected between Elizabeth of York and Henry Tudor, the Lancastrian pretender. The queen-dowager, Margaret Beaufort and some of the Kentish leaders were at the centre of this wider conspiracy, and from all accounts Buckingham was only drawn in by their ally, and his prisoner, Bishop Morton. In the last analysis Buckingham probably decided to join the insurrection because he believed that it had the

Sir John Cheney, later Lord Cheney (died 1499); effigy in Salisbury Cathedral, wearing Garter robes and SS collar.

strength to succeed, and because he knew that otherwise it would destroy him in its wake.

Certainly the rebellion of the autumn of 1483 represented a formidable challenge to the king, and as he cut back across the midlands he must have been wondering how far the conflagration would spread. If Buckingham had raised the standard of rebellion, other lords less implicated in the regime might follow suit. Lord Stanley was of doubtful loyalty. His wife was a conspirator, and it seems that his son Lord Strange, after receiving appeals from both sides, mobilised a massive force of family retainers and levies, without making his intentions known.[15] Richard ordered a general muster at Leicester, and was doubtless much relieved when the Stanleyites fell in behind his northern army. Indeed it must have soon become apparent that for all its political strength, the rising was militarily weak. Its strategy was sound in theory. The rebels in the Home Counties would secure London and release the queen and princesses, while Buckingham and Dorset would raise armies in Wales and the West Country to support the invasion of Henry Tudor. Lacking in centralised direction, however, the insurrection misfired. The rising in Kent broke out too early, and was unable to secure its crucial objectives. Buckingham proved a weak straw, scarcely able to raise his own tenantry, while Dorset could not even provide a safe landfall for the exiles. For their part Richard and his allies acted decisively and with sound strategic sense. At the first whiff of trouble the duke of

Great Seal of Richard III (engraving from Sandford's Genealogical History*).*

Norfolk moved to defend London and to break the back of rebellion in the south-east. Humphrey Stafford of Grafton similarly contained Buckingham by seizing control of the Severn bridges. As the king's army pushed south-westwards from Leicester, the rebels lost heart. Betrayed ignominiously by one of his own servants, Buckingham was brought in chains to Salisbury, where he was summarily executed on All Souls day. Forced marches brought the king rapidly to the south coast, and within weeks he was mopping up the last pockets of resistance in the West Country. Buffeted by storms in the channel and dismayed by the failure of his allies, Henry Tudor sailed despondently back to the continent.

Despite its poor military showing, the rebellion had grave consequences for Richard III. At one level it had proved too easy, and his experience might well have led him to over-estimate the potency of his call to arms and to under-estimate the resolution of his opponents at Bosworth two years later. On the other hand in his moment of triumph the king might not have fully counted the costs of the rising. On reflection it must have been painfully apparent that his government, whatever its strength militarily, had been shown to be very fragile in political terms. Buckingham earned his just deserts, and there was a grim satisfaction in that, but it could not have been overlooked that the regime had lost one of its most powerful props. His two other chief enemies, Henry Tudor and the marquis of Dorset, had escaped to fight another day. Bishops Morton and Courtenay likewise had fled abroad. Probably even more unnerving the king knew that he had lost at a stroke almost all the knights and squires from southern England on whose loyalty and service the Yorkist monarchy had depended for a generation. Brown and St Leger were captured and executed, but many others joined the swelling band of refugees in Brittany. Without waiting for formal acts of attainder, the king confiscated their lands, inevitably spawning a large, new and unusually distinguished class of disinherited dissidents. Facing total destruction, the opponents of Richard III could not be expected to lessen their resolve. Rallying around the exiled Lancastrian pretender they were in a better position to sink their differences, coordinate their plans, and to learn from their experience.

Of course, the victory added considerably to the king's reserves of patronage The forfeitures of Buckingham and many other notables released a flood of honours, posts and properties across the length and breadth of southern England. While still on campaign the king doled out valuable prizes to his comrades-in-arms. A large proportion of the early grants, plundered from Buckingham, went to the Stanleys and their retainers, whose military support, however grudging, was probably critical. The names of the king's northern friends and retainers likewise figure prominently in the grants, with men like Lord Scrope of Bolton, Sir Richard Radcliffe, Sir Thomas Markenfield, Sir Ralph Ashton and Robert Brackenbury richly endowed in the southern counties. Although a number of northerners like Lord Fitzhugh, Sir John Huddleston and Halnath Mauleverer already had interests in the south on which to build, and although a number of southern loyalists like Lord Dinham and John Sapcote also benefited, there does seem to have been, as the Crowland chronicler alleged, a systematic policy of implantation. When the honour of Tonbridge, Kent was granted to Sir Marmaduke Constable the inhabitants were informed that the Yorkshire knight was 'to make his abode' in the locality and 'to have the rule' of the men of the lordship.[16] It was a bold, almost revolutionary strategy, but it seems to have been less a product of policy than desperation. The distribution of so much largesse while still on campaign indicates that in terms of bargaining-power his supporters had the upper hand. Such a view is confirmed by the evidence that he bent over backwards to rehabilitate proven traitors like Bourchier, Hungerford and numerous others. His treatment of Margaret Beaufort was likewise generous: her person and her estates were simply committed to the custody of her husband. For all the hostility and opprobrium it engendered, it might well be that his military style plantation of southern England was less a high-handed and vengeful act of tyranny than a confession of political bankruptcy.

As 1483 came to a close, Richard III must have hoped that the last major challenge to his throne had been defeated. Even when intelligence arrived of his enemies gathering in exile to swear allegiance to Henry Tudor, it might not have greatly disturbed his composure. After his easy triumph, the rulers of Europe, not least the duke of Brittany, were inclined to take his government more seriously. Indeed on the continent the general view seems to have been that he had attained a position of strength unprecedented in recent English history.[17] The magnificence of his court added conviction to his status as monarch, even if it laid him open to the charges of licentiousness that he had levelled at his brother. Likewise the reserves of patronage available to him enabled him at first to live grandly, to reward his supporters, and be generous to the uncommitted, without having to resort to unpopular financial exactions. He could look forward to the opening of his first parliament, postponed from November on account of the disturbances, in which he intended to affirm in the most solemn and authoritative way his title to the throne, and to give statutory authority to the punishments meted out to the rebels. More important it would be the occasion for showing his qualities as a ruler, for conciliatory gestures, for appeals for moral reform, and for legislation to promote the 'common weal'. What he had no means of knowing was how long it would take for the wounds of 1483 to heal, whether infection had taken deep root and whether the drastic surgery he had applied had attacked the symptoms but aggravated the disease.

Signature of Richard III.

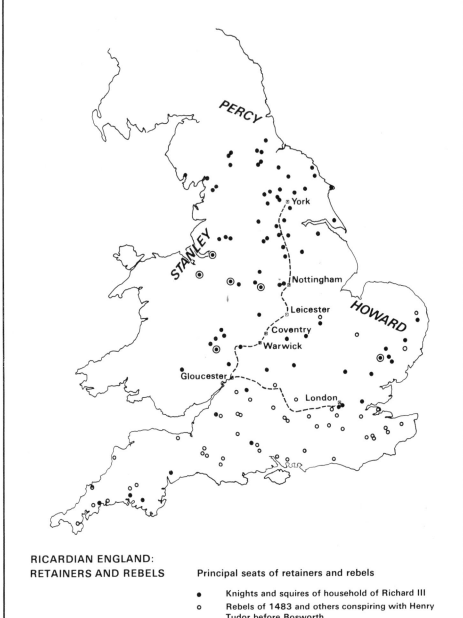

RICARDIAN ENGLAND:
RETAINERS AND REBELS

Principal seats of retainers and rebels

- ●   Knights and squires of household of Richard III
- ○   Rebels of 1483 and others conspiring with Henry Tudor before Bosworth
- ⊙   Men in both categories
- ----   Itinerary of Richard III July to September 1483
- PERCY   Noble families with regional power-bases

Information drawn from Horrox & Hammond, *British Library Harleian Manuscript 433*, IV, and Edwards, *Itinerary of Richard III*.

4 Kings, Pretenders and Powerbrokers

It is not just the magic of Shakespeare which tends to telescope Richard III's reign into a number of acts culminating at Bosworth. After the usurpation, rebellion and settlements of 1483–4, there is a sense in which the nation was waiting for, almost counting time towards the final climax and resolution. It is almost as if the main political actors found themselves frozen in the positions that they had found themselves over the winter. For the king it was a dogged determination to maintain himself on the throne in the face of all misfortunes. For his close friends and supporters it was a steadfastness born of loyalty, complicity or gross material interest. For many others it was a numbness born of incapacity or a paralysis bred of fear. For the exiles it was the listlessness of waiting, hope against hope. Of course, the mundane life of England continued in its own humdrum fashion. William Caxton even felt that he could tempt the English reading public with a second edition of *The Canterbury Tales* as well as his *King Arthur* at this time. Yet the impression of listlessness is not simply derived from chronicles written up in hindsight. In the last eighteen months of Richard III's reign the volume of chancery business declined dramatically. Judging from extant private muniment collections, too, it seems that the nobility and gentry were less active in making land settlements at this time. While it would be rash to place too much reliance on arguments from silence, it is hard to escape the impression that 1485 in particular was a time of political uncertainty, a time of postponing decisions, a time of watching and waiting.

*   *   *

His face somewhat world weary and his small frame tense with nervous energy, the king holds centre stage in this still life.[1] The earliest portraits of him give the lie to the Tudor image of the villainous hunchback, and present a man with a sensitive rather than brutal face, and a handsome, trim physique, even if with a hint of a droop in one shoulder. At the time of his accession he was only thirty-one years old, but the innocence of childhood must even then have been a distant memory. Of course, there is precious little truth in the 'black legend' of his life before 1483. One of Shakespeare's more derisory calumnies is to assign Richard a prominent role in the blood-letting at St Albans in 1455, when in truth he was a two-year-old toddler. What is clear is that his childhood must

Middleham, Yorkshire, residence of Richard of Gloucester 1472–83 while ruling the North for Edward IV.

have been cruelly cut short and his development permanently scarred by the vicissitudes of the 1450s and 1460s. The most formative years of adolescence were spent in the household of his mother's kinsmen, the Nevilles, at Middleham castle. It was here he met his future bride, the daughter of Warwick the Kingmaker, and developed lasting friendships with the young nobles and gentlemen who gravitated around the house of Neville. Yet he proved steadfast in his loyalty to Edward IV when their other brother George duke of Clarence joined Warwick in the rebellions of 1469–70. The young duke of Gloucester played a prominent role in winning back the kingdom for Edward in 1471, but there is no early evidence that he was responsible for any of the battlefield executions, or for the subsequent murder of Henry VI. Through the 1470s he served the crown faithfully as lieutenant in the north and chief field commander, and even in retrospect it is impossible to find evidence of any higher ambition. Whatever his private feelings about Clarence, he pleaded for his life in 1478. On the death of Edward IV there was no general suspicion of his motives, and even after his usurpation of the throne there seems to have been a willingness in many quarters to believe the best of him.

Once king of England, Richard III set out to win the hearts and minds of his subjects. He brought to the tasks of kingship many sterling qualities. In contrast to his brother he could present himself as a virtuous Christian prince and champion of the church. His strictures against immorality at court and his zeal for the reform of public morals, though advantageous politically, were not wholly cynical. From his personal prayers and his taste in books it is known that he was a man of deep religious sensibilities.[2] He was a generous patron of the church: he even stimulated the cult of Henry VI by translating his remains to Windsor. His appointments to church livings were impeccable. Some of the most learned and reform-minded churchmen of the time seem to have entertained great hopes of him, and their role in winning public acceptance of his coup might have been crucial. Though less physically imposing than his predecessor, he had a regal bearing, and from all accounts looked a true son of the house of Plantagenet. His lack of inches was more than compensated by his prowess in arms, and no one could doubt his capacity to lead the realm in war. According to a European visitor to his court, he had a deep-seated desire to crusade against the Turks, who were then making savage inroads into Christendom.[3] He had all the makings of a great soldier-king. Far from being mean, jealous and vindictive, he was a man of real magnanimity and generosity. He was loyal to his friends, and forgiving of his enemies. Initially at least he was lavish in the distribution of honours and largesse, and made a show of refusing grants made by the towns he visited and abolishing the notorious 'benevolences' by act of parliament. Above all he was able to represent himself as the champion of justice. Doubtless he was most at home with the rough-and-ready, equitable adjudication associated with 'good lordship'. On his first summer progress he listened to the suits of poor people, and was commended for redressing many long-standing wrongs. He knew the realities of court procedure at the local level, and took measures to combat the problems of corruption and intimidation. As well as a practical concern for 'the administration of justice whereunto we be professed', he showed considerable interest in the finer aspects of jurisprudence. His legislation won grudging admiration in Tudor times, and on occasion at least he had lengthy consultations with the judges at Westminster on the reform of the land law.[4]

This review of the very real qualities which he brought to the task of kingship merely underlines the magnitude of Richard III's failure. It would be easy to claim that the just and generous ruler degenerated over the course of his reign into a savage and lustful tyrant, but the problems seem to have been there at the outset. Soon after he left London the dangerous rumour that he had ordered the murder of the princes in the Tower spread abroad, following his glorious progress across the midlands and then to the north like a long, dark shadow. The strength of repugnance was such as to precipitate a general rising in all the counties lying south of the line marked by his itinerary, which welded together in a formidable combination the old Yorkist establishment and the Lancastrian diehards in exile. Inevitably the challenge of the rising pushed the king further along the dangerous path towards military rule and 'tyranny'. The basic necessity of making the southern counties governable, as well as the need to find the means to commit his allies more firmly to the regime, dictated an ambitious programme of confiscation and resettlement, which only added to the resolve

Garter stall plate of Francis, Viscount Lovell, from St George's Chapel, Windsor.

and ammunition of his enemies. Apparently triumphant in the winter of 1483–4 Richard III was no nearer translating his undoubted military superiority into political dominance than he had been at his usurpation. Perhaps he lacked time to entrench himself, to win over the malcontents, and to secure through good government the hearts of the people. There were moments when he came close to eliminating the threat from his opponents: the queen-dowager lost the will to resist, and made her peace, while Henry Tudor was almost extradited from Brittany. For each step forward, however, there was a corresponding rebuff, not least a succession of personal tragedies which dogged the king.

From early 1484 there are unmistakable signs that the regime of Richard III was crumbling. The parliament which assembled to ratify the title of the king and to give legislative form to the measures which he hoped might secure his reputation can scarcely have been an impressive representation of the community of realm. There are no records of its membership, and its choice of William Catesby (a prominent adviser of the king but with no previous parliamentary experience) as speaker hardly inspires confidence. The need to rehearse the legitimacy of his title not only in parliament but also in the city hall and all the county towns of England is also telling. The number of attainders

Edward of Middleham, Prince of Wales (died 1484); effigy at Sheriff Hutton, Yorkshire.

passed against rebels was unprecedented in a single session: one hundred, as opposed to one hundred and forty for the whole of Edward IV's reign. The morale of the king and the prospects of his line were shattered in April 1484 by the sudden death of Edward prince of Wales, the king's only legitimate son and the focus of all his ambitions. Though fear gripped the realm, the enemies of the regime gained heart. The circle around the king became perceptibly thinner, not least as the flow of royal patronage was reduced to a trickle. Three of the king's chief counsellors, Sir Richard Radcliffe, William Catesby and Viscount Lovell, were publicly lampooned as 'the rat, the cat and Lovell the dog', who ruled all England under the 'hog'. More seriously the author of this doggerel, William Collingbourne, was engaged in conspiring to bring Henry Tudor to England. There seem to have been a number of other plots uncovered from late 1484, often involving men who had only recently been pardoned for their rebellion in 1483. Bankrupt financially, politically and morally, the regime resorted to ever more arbitrary and desperate expedients, including a resort to 'forced loans' from churchmen as well as prominent laymen, losing all claims to be more than a thinly disguised tyranny.[5]

Through a heroic act of will Richard III steeled himself to his fate. Given what is known about the spiritual climate of the age, as well as what is known of his own attitudes and actions, he cannot but have been ravaged by self-doubt and guilt. Even if he had not been directly responsible for the deaths of his nephews, it is probable that he held himself in some measure culpable. Though normally eager to refute, on oath or otherwise, even the grossest allegations, it is significant that there is no record of any public denial of the murder. The king might at first have hoped that the crime would be seen as a grim necessity in dangerous times, perpetrated at the instance of the dead Buckingham, and would be forgotten once the realm was offered the blessings of peace, stability and justice. Perhaps many people did succumb to this sort of moral cowardice in the first half of his reign, and it might explain the bitterness of their subsequent repudiation of him. Yet even before the reign was a year old the king began to appear to his subjects, perhaps even to himself, as a man marked down for divine retribution. The king was devastated by the death of his son, and the tragedy might well have placed an intolerable strain on his relationship with his wife, for there seems to be no expectation of further fruit from their union. By the end of 1484 it was alleged that the king wished to put her away, and marry his niece, Elizabeth of York. When Queen Anne died early in 1485 there was talk that she had been poisoned. On the prompting of his chief counsellors Richard denied on oath having any designs on his niece, but ugly rumours continued to circulate, even in the hitherto loyal north. As the king's charisma hæmorrhaged away, and as dynastic failure compounded the wretchedness of his position, there can have been few men who had confidence in the future of the regime. All that was known was that Richard had the martial skills and the military power to hold the realm in thrall, and that his opponents were weak, divided and untried. Frustrated by his lack of opportunity to meet his enemies and prove his title on the field of battle, eager both for his own and his subjects' benefit to have divine judgement pronounced upon him, the king seems to have yearned for the ultimate trial by combat. In the summer of 1485, as he took up his position at Nottingham castle, 'the castle of Care', it must have seemed that he had been waiting an eternity for this crucial encounter.

*   *   *

Fretting in exile, waiting for his destiny to be revealed, Henry Tudor looked back on a whole lifetime spent in limbo. His ancestry had offered no sure prospects, but endless potential for adventurism. His paternal line stretched back, in imagination at least, to the great Welsh chieftain Cadwaladr, but in more recent times it had been embodied in a proud, but relatively undistinguished Welsh gentry family whose principal seat was at Penmynydd in Anglesey.[6] His great-grandfather was a younger son of Tudur ap Goronwy, who along with his brothers sought his fortune in the service of the Black Prince and Richard II. After the usurpation of 1399 they threw in their lot with Owain Glyn Dŵr, and for a time suffered forfeiture of their lands. The new prince of Wales, the future Henry V, however, worked hard to win Welsh acceptance for the Lancastrian dynasty, and it is not really surprising to find as a page in his household Owain ap Maredudd, known under the English name of Owen Tudor. What is more remarkable is the subsequent career of this dashing and smooth-talking courtier. Around 1430 polite society was outraged to discover

SOVVENT ME SOVVIENT

Margaret Beaufort (1443–1509), mother of Henry VII by her first husband Edmund Tudor, Earl of Richmond, she later married Thomas Lord Stanley.

that he had secretly married Catherine of Valois, the widow of Henry V, and sired sons. For a time the future looked black for the children of this *ménage*, with Owen arrested and Catherine packed off to a monastery. Fortunately the gentle young Henry VI took a shine to his new Tudor half-brothers, making two of them peers and granting them modest patrimonies. Jasper, earl of Pembroke was to repay the debt of gratitude with over fifty years of unstinted service to the house of Lancaster. Edmund, earl of Richmond died young in 1456, several months before the birth of a son who would be named in honour of Henry VI and would ultimately prove his avenger. His widow, still but a girl, was Margaret daughter and heiress of John Beaufort, duke of Somerset. Despite the father's connections with the king, it was the mother's line which would be crucial in giving the posthumous child a claim to the throne. Descended from an irregular union between John of Gaunt and Catherine Swynford, the Beauforts had been legitimated but specifically barred from the royal succession in Richard II's time. Nevertheless their royal blood and their close kinship were widely recognised, and it seems likely that at the court of Henry VI they would have been favourites for the succession in the event of the failure of the main line of the house of Lancaster. In the event the blood-letting which destroyed Henry VI and his son also extinguished the Beauforts in the male line, leaving young Henry Tudor as the forlorn hope of the diehard Lancastrians.

Temperamentally Henry Tudor was not cut out for the life of an adventurer, and in later life he would embrace a regimen of dull routine like a long sought prize. His early life was scarred by personal misfortune and privation. He was born in January 1457, his father dead and his mother only fourteen years old. For a while the pair resided under the protection of Jasper Tudor at Pembroke castle, but any hopes of domestic tranquility were shattered by the vicissitudes of politics. The Yorkist triumph in 1461 assured the local advancement of Lord Herbert, who not only took the earldom of Pembroke but also the wardship of Henry Tudor. Deprived of his uncle, who was to spend most of the next two decades in exile, the young boy also lost the comforting presence of his mother, the remarkable Lady Margaret, countess of Richmond, who took a second husband in 1464. Little is known of Henry at this time, but he seems to have been generally well treated in the Herbert household. Between 1469 and 1471 the twists and turns of national politics presumably raised and dashed his hopes alternately. In 1470 Jasper Tudor was a prominent member of the unholy alliance which restored Henry VI to the throne, and it is possible that Henry was for a time united with his mother and presented at court. His time in the sun was all too brief, and after the collapse of the Lancastrian regime in 1471 his uncle hurriedly arranged their escape to France. Ill-fortune landed them on the Breton shore, and they were taken into custody by Francis II, duke of Brittany.

For over a decade Henry Tudor, styling himself earl of Richmond, served as a bargaining-counter in a three-cornered game of war and diplomacy involving England, France and Brittany. Struggling hard to maintain himself against French interference, the duke of Brittany needed to oblige Edward IV, and was inclined to hand over the Lancastrian pretender or at least keep him in close detention. At one stage Henry was actually surrendered to English agents, and was only saved by some quick thinking on his own part and a fortuitous change

Henry VII (1455–1509); bust by Pietro Torrigiano, about 1508–9.

of heart at the ducal court. Almost certainly the Yorkist monarchy was not so much concerned with securing the exile, who at first presented no real threat, as with preventing his fleeing to France, where he could have become a real source of mischief. The deaths of both Edward IV and Louis XI in 1483 left the duke of Brittany more room to manœuvre, and when the English rebels called on Henry to be their king, the Breton government provided him with transport and arms. The enterprise was a fiasco, with the pretender's flotilla dispersed by gales and his allies put to flight. It was in an atmosphere of defiance rather than of optimism that at Rennes cathedral on Christmas day 1483 Henry Tudor, now joined by many distinguished refugees, solemnly promised to marry Elizabeth of York and laid formal claim to the English crown.

The total triumph of Richard III not only destroyed his immediate prospects but also threatened to jeopardise his Breton sanctuary. The duke of Brittany himself felt honour-bound to protect his guest, but by summer the hard-headed chancellor Pierre Landois was willing to meet English demands. Fortunately appraised of the extradition plans, Henry and a few companions made a daring bid for the French border, and were soon followed by the rest of the English exiles. Charles VIII of France gave them a royal welcome, and for some months they followed the court in its itinerary. While the French regency council greatly relished the irritation that harbouring them caused the king of England, however, it was chary of making any large-scale commitment to their schemes. Even for the most hawkish of French ministers, the prospects of the penniless and inexperienced pretender's toppling Richard III from his throne must have seemed very slim. Concerned to prevent the English lending support to Brittany, the French presumably saw greatest advantage in maintaining the threat rather than hazarding the reality of an invasion. Henry must have been frustrated by the irresolution of the French court and by the slipperiness of royal diplomacy. Nevertheless there were real strengths to his position in France. He was now treated as the rightful heir to the English crown, and could maintain a sort of court in exile. If still without resources he seems to have been rather more credit-worthy. More important he was freer and better-placed to communicate with his allies in England, and during his year in France he was able to receive not only messages and money from his well-wishers but also a steady stream of recruits to his cause.

*   *   *

From the small circle of family retainers who had shared the long decade of exile in Brittany, the entourage of Henry Tudor had grown into a company several hundred strong by the time of the escape to France. Apart from his uncle Jasper Tudor, none of the original exiles were men of note, though some of the names are known from subsequent rewards. It was the circumstances of 1483 which dramatically altered the size, standing and mood of this group. Soon after the usurpation of Richard III, Sir Edward Woodville, former admiral, seems to have made contact with the Tudors, and by the late summer other gentlemen were beating a path to their door. Thus Hugh Conway and Thomas Romney were sent by Margaret Beaufort and other conspirators to involve Henry Tudor in the rising in southern England. The collapse of the rebellion in November led many notables to seek refuge on the continent. Though some like Bishop Morton and John Haliwell established bases elsewhere, most sought out the Lancastrian pretender. The West Country contingent, including the marquis of Dorset, the bishop of Exeter, the claimants to the earldom of Devon and the barony of Welles, Sir Edward Woodville, Sir Giles Daubeney, Sir William Berkeley and many other squires, most naturally found a Breton landfall. Many of the leading rebels from the south-east, however, also seem to have made their way to Rennes by Christmas 1483. Such young exiles as Richard Guildford and Edward Poynings had a close personal attachment with Henry Tudor from this time.

From his more secure and accessible quarters at the French court, Henry

'Henry VII Tower', Pembroke Castle, birthplace of Henry Tudor.

Tudor was able to make significant additions to his following. It was possible to begin to tap systematically the growing fund of good will towards him in England. In the course of 1484 Sir Richard Edgecombe, John Risley, William Brandon and other conspirators left their homes to join him. Hugh Conway and Christopher Urswick, both in the service of Margaret Beaufort, stayed on at his makeshift court. Through this same connection came Thomas Savage, a civil lawyer, whose recruitment was the more appreciated in that his lineage was one of the most powerful in Cheshire and he was the nephew of Lord Stanley. Other members of the overseas student community enlisted, the most notable being the learned Richard Fox. At the same time English merchants trading on the continent could be drawn in to provide money and arms: William Bret, a draper of London, purchased armour for the rebels in France.[7] Even more important for the invasion plans was the ability of the exiles to win support among the English soldiers in the garrisons in the march of Calais. Thus the captain of Hammes castle, James Blount, and his lieutenant, John Fortescue, defected to Henry Tudor soon after his escape to France, bringing with them not only a much-needed contingent of professional soldiers but also an even more welcome recruit, their former prisoner the earl of Oxford.

John de Vere, the earl of Oxford, was the head of the oldest surviving noble house, and could not but add immense lustre to the rebel cause. For several centuries his lineage had played a distinguished role in the life of the nation, and in some areas at least theirs was a name with which to conjure. Even with the real earl in custody, a pseudo-earl had been able to cause the Yorkist authorities in Essex some disquiet in the 1470s. Indeed the thirteenth earl had a reputation in his own right. After the execution of his father and brother by Edward IV in 1462, young John de Vere had been allowed to win his way back to favour with the new regime, but predictably he seized the opportunities presented him by his brother-in-law Warwick to turn the tables on the Yorkist king, playing a leading role in the invasion from France which secured the 'readeption' of Henry VI. Escaping from the carnage at Barnet in 1471, he remained a thorn in the side of the Yorkist monarchy by staging a number of armed incursions from the coast and by his capture of St Michael's Mount, which he held over the winter of 1473–4. After his surrender he was imprisoned at Hammes, where he won the respect of his custodians. Rather significantly Richard III, aware of the danger of his escaping to join the exiles in France, commanded his return to England in November, but his orders either prompted the escape or arrived too late. According to Jean Molinet, Lord Stanley engineered the defection of Blount, who as a former retainer of Lord Hastings, might well have needed little encouragement. At least there can be no doubt that in throwing in his lot with Henry Tudor, the earl of Oxford, the last great champion of the house of Lancaster, added considerably to the credibility of the pretender's cause both in France and in England. Of course, he could not have contributed financially to the enterprise: his patrimony had been confiscated, with the lion's share granted to the duke of Norfolk. At the same time his following in East Anglia must have become somewhat attenuated over the years. Yet Oxford was an appealing figure, with real political gifts, and it seems probable that families like the Pastons wished him well. Of more immediate significance he was a seasoned and

John de Vere, Earl of Oxford (died 1514); drawing by Daniel King (1653) of an alabaster effigy destroyed in 1730.

Oxford's signature.

a spirited commander. At Barnet his inspired generalship on the left wing had driven his opponents from the field, and his military reputation had been further enhanced by his exploits at St Michael's Mount. Without Oxford to command in the field, it is hard to imagine Henry Tudor daring to venture into the heart of England and to meet his royal adversary in battle.[8] Certainly Richard III appreciated the potential value of Oxford to the rebel movement, and it was probably in response to news of the escape that on 3 December he issued his first proclamation denouncing Henry Tudor and his associates as traitors who had put themselves under the obedience of the French king and who plotted the destruction of the realm.

There is precious little evidence from which to reconstruct the atmosphere in the camp of Henry Tudor in the first half of 1485. As the months dragged on it must have been hard to maintain morale. A great deal probably depended on gauging the changing mood at the French court, and assessing the latest intelligence from England. Some of the young gallants probably enjoyed their time in Paris, others seem to have been joined by their wives. William Brandon's eldest son was born in exile, and was named Charles, presumably in honour of the king of France. There were moments of great exhilaration, as when the earl of Oxford rode into the camp, but also times of great despondency, as when Richard III managed through the queen-dowager to tempt the fickle marquis of Dorset to come in out of the cold. Doubtless there was a great desire simply to see some action, and the chroniclers naturally batten on to their few exploits; their relief of the garrison at Hammes, for example, or Humphrey Cheney's dramatic recapture of Dorset. At times the exiles must have despaired of ever seeing their homes again, and though schooled in misfortune Henry Tudor found some of its blows hard to bear. According to Polydore Vergil, the news that reached him, perhaps as late as early summer 1485, that Richard was going to marry Elizabeth of York, 'pinched Henry by the very stomach'. Though he gamely looked around for other advantageous matches, he must have known that he depended on this alliance with the White Rose for a great proportion of the support he hoped to gain in England.

*   *   *

In the summer of 1484 Richard III appeared unassailable. With his chief enemies dead or languishing in exile, and with the queen-dowager and other malcontents bowing to the inevitable and making their peace, he seemed to foreign observers the most powerful English monarch in generations. While Henry Tudor was harried from his Breton bolt-hole, and haggled with the French king for men and money, King Richard had at his disposal the immense resources of the kingdom. Commissions of array could raise, at short notice and at the rate-payer's expense, large contingents of reasonably well-trained and well-equipped foot-soldiers to assist the king in the defence of the realm.[9] Most of the chief magnates would have felt honour-bound to provide private retinues of men-at-arms, and there were specific obligations of this sort on the numerous office-holders and annuitants in the country as well as on the 'knights of the body' and other fee'd men of the household. An established monarch and anointed king would seem to hold all the best cards. His ability to deploy them, however, inevitably depended on the quality of his relations with his subjects and the circumstances of the hour. It might well have been advantageous to the king in terms of his raising the militia, for example, that the threat posed by Henry Tudor took the form of a foreign-backed invasion rather than a regionally based insurrection. On the other hand, since commissions of array were often led by local magnates, the king's standing with them remained crucial. It is here that there are real question marks over the strength of the Ricardian regime. While it is fairly easy to identify the small circle of exiles who were firmly committed to Henry Tudor, it is rather more difficult to name with certainty the lords and gentlemen who would stand up and fight for the king.

It is generally assumed that Richard III relied to an inordinate degree on the network of friends and retainers he had built up in the north as heir of the Nevilles and his brother's lieutenant in the region. The company which he brought to London in May 1483, the military following which menaced the capital at the time of the usurpation, and the army which suppressed the rebellion in November, were composed almost entirely of northerners. The names of many of their captains are known, because the king used them as his agents, lavished rewards on them, and advanced them to high office. Sir Thomas Mauleverer, Sir Christopher Ward, Sir Thomas Everingham, Sir Thomas Broughton, Sir Marmaduke Constable and many others were granted lands and offices confiscated from the rebels and implanted as loyal agents of the regime in the disaffected south. Two Yorkshiremen Edward Redman of Harewood and Edward Frank of Knighton served as sheriffs of Somerset and Dorset, and Oxfordshire and Berkshire respectively, while other north-country squires held the shrievalties of Kent, Wiltshire, Gloucestershire and Devon. Some like Sir Richard Radcliffe, Sir Ralph Ashton, Robert Brackenbury and Thomas Metcalfe attained an eminence in affairs of state wholly incommensurate with their relatively undistinguished backgrounds. Along with Sir Robert Percy, controller of the household, such men constituted the loyal and experienced nucleus of the king's affinity. Though less dependent on royal favour, a number of northern peers also seem to have been closely associated with the Ricardian regime: Lovell, Scrope of Bolton, Scrope of Masham, Fitzhugh, Dacre and Lumley. The first two seem to have been particularly close to the king. Francis Lovell, Viscount Lovell, was the king's chamberlain, and John Scrope, Lord Scrope of Bolton was a royal councillor. In addition they served the regime in south-central England and the West Country respectively, where their interests were hugely augmented by grants of forfeited properties.[10]

Even though the king's affinity was originally based on the circle of lords and gentlemen which gravitated around the house of Neville, it must not be supposed that it was ever entirely northern. Even before his accession Richard had territorial interests and well-wishers in most parts of the midlands and eastern England. Despite his strong northern connections, Lovell had his principal seat in Oxfordshire and held land in half-a-dozen other counties. Another member of this network, Lord Zouche, had his main estates in the north midlands, while Fitzhugh had interests in the south-west even before the grants of forfeited lands. John Kendal, Richard's secretary, was from Warwickshire. From the beginning of his protectorate onwards, Richard was naturally able to extend dramatically the network of his supporters. The unscrupulous Leicestershire lawyer William Catesby betrayed Lord Hastings, his old patron, to clamber onto the protector's bandwagon, and rapidly established himself in the inner circle of royal counsellors. Ambitious men from other parts of the realm, like Sir James Tyrell from Suffolk, followed suit, no doubt strengthening Richard's resolve to take the throne. Indeed the lords who tarried in giving their support to the new regime soon found their local rivals gaining influence at their expense. Lord Stanley was lucky to escape with his life, when a disaffected Lancashire gentleman who had joined the protector's retinue came near to mortally wounding him at the time of his arrest. As the opponents of Richard III showed their hands and were steadily eliminated, their lands and offices became available for the men who had helped to pull them down. The Woodvilles had many enemies, who inevitably benefited from their discomfiture. A prominent role in the defeat of the duke of Buckingham was taken by Humphrey Stafford of Grafton, who likewise had high hopes of advancing himself through the fall of his distant cousin. Other southerners who provided local support were Sir Richard Charlton, Sir Henry Bodrugan, Sir Alexander Baynham, John Sapcote and Morgan Kidwelly. Richard also made a great deal of progress in associating, at least formally, with his government most of the peerage from the midlands and the south. Lords Dudley, Dinham and Grey of Codnor all served as privy counsellors, while Maltravers, Ferrers of Chartley, Grey of Powys and others actively worked for the government. As regards the upper aristocracy, the ageing earls of Arundel and Kent lent their names to the regime, while Viscount Lisle and the earls of Huntingdon, Nottingham, Surrey and Lincoln seemed committed, as also were the dukes of Norfolk and Suffolk, the only two men of this rank. Almost all these peers had benefitted immensely from the regime, and stood to lose a great deal if the king were overthrown. A number were relatives of the king: Huntingdon was his son-in-law, Suffolk his brother-in-law, and Lincoln his nephew and possible heir.[11]

How far the king managed to weld such unpromising elements into a political establishment is difficult to determine. Obviously he was more successful north of the Trent, where he had proved his qualities of 'good lordship' before 1483. His generous patronage of individuals, religious houses and towns in the region certainly bore fruit, and his arrangements for the council of the north were well received among the general populace. Yet it might well be that following the Crowland chronicler's lead recent scholars have tended to over-estimate the regional bias of his government. The ruling elite, in so far as it can be identified from membership of the council and so on, was as much 'midland' as 'northern'. In terms of loyalty to the regime, Richard's old northern power-base certainly looked less convincing in 1485 than two years earlier.[12] The death of Queen Anne strained his relations with some of the old Neville connection who entertained suspicions of murder. There were other grounds for disillusionment. In providing some northerners with lavish patronage, the Ricardian regime antagonised others, and the establishment of an outsider, John de la Pole, earl of Lincoln, as the king's chief lieutenant in the north, must have raised hackles in some quarters. In any case the two most powerful and independent-minded northern magnates, the earl of Northumberland and Lord Stanley, seem never to have been unreservedly committed to the king. Whatever his views on northern developments, it is a fact that Richard never ventured more than a few miles north of Nottingham in the last thirteen months of his reign. Doubtless he still felt most vulnerable in the midlands and the south, and indeed his power-base in most counties south of the Trent was alarmingly narrow. The gentry who were prepared to collaborate in the region were, where not hated outsiders, men of dubious value, like the lawless Sir Henry Bodrugan in Cornwall or the pushy Morgan Kidwelly in Dorset. Despite his efforts with the southern peerage, most were unwilling or unable to deliver the goods in terms of political support. Some, like Arundel, were no more than formally

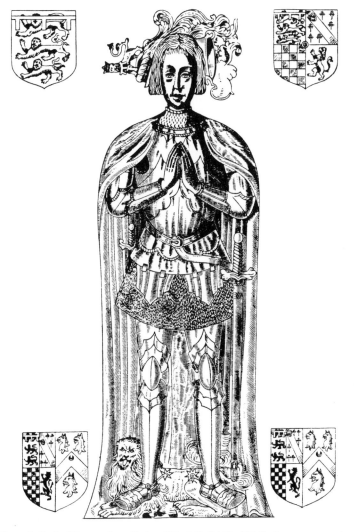

Thomas Howard, Earl of Surrey, later Duke of Norfolk (1443–1524); from an engraving of a lost brass at Lambeth.

Surrey's Signature

committed, others, like Nottingham, were amiable lightweights, while others, like Lisle, were playing a double game.[13] For all his status and royal connections, Suffolk seems to have withdrawn from public life, leaving his son Lincoln to take his place at court. In any case most of the lords from the south and the midlands were not militarily powerful. In fact the only southern magnate with the landed wealth, territorial power-base and martial prowess to commit large numbers of troops was the duke of Norfolk. He can thus be placed along with the two semi-independent northern magnates, Northumberland and Stanley, as arbiters of the fate of England in the summer of 1485.

*   *   *

In terms of rank and power John Howard, duke of Norfolk and marshal of England, stood supreme.[14] Still his royal blood and illustrious title belied his new nobility. At the beginning of the fifteenth century the Howards were Suffolk squires, and for all their talents they owed their change in fortunes to the marriage of Robert Howard to a daughter of Thomas Mowbray, duke of Norfolk. John Howard was the fruit of this union, and seems to have been a man of ability and drive. With the assistance of his Mowbray kinsmen he had made a career for himself in soldiering, local politics and eventually at court. He saw action in the French wars, and was possibly captured in the fateful expedition of 1453. His military ambitions temporarily frustrated, he channelled his energies into East Anglian affairs, and the consternation which his interventions caused in many quarters is eloquently recorded in the Paston letters. The triumph of the Yorkists, which temporarily ruined the De La Poles and the De Veres, the other main powers in the region, left the field clear for the Mowbrays and John Howard, their chief lieutenant. It also brought opportunities for further advancement. Edward IV saw the value of a man like Howard, and drew him into the royal service. In 1467 he was appointed treasurer of the royal household, and at about the same time he was raised to the peerage. He returned this trust and consolidated his achievement with unwavering loyalty during the upheavals of 1470–1, and a distinguished record of service to the king, both at the council-table and on campaign, through the remainder of the reign. Predictably enough, he was appointed one of the executors of the king's will.

If Howard had run true to form in 1483, he would have been one of the most reliable supporters of Edward V. Instead he threw in his lot with Richard of Gloucester, even when it became apparent that he was angling for the crown. Two sets of explanations have been proffered for his behaviour. It has been surmised that Howard and the protector were men of the same ilk, if not friends. Both were soldiers, indeed comrades-in-arms, and shared a disdain for the frivolities of the court, particularly as embodied in the queen's party. Yet there is no evidence of any real personal closeness between the two men, who in any case were of entirely different generations. A more cynical theory stresses the role of frustrated ambition. The deaths of the last Mowbray duke of Norfolk in 1475, and his only daughter, Anne, in 1481, had made Howard joint-heir to the Mowbray titles and lands. Rather mean-spiritedly Edward IV had created a

John Howard, Duke of Norfolk (c. 1420–85); from a stained glass portrait once in Tendring Hall, Suffolk, engraved in Dallaway's History of Sussex.

life-interest in this inheritance for his second son, Richard, who though a child had been 'married' to Anne Mowbray. Though the affair did not supply, as some have alleged, a compelling motive for Howard to take on himself the murder of the princes in the Tower, there can be no doubt that it played a significant part in determining his allegiance. Since two days after his accession Richard III granted Howard the dukedom of Norfolk, it does seem likely that the two men had made some sort of prior deal. Other marks of signal favour followed thick and fast. Norfolk was given, in addition to his share of the Mowbray inheritance, forty-six manors confiscated some time ago from the earl of Oxford, and twenty-five manors, all in East Anglia, taken from Earl Rivers. Meanwhile his eldest son Thomas Howard was made earl of Surrey and was granted an annuity of over one thousand pounds.

Whatever his motivation, Norfolk was from the outset a major pillar of the Ricardian regime. Given his political experience and reputation in the capital, his presence among the men taking power in summer 1483 must have added considerably to public confidence in the regime. In fact the contribution of the Howards to the new dispensation involved more than mere moral support. While the son apparently played a role in the ensnarement of Lord Hastings, the father was given soon after the accession a wide-ranging military command over all the eastern counties. Indeed, while the king toured points west and north, Norfolk kept the Home Counties secure: his prompt military action in defending London in October denied the rebels their best chance of victory. Throughout 1484 the Howards were active on the council and on royal commissions, while a list in their household accounts of a thousand men whom they had ready for royal service indicates their preparedness to fight again for the king. Yet in 1485 it might have caused Richard III some disquiet that they were increasingly eschewing court life in favour of their country mansion at Framlingham. In facing the challenge from Henry Tudor and the earl of Oxford, Richard doubtless found most comfort in the fact that the Howards had almost as much to lose as he himself from a successful invasion. Still, if Norfolk faltered, the vulnerable south-east coast, the Home Counties and London itself would be in grave jeopardy.

*   *   *

Another power-broker in 1485 was Henry Percy, earl of Northumberland.[15] For over a hundred years the house of Percy had been pre-eminent in wealth and standing in the far north, and had added to its power through its control of at least one of the wardenships of the Scottish marches. Among the clannish and violent border communities the Percys had built up impressive military followings. Ballads and poems extolled their victory over the Scots at Otterburn, the gallantry of Harry Hotspur at Homildon Hill, their king-making role in 1399 and their rebellion of 1403–8. In Tudor times local men would look back nostalgically to a 'golden age' of Percy power and provincial achievement, and recall the old adage that Northumberland knows no king but a Percy. Yet it would be mistaken to assume that the house of Percy had prospered during the civil strife of the fifteenth century. On the contrary, it was nearly destroyed in the wars and political upheavals. The collapse of their rebellion in 1408, and the long minority which followed it, set a woeful pattern. At the battle of St Albans in 1455 the third earl of Northumberland was cut down in his prime, leaving Henry, then only a small child, as his heir. The Yorkist victory in 1461 was catastrophic: the fourth earl was attainted, and in the north the Nevilles attained a new hegemony, with the earldom of Northumberland revived for the benefit of a brother of Warwick the Kingmaker. During the crisis of 1470, however, with the Nevilles in rebellion against the Yorkist monarchy, Edward IV was only too eager to restore the earldom, and after the collapse of the 'readeption' regime in 1471 Percy could hope to rebuild his family fortunes in the north. The earl of Northumberland served the king well, not least in the French expedition and the Scottish wars. Even then he was not allowed to have it all his own way. Richard duke of Gloucester took over the Neville connection in Yorkshire and the west march, and was naturally regarded as the king's chief lieutenant in the north.

In the turbulent politics of northern England, Richard and Northumberland shared a common background, and must have grown to know each other well. At times the two magnates, vying for regional leadership in a continuation of the old

Garter stall plate of Henry Percy, Earl of Northumberland, from St George's Chapel, Windsor.

Neville-Percy feuds, came close to blows. Perhaps more remarkable than the predictable rivalry, however, is their successful resolution of some of the differences in 1474 in an unusual power-sharing agreement. Probably this pact is more a testimony to Richard's than Percy's statesmanship, but it does at least document their ability to work together for common goals. In the short reign of Edward V this collaboration proved significant. The earl of Northumberland maintained a united 'northern' front with Richard, and put his weight behind the protector's bid for power. It also seems that he took responsibility for the detention, 'trial' and execution of Rivers and his friends. Shortly afterwards he came to London with his retinue to participate in the coronation. His motives in supporting Richard can be well imagined: he could reasonably expect not only honour and advancement from the new king but also more room for manœuvre in the north. Whether any specific promises were made is hard to discern. On 10 May the protectorate granted him the wardenship of the middle and east marches, and after his accession Richard III confirmed him in this office. Yet the wardenship was no more than his due, and the term of his appointment, for one year only, could not have been encouraging. Still Northumberland continued to serve the regime well. He played a prominent role in the royal reception at York, and joined with the king in the suppression of the rebellion in autumn 1483. In the aftermath of this revolt he gained more valuable prizes, including the office of steward of England and the valuable lordship of Holderness, both forfeited by Buckingham. In 1484 his mother died, leaving him in possession of the Poynings inheritance in southern England. At this stage the house of Percy must have appeared one of the chief pillars of the regime.

In the last year of Richard's reign, however, there are signs of a weakening of commitment. If ever he had hoped that the departure of the heir of the Nevilles for the south would leave him an undisputed hegemony in the north, such dreams must have been finally dashed in summer 1484, when the king set about instituting the council of the north. Although Northumberland was given a leading role in this new scheme, it could not but serve as a straitjacket to his dynastic ambitions, not least because pride of place was accorded to the king's nephew, the earl of Lincoln. Indeed Northumberland might well have found his power-base in the north eroded in more subtle ways. With the king offering glittering prospects to many northern gentry, he must have found his 'good lordship' increasingly at a discount, and quite a number of his retainers now found their way into the royal service. Perhaps some word of his disillusionment reached Henry Tudor, for at some stage in early summer 1485 the pretender tried to sound him out as a possible ally. Northumberland was in an unenviable position. If his main grievance was that his own following was being seduced by royal patronage he could not even be sure that his retainers would follow him into treason. In such circumstances it would be foolish to jeopardise what gains he had made from the regime, and what credit he continued to enjoy at court, through open involvement in the hazardous enterprise of Henry Tudor.

*　　*　　*

The third more or less independent power-broker in the reign of Richard III

Possibly Thomas, Lord Stanley (died 1504) and his first wife Eleanor Neville; alabaster effigies at Ormskirk, Lancashire; the effigy could be of Thomas' father, also Thomas.

was Thomas Stanley, Lord Stanley.[16] Like the Howards, the Stanleys were a new noble family. A younger son of a Cheshire gentry family, Sir John Stanley, Lord Stanley's great-grandfather, had made his name as a soldier-of-fortune, and prospered in the service of Richard II. As controller of the wardrobe from 1397 he was responsible for the recruitment of the king's notorious Cheshire guard, but in 1399 he had no difficulty in transferring his allegiance to the Lancastrian dynasty. Building up an impressive patrimony in the north-west, the first Stanley of Lathom was able to establish himself as a sort of broker between the crown and the famous fighting men of the palatinates of Chester and Lancaster. It was a role further developed by his son, another John, who through his 'good lordship' gave the lineage a sound regional power-base, and by his grandson, Thomas, who consolidated and expanded the connections with the court. During the personal rule of Henry VI Sir Thomas Stanley became controller of the household, and in times of crisis like Jack Cade's revolt in 1450 the court looked to him to provide loyal troops from the north-west. During the faction fighting of the 1450s, the recognised military potential of Cheshire and Lancashire added immensely to the stature of the lineage able to harness it, and Thomas Stanley was raised to the peerage in 1456. It also brought its dangers, as dissatisfied dynasts sought to by-pass the brokership of the Stanleys. The greatest danger came in 1459 when Queen Margaret made a bid to recruit directly in Cheshire, and when the Yorkists who were also mobilising sought assistance from the Stanleys. To add to the dilemma, Lord Stanley died in the same year, leaving his young son and namesake to weather the storm as best he could. The battle of Blore heath, in which the chivalry of the north-west were engaged on both sides, could have spelt disaster for the house of Stanley. Through audacious brinkmanship, however, the young Lord Stanley held his main retinue and some of the county levies some miles off from the encounter. He then had the nerve to congratulate his Neville kinsmen on their escape and to ride out the storm emanating from the court.

The battle of Blore heath set the pattern for Lord Stanley's career. Narrowly missing being attainted in 1459, he kept his head down during the upheavals of 1460–1, but was quick to share in the fruits of the Yorkist victory. In the crises of 1470–1 he flirted with the Nevilles, played some role in the 'readeption' of Henry VI, but again disappointed his allies by making no effort to resist the return of Edward IV. On the whole historians have disapproved of his shifty trimming, and there can be no doubt that his primary concern was dynastic aggrandisement. His second marriage to Margaret Beaufort brought him a wife of great wealth as well as of rare breeding and accomplishment. Meanwhile he had matched George, his eldest son, with the heiress of Lord Strange of Knockin, providing him with an independent title and endowment in north Shropshire. It was doubtless part of family strategy, too, that his younger brother, Sir William Stanley, flew the kite for the Yorkists in the whirling times of 1459–61 and 1470–1, and won advancement on his own account, with one prize being the hand of the widowed countess of Worcester. Yet such policies were not incompatible with the interests of wider communities. Far from squandering the blood of his retainers, Lord Stanley was able to advance their careers through his sound leadership. In moments of national crisis, instead of compounding divisions through diehard commitments he was able to put his weight behind political stability. Probably more than any other magnate in the last quarter of the fifteenth century, Lord Stanley had the trust of his retainers and the love of his 'country'.

There can be no doubt that Richard III feared him more than anyone. In the 1470s the duke of Gloucester and Stanley contested spheres of influence in the far north-west, and according to local tradition when it came to blows the Stanleyites had been triumphant.[17] In 1483 Richard had Lord Stanley arrested along with Hastings, but according to Vergil feared to move against him for fear of Lord Strange mounting a rebellion in the north-west. Instead the new king determined to keep Stanley under close scrutiny, and at the same time seek to bind him to the regime by fair dealing. The loyalty of the Stanleys, forced or otherwise, during the autumn rebellion of 1483, and their part in the suppression of the revolt, were richly rewarded: family members and clients were granted estates and offices right across the realm, Sir William Stanley was appointed chamberlain of north Wales, and Lord Stanley himself was made constable of England. Supreme in the countryside between Shrewsbury and Lancaster, and prominent throughout north Wales and parts of the midlands, the Stanleys at this time could only have been rivalled by the Howards in wealth and influence in the kingdom. In 1485 their actions would be crucial, if not decisive.

The house of Stanley can never have been deeply committed to the Ricardian

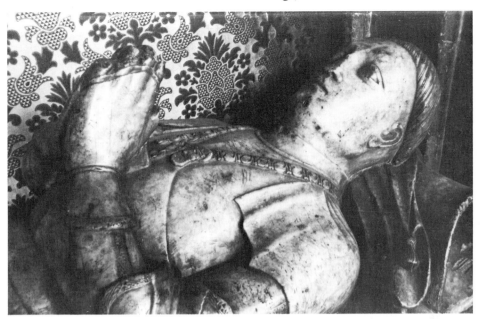

Sir John Savage; effigy at Macclesfield, Cheshire.

regime. Obviously in June 1483 Lord Stanley was regarded as a potential opponent, and the attack on him could have done little to win him over. It is possible that after initial hostility he threw in his lot with the usurper, and it is true that the Stanleyites came in behind the king to defeat Buckingham's rebellion. On the other hand, there are signs that his heart might have been elsewhere. His wife, Margaret Beaufort, was one of the chief conspirators, and Lord Strange might have initially mobilised in support of the rebellion. His own freedom of manœuvre was limited by his presence in the king's entourage in the north. His position in the royal household would remain a problem throughout the reign, but he does seem to have found ways and means to assist his stepson, Henry Tudor. He might have been the ultimate source of the intelligence which prompted the pretender's escape from Brittany, and Jean Molinet claimed that he was responsible for engineering the defection of the captain of Hammes and the release of the earl of Oxford. The ballad tradition doubtless exaggerate as well as over-dramatise his role in bringing Henry Tudor to England, but a wide range of sources stress the importance of his encouragement and promises to the enterprise. His wife was certainly deeply involved in the preparations and planning, his nephew, Thomas Savage, was actually with the pretender, and his brother, Sir William Stanley, and his other nephew, Sir John Savage, were also implicated. At the same time nothing is more certain than that the king mistrusted the Stanleys. Unhappily for his peace of mind he also needed them to raise the men of the north-west on his behalf. As the day of reckoning drew nigh he allowed Lord Stanley leave to return to Lancashire, but only on condition that his son Lord Strange took his place to serve as a hostage for his good behaviour.

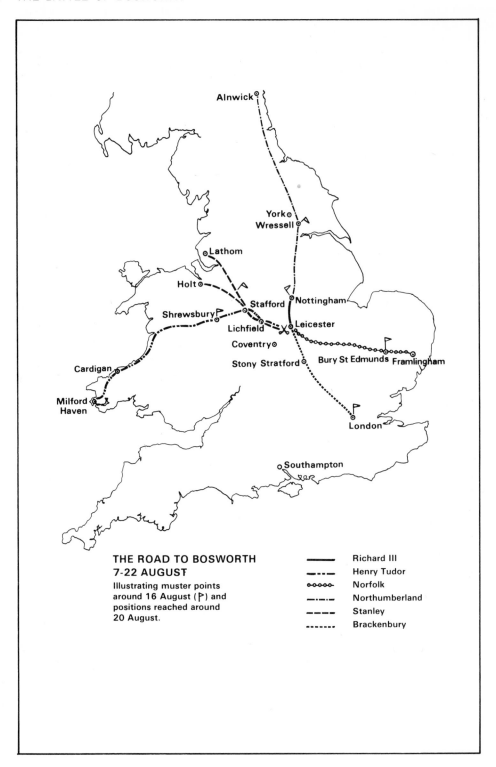

**THE ROAD TO BOSWORTH
7-22 AUGUST**

Illustrating muster points
around 16 August (⚑) and
positions reached around
20 August.

———	Richard III
—·—·—	Henry Tudor
∘∘∘∘∘	Norfolk
—··—··—	Northumberland
— — —	Stanley
·······	Brackenbury

5 The Road to Bosworth

Between 1483 and 1485 it is tempting to see all roads leading to Bosworth. This quiet market centre, in the heart of *champion* England, seems almost to have exercised a gravitational pull on the actors in the tragedy of Richard III. Twice in the first months of his reign the king passed through this part of Leicestershire. In August 1483 the royal progress took him along the road from Warwick to Leicester, where he rested on the very day on which two years later he would march out from the town to his destiny at Bosworth. Presumably the inhabitants of Market Bosworth and other neighbouring villages lined the road to salute his cavalcade, unless perhaps the sinister rumours from London had begun to catch up with the king, sowing seeds of unrest in the neighbourhood. The lord of the manor of Bosworth, John Harcourt, was an active conspirator, and though he resided in Oxfordshire he doubtless had his agents in the locality. The next time the king passed through Leicestershire on this road, it was in the opposite direction and in quite a different mood. News of the duke of Buckingham's rebellion had interrupted his leisurely perambulation in the middle of October, and he hurriedly retraced his steps southwards. Leicester was selected as the venue for the troops he was mustering, and on the town converged, not for the last time, the king's trusted northerners, loyalists from the eastern counties, and the powerful Stanley affinity from the north-west. Foraging far and wide, the king's 'scourers' probably visited Bosworth, and if Harcourt's treason was already known his barns would have been emptied with special relish. The estate was subsequently granted to Sir Marmaduke Constable, one of the king's northern captains. Even as the royal host moved south towards Coventry, however, Richard was still anxiously weighing the seriousness of the movement. Almost certainly he was already surveying the Leicestershire landscape with the keen eye of a military strategist.[1]

The green, undulating countryside around Bosworth, radiant in summer but bleak and windswept in winter, was scarred by a series of broad thoroughfares, not unakin to long flood-plains in parts where travellers fanned out to avoid pot-holes in the dry season and mires in the wet. A league to the south of the battlefield ran the ancient highway known as Watling Street, which linked London with north Wales, and a little to the east was another old road, Fosse Way, which stretched from the southern coast to the north midlands. Along such thoroughfares armies had moved from Roman times. There had been action in

Nottingham Castle, a drawing of the castle as it was in the fifteenth century, based on recent excavations.

this region in 1471 when the Kingmaker had taken refuge behind the walls of Warwick castle and Edward IV and Richard had established their base at Leicester. Nevertheless far more common than the movement of armies of soldiers in the fifteenth century were the droves of cattle and sheep from the rich Leicestershire pastures to the great markets of Coventry and London. Indeed the region, itself lacking navigable rivers, was criss-crossed with roads, for the most part of dubious quality, which served to link up the riverborne traffic of the Thames, Severn and Trent systems. For all its heavy soil and cloddish aspect of its lowlands, and its bleak and windswept uplands, this part of Leicestershire was no backwater, but a place to feel the pulse of the nation. Whatever movements were afoot, their stirrings would be felt in this crossroads of the kingdom.

The political geography of Ricardian England made the crossroads a cock-pit. For long months at a time Richard III made his operational headquarters on the rocky eminence of Nottingham castle, whence he could look out over the open fields of the north midlands. He developed almost a sentimental attachment to what he termed his 'Castle of Care'. He built a new tower and refurbished the royal suite. He also was able to indulge his passion for hunting in neighbouring Sherwood forest. Yet there were sound strategic reasons for making Nottingham the citadel of his realm, which had been well appreciated by his brother before him.[2] In so far as his power-base lay north of the Trent, he was in a position to assemble the bulk of his personal retinue within a few days. From this vantage-point, too, he could keep a wary eye on his dubious allies in the north-west, and shepherd in his partisans from East Anglia. Leicester, a comfortable day's march to the south, was the natural rendezvous for them. Admittedly he was rather remote from the disaffected southern counties, but their will had been largely broken in the suppression of the rebellion of 1483. Of all the regions, it must have seemed that the midlands was the most unstable, and its control most crucial. The civil wars and the vicissitudes of politics had left it a dangerous no-man's-land.[3] The great Beauchamp connection, in so far as it had survived the ambitions of Warwick and the follies of Clarence, could only look to Clarence's unpromising progeny. The heirs to the Staffords, dukes of Buckingham, and the Talbots, earls of Shrewsbury, were still children. The remarkable Hastings and Grey-Woodville machines had been dismantled. Only a few minor peers, like Ferrers of Chartley, Grey of Codnor and Zouche, worked actively for the regime in the region. This lack of aristocratic leadership emphasised the need for a strong royal presence, especially since there was little love for the king in the many manor-houses where the names of Stafford, Hastings and Grey were still revered. Richard knew that the midlands would be where his kingdom would be won or lost.

It is scarcely surprising then to find, as intelligence reached England of Henry Tudor's preparations for invasion, that the king moved to take up his vigil at Nottingham castle. After an unprecedented six months' sojourn in the environs of Westminster, he set out for Windsor on Ascension day, progressed to Kenilworth for Whitsuntide, and took up residence in Nottingham in early June. He was to remain at this strategic site for two and a half months, maintaining an open household for the local notables, and hunting from Beskwood lodge, but for the most part simply watching and waiting. It was from this base that on 21 June he instructed the chancellor in Westminster to make proclamation throughout the realm that the former earls of Oxford and Pembroke and other traitors, having failed to gain Breton assistance for their 'unnatural and abominable' plans had gone over to the obedience of France, and 'to abuse and blind the commons' of England had chosen as their leader Henry son of Edmund Tudor, who through 'his ambitious and insatiable covetousness' had taken upon himself the royal title. The following day he set in train preparations for the mobilisation of the realm. Reporting that 'our rebels and traitors, in association with our ancient enemies of France and other strangers, intend hastily to invade this our realm purposing the destruction of us, the subversion of this our realm, and disinheriting of all our true subjects', he ordered his officers to muster the able-bodied men in their bailiwicks, to see them well-horsed and harnessed, and to have money collected for their wages. In a rather more urgent and menacing tone, he commanded all knights, squires and gentlemen to hold themselves ready to support the king at an hour's warning 'upon the peril of losing of their lives, lands and goods'. To ensure smooth and rapid mobilisation, nobles and other captains were strictly enjoined to put aside their own quarrels and to assist each other in the royal service, and the sheriffs were ordered to reside in their county-towns in readiness for the king's signal.[4]

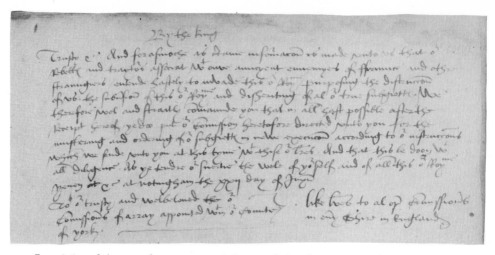

Commission of Array to the county commissioners ordering the mustering of troops, dated from Nottingham on 22nd June 1485 (BL Harleian MS 433, folio 220).

The kingdom had been in a state of vague war-preparedness for some time. The proclamation against Henry Tudor largely repeated the one issued the previous December, at which time the current commissions of array had also been appointed.[5] More recently, Richard had pursued various means to raise money, including 'forced loans' from churchmen and pawning jewels and silverware to London merchants. Prior to leaving the capital, he had made further military dispositions. Sir Robert Brackenbury was left in command of a sizeable force at the Tower of London. The duke of Norfolk, in residence at Framlingham in Suffolk, was ordered to have his forces in readiness, and keep a wary eye on the eastern approaches to the capital. Rather more reluctantly, Lord Stanley was given leave to withdraw to Lathom in Lancashire to marshal the men of the north-west. Viscount Lovell was sent to Southampton to superintend naval preparations for the defence of the southern coast. Presumably he was asked to keep an especially close watch over the small Hampshire port of Milford-on-Sea, where according to prophecy or report the pretender intended making land-fall. The possibility of a landing at Milford Haven in Pembrokeshire or elsewhere in south Wales was not overlooked either. In general terms the king relied in this region on his son-in-law the earl of Huntingdon and the latter's energetic brother Walter Herbert, but he had also cultivated some of the local gentry. Rhys ap Thomas was paid large sums to raise loyal Welsh troops, while Richard Williams was entrusted with the command of the castles at Pembroke, Tenby, Haverfordwest, Manorbier and Cilgerran. Extensive repair work was done on Pembroke's fortifications at this time, and along the Pembrokeshire coast, as elsewhere in Britain, beacons were prepared to signal the news of an invasion from hill to hill across the realm.[6]

* * *

Presumably what galvanised the king into unseasonable action around midsummer was definite intelligence of imminent invasion. Little is known of the chronology of Henry Tudor's preparations, and the date of the proclamation provides a clue as to when the pretender began in earnest to assemble men, arms, ships and supplies at Rouen. It is probable that he had struck the best bargain he could with Charles VIII's government, and set up his operational headquarters in the Norman capital as early as spring. He seems to have been there when he received news of Queen Anne's death and the king's plan to marry Elizabeth of York. Through April and May there must have been a constant stream of messages back and forth across the Channel, as Henry Tudor made his last bids to secure new allies and commit old well-wishers. *The Song of Lady Bessy* gives 3 May as the date of a crucial meeting at which Lord Stanley, Sir William Stanley and Gilbert Talbot firmly committed themselves to support Henry Tudor, and less plausibly alleges that it was this offer, carried by Humphrey Brereton, which prompted the pretender to make his last appeal for increased French support and to set in train the invasion plans. Certainly some time early in June a final decision to go ahead with the invasion must have been taken by the pretender and his allies. Rather interestingly it seems to have been at this time that a number of distinguished sympathisers, like Peter Curteys, keeper of the wardrobe, slipped into sanctuary, presumably on the advice of agents like Robert Skerne.[7] By the end of June all of England must have sensed that the game was afoot.

For Henry Tudor it was a last ditch effort to build up his fighting strength, and to find arms, transport and provisions. His entourage formed the nucleus of the army. The earl of Oxford and the earl of Pembroke were experienced commanders, and both had taken part in successful invasions of England. Sir Edward Woodville, former admiral of England, must have been able to give valuable advice on naval matters. The bishop of Exeter was no mean warrior, and several other exiles, like Giles Daubeney and Richard Edgecombe, were talented soldiers. Young Richard Guildford seems to have developed some flair for ordnance. Meanwhile James Blount and the defectors from the Hammes garrison provided a backbone of professionalism. Yet all told, the English contingent was less than five hundred strong, and even this figure would be an over generous estimate of its fighting strength: the unreliable marquis of Dorset was left behind in France as a surety for a loan. Indeed it needs to be stressed that the expeditionary force was composed predominantly of French and other foreign units. Although there is some doubt as to how much assistance Charles VIII actually provided, it is likely that as many as 2,000 mercenaries set sail with the exiles. The most prominent of their captains, Philibert de Chandée, seems to have been a close friend of Henry Tudor, and was to make his career in England. There is a strong tradition that Bernard Stuart and Alexander Bruce also took part with detachments of Scotsmen who were serving in the French army. Of particular value was a unit of gunners and arms specialists which the exiles were able to recruit: some like Ralph de Ponthieu, a brigandiner and maker of plate-armour, remained in the royal service after Bosworth. More dubious were the Frenchmen who enlisted out of desperation, some of whom were apparently delivered from Norman gaols. All in all, the pretender might have wished for a larger army, but as Commines observed limited transport and supplies in any case imposed a low ceiling[8].

Henry Tudor worked on the assumption that his invading force had only to establish a beach-head, and that his arrival would provoke a chain of risings on his behalf across the country. Margaret Beaufort had worked hard for her son, raising money and conspiring with other possible allies. Her husband, Lord Stanley, had given assurances of support from the north-west, and Gilbert Talbot, a name with which to conjure in the north-west midlands, was also on his side. Elsewhere in England it would be unwise to expect too much. A bid to turn to advantage the disaffection of the earl of Northumberland had thus far met with no success. The good will of the southern counties from Land's End to the Thames estuary was generally assured, but with the more prominent sympathisers in exile or under close watch it would be hard to make progress in military terms. More fruitful might be the discontents of the midlands, which had still to find expression from 1483, to say nothing of later developments. Here again there was a leadership problem: as in the southern rising of 1483 a great deal would depend on the willingness of a whole series of independent-minded knights and squires to make their own stand. Indeed with the king keeping guard at Nottingham, the prospects of making any headway in the midlands, or even effectively co-ordinating with the Stanleys in the north-west must have seemed bleak. To convert good wishes in England into armed support, Henry Tudor knew that he would have to penetrate to the heart of the kingdom and beard the lion in his den. His gateway would be Wales.

From the start Wales must have loomed large in the plans of Henry Tudor. His blood was only a quarter Welsh, but his roots were almost entirely in the land of St David. It was this part of Britain, most particularly the ruggedly beautiful Pembrokeshire coast, which alone he knew well and where he himself was known. It was in this region too that his uncle Jasper Tudor, earl of Pembroke, still had considerable credit. Of course, two decades of Yorkist rule had changed the political complexion of south Wales. The Herberts were the dominant lineage, but a number of other Welsh gentlemen had also prospered through service to the Yorkist monarchy. Nevertheless the Tudors had high hopes in the area, and their agents, most notably the Morgan brothers, Trahaiarn and John, worked assiduously to raise support. Although the earl of Huntingdon could not be drawn into the enterprise, the word was that the influential Walter Herbert and Rhys ap Thomas might be brought on side. At the very least the secluded inlets of the Pembrokeshire coastline provided the sort of beach-head that the puny expeditionary force required: remote from the king's centres of strength, secure in the good will of the local populace and giving immediate access to countryside in which a fledgling army might build its strength undisturbed. From the first it seems to have been planned to head northwards rather than immediately westwards. According to the ballad tradition, Henry Tudor arranged at the outset to push through to Shrewsbury, where he hoped his allies from north-west England would meet him.[9] On this path it would be possible to tap the rich veins of support promised by chieftains in the heartland of Wales and to make early contact with Sir William Stanley, chamberlain of north Wales. Presumably it was felt too that it would take time

Sir Rhys ap Thomas (died 1525); effigy in St Peter's Church, Carmarthen.

for the pretender to rally support in England, and that the longer his standard was kept raised, the more his supporters would be willing to rally to it.

It is hard to assess the contribution of Welsh national sentiment to the cause of Henry Tudor at this time. It is uncertain whether the young prince spoke or understood Welsh, but in his early years of exile his association with Wales might well have been the one firm centre in his growing sense of his own identity. Since at the Breton court at this time there was considerable interest in Celtic culture, his pride in his Welshness can only have been encouraged.[10] Meanwhile, across in the land of his fathers, there were powerful currents of patriotic feeling waiting to be canalised. For hundreds of years, the bards had kept alive the hopes of a defeated people with songs and poems extolling the glories of long dead heroes and issuing prophecies of a golden age to come. Henry Tudor was by no means the first claimant to the English throne to act as a focus for Welsh messianic hope. Ironically the house of York, through their descent from the Mortimers, had kindled similar expectations a generation earlier. Yet, in respect of background at least, Henry Tudor was a far more credible candidate, and seems to have been determined to exploit to the full his Welsh associations. Though the Red Dragon does not seem to have been an intrinsically Welsh emblem, there can be no doubting its magnetic power as a symbol of national revival. Many of the Welshmen who promised their support were doubtless motivated solely by the prospects of their own advancement, but there is clear evidence as well that the cause of Henry Tudor stirred the deepest aspirations of a stubbornly proud race.

The small flotilla set sail from the Seine estuary on 1 August. The date of departure was probably determined by the weather, and unlike the abortive invasion attempt in 1483 the convoy was to be gently wafted to its predetermined destination rather than broken up, and smashed against the well defended coast of southern England. Whether the timing of the expedition fitted with the arrangements of Henry Tudor's English allies is another matter. The king's proclamation of 21 June did not assume a sudden attack. His commands were after all only to establish a general preparedness for the defence of the realm. It is hard to know what to make of the evidence of *Lady Bessy* that Henry Tudor told the Stanleys to expect him about Michaelmas, which would make his invasion a month premature. Apart from the obvious need for time to raise men and money for the scheme, it might well have been sound strategy to wait for the summer sun to bake hard the muddy passes though central Wales. Again the plans as communicated to the allies might have been predicated on favourable weather conditions. One passage in the ballad account has Sir William Stanley deducing Henry Tudor's descent on Britain from the direction of the wind.[11]

It was the afternoon of Sunday 7 August that the young adventurer, styling himself Henry VII, king of England and prince of Wales, saw for the first time in almost fifteen years the magnificent Pembrokeshire coast line. He waited for sunset before entering the broad inlet known as Milford Haven, and put in at Mill Bay, the first cove on the western side. Setting foot on his native ground, he knelt down and prayed, beginning with the words of the psalm, 'Judge me, O Lord, and determine my cause'. In the mean time his men disembarked and established a beach-head, and while some set about unloading horses and equipment, others clambered up the cliffs towards Dale castle. A local tradition has it that Henry himself climbed up near Brunt farm, which took its name from his remark that it was a 'brunt' place, meaning in English hard terrain, or in Welsh a foul spot. Within a few hours his troops must have taken Dale, and with no resistance being encountered were able to settle for the night in relative comfort and safety.[12]

After all the patient waiting for over a decade, and indeed the mounting excitement of the past week, the reception at Dale must have been an anti-climax. There were no allies to meet him: the tradition that Rhys ap Thomas welcomed him on his arrival must be discounted. Indeed he learnt more about the strength and organisation of his enemies than he did about the movements of his friends. With the news of his landing flashing from beacon to beacon, he must have been all too aware that his arrival was public knowledge, and it would be all of a week before any of the more important allies would show their hands. Perhaps there was some hospitality from the local gentry, but no really encouraging signs. All that is recorded of the first evening and morning in Wales is that Henry Tudor boosted the morale of his army by knighting a number of his companions: Philibert de Chandée, Edward Courtenay, John Cheney, Edward Poynings, John Fortescue, James Blount and the Welshman David Owen. Indeed the first two days brought much cause for consternation. On 8 August the company advanced undisturbed to Haverfordwest, and a few miles further on Jasper Tudor received messages of support from the town of Pembroke, but there were alarming reports that Rhys ap Thomas was raising men for the king, and that Walter Herbert was preparing to strike against them from Carmarthen. The immediate panic quickly subsided, however, when a local gentleman named Griffith brought into the rebel camp a section of the Carmarthenshire muster. As the small army headed north from Cardigan without any significant reinforcement, Henry Tudor knew at least that he was to have his chance finally to show his mettle.

Even if he still lacked credit as king of England, the young adventurer was now entering his inheritance as prince of Wales. Advancing along the coast road to Llanbadarn, and then striking inland at Machynlleth, his progress took him through countryside which had never seen royalty since the days of Welsh independence,. save perhaps for a brief glimpse of the doomed Richard II as he rode panic-stricken across Wales shortly before his deposition in 1399. Doubtless from the first night at Dale the numerous clerks in Henry's entourage rounded off a hard day on the road with quill-pushing late into the night, as letters were penned urging kinsmen and friends to rally to the Tudor banner. 'Right trusty and well-beloved, we greet you well', the would-be king wrote to a distant cousin John ap Meredith of Eifionydd in Gwynedd, 'and whereas . . . through the help of Almighty God, the assistance of our loving and true subjects, and the great confidence that we have to the nobles and commons of this our principality of Wales, we be entered into the same, purposing . . . to descend into our realm of England . . . We desire and pray you, and upon your allegiance strictly charge and command you that, immediately upon the sight hereof, with all such power as ye may make, defensibly arrayed for war, ye address you towards us . . . wheresoever we shall be, to our aid . . . and that ye fail not hereof as ye will avoid our grievous displeasure, and answer it unto your peril'. Such letters were not without fruit, and judging from the provenance of the Welsh gentlemen and yeomen later rewarded for their efforts his army attracted small companies of recruits at each stage along the road: men like Owen Lloyd of Cardigan, and Philip ap Rhys of Mabwynion. Henry Tudor had even more compelling wordsmiths working for him. The writings of the Welsh bard, Robin Ddu, had already prepared the way for him in many districts: '*Y mae hiraeth am Harri/Y mae gobaith i'n hiaith ni* (We look forward to the coming of Henry; our nation puts its trust in him)'. According to local tradition, he was received at Mathafarn just outside Machynlleth by the famous poet Davydd Llwyd, who with a little prodding from his wife prophesied triumph for the Tudor cause.[13]

Prophecies along with promises had to suffice for two more days: not until Henry Tudor reached Welshpool would his appeal to his countrymen to arms show more than modest success. The movements and intentions of Rhys ap Thomas and Walter Herbert, who in addition to their own retinues had mustered the men of the southern counties, were a particular cause for consternation. Theoretically, they were still loyal to Richard III and were flanking the rebels' advance along inland routes. On the other hand the manœuvre might have been designed to suggest to the king that the insurrection was being contained while in reality the movement was gaining strength. It certainly enabled Rhys to keep his options open longer, and to add to the value of his ultimate commitment. Allegedly Henry was forced to promise him the lieutenancy of Wales. Even so he must have been greatly relieved to see the

Welsh Bridge, Shrewsbury, across which Henry Tudor and his men would have marched.

famous Black Raven standard fall in behind his own Red Dragon, either at Newtown or further along the road to Welshpool. Rhys's company from south Wales must have doubled at a stroke the Welsh contingent, and included many men who were later rewarded for their pains, such as Adam ap Evan, Morris Lloyd of Wydegada, and Philip ap Howel, whose wife had formerly been Henry Tudor's nurse. At the same time, or perhaps a little later, Walter Herbert joined the swelling host with a company from south-east Wales. Finally on Long Mountain, outside Welshpool, there was a gathering of the clans from north Wales, including kinsmen of the pretender. Among the more notable chieftains were Richard ap Howel of Mostyn and the formidable Rhys Fawr ap Maredudd, whose exploits at Bosworth were to pass into Welsh legend. On 15 August no longer a puny band of adventurers but a substantial army pushed down the Severn valley into England, and demanded the surrender of Shrewsbury.

*   *   *

News of the landing of Henry Tudor reached Richard III remarkably quickly, indeed within four days of the land-fall. One at least of the king's agents in south-west Wales, Richard Williams, constable of Pembroke, remained loyal to the king, and was doubtless responsible for getting the news to Nottingham. Apparently the first report was that the rebels had landed at Angle, on the eastern rather than the western side of the haven.[14] While it is possible that a detachment was sent in this direction, it is more likely that the king's agents were simply mistaken in their assumptions. If the source of their intelligence was the lighting of the beacons, it is easy to see how the signals could have been misread. More probable still is that the flotilla was seen approaching the haven in the late

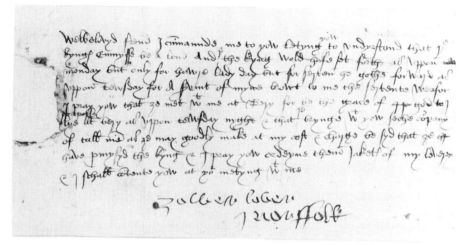

Letter from the Duke of Norfolk to John Paston, commanding him to meet him at Bury St Edmunds with armed men raised for the King; written in August 1485 and signed J Norffolk (BL Additional MS 43490, folio 53).

afternoon, and that Angle was the assumed destination. Such an hypothesis has the additional merit of allowing more time for Richard Williams to consider the position, to realise the impossibility of preventing a landing, and to dispatch a messenger across two hundred miles of difficult terrain to Nottingham.

The king received the news at Beskwood lodge on 11 August. Immediately stung into action, urgent summonses were sent not only to the sheriffs and commissioners of array, but also to a large number of individual lords and gentlemen. There survives a letter from this time to Henry Vernon of Haddon, Derbyshire, which instructed him in the firmest of tones to bring immediately his promised quota of men-at-arms, properly horsed and harnessed, under pain of forfeiture. In their turn the king's chief lieutenants wrote to their own retainers. The duke of Norfolk, who could not have received his orders much before 13 August, rapidly arranged for his men to assemble at Bury St Edmunds on the evening of 16 August. He instructed John Paston to meet him there with 'such a company of tall men as you can easily make up at my expense, as well as what you have promised the king'. William Allington, commissioner of array for Cambridgeshire and likewise under strict orders to mobilise, wisely made his last will on 15 August.[15]

It is a problem to square this unequivocal evidence of the king's swift and purposeful preparations with Polydore Vergil's testimony that his early response to the invasion was nonchalant and contemptuous. It certainly added to the drama and piquancy of his account to portray the king braying over the puniness of the rebel challenge and claiming that it could be adequately met by the royal forces in Wales. On the other hand, the story might well reflect one of a number of changes in mood in the royal camp at Nottingham. After all, it would be absurd to assume that a communications-system which could bring one letter two hundred miles in four days, could not bring others in their wake. The first report might have simply reported the descent on Angle, perhaps postscripted with anxious speculation about the size of the rebel army and the vulnerability of Pembroke. Subsequent intelligence, perhaps brought by Williams himself, must have been more reassuring: there had been no general rising; the small rebel army had been deflected northwards, and were being shadowed by loyalist troops. Letters from Rhys ap Thomas and Walter Herbert would have likewise fostered the illusion that the rising was a derisory affair. Perhaps it was in this relaxed frame of mind that the king decided not to dishonour the feast of the Assumption of the Blessed Virgin Mary, celebrated on 15 August, with unnecessary military manœuvres.[16] It is not hard to imagine the king's rage when, perhaps on this very day, he learnt that Henry Tudor had been joined by the men who were allegedly dealing with him, that their joint army had entered England unopposed, and that Shrewsbury had opened its gates to receive them.

By this stage the king must have begun to sense treachery in other quarters. It is probable that throughout summer he had in his entourage a considerable company of lords and knights. A select party of Ricardians, including Viscount Lovell, Lord Scrope of Bolton, Sir Richard Radcliffe, Sir William Catesby, Sir Thomas Mauleverer and Edward Frank, had been at Woburn on 20 June, and had probably joined the king soon afterwards. The earl of Lincoln, Lords Scrope and Strange witnessed the surrender of the great seal at Nottingham on 1 August, and Sir Marmaduke Constable and Sir John Babington seem to have been in town on 5 August.[17] Yet little progress could have been made by the feast of the Assumption in the general mobilisation ordered five days earlier. Perhaps Norfolk had been prompt in giving assurances of his immediate action, but the two other chief power-brokers, the earl of Northumberland and Lord Stanley, could be seen to be dragging their feet. Since Northumberland had the chief responsibility for mustering the levies of the northern counties, the request on 16 August from the loyal citizens of York as to the king's military needs indicated a gross dereliction of duty. Almost certainly he had determined to keep his options open, and was deliberately trying to minimise the number of royalists in his contingent. Lord Stanley was showing no inclination to hurry to the king's banner, even though his dilatoriness was putting his son's life in jeopardy.[18]

*   *   *

Henry Tudor's first few days on English soil could not have been particularly encouraging. After a show of resistance from its bailiff, John Mitton, Shrewsbury opened its gate to him. Probably the town had been asked to admit the rebels by Sir William Stanley or Gilbert Talbot, but there was no reception party for the pretender. His position was precarious in the extreme. There were no signs of a rising on his behalf, and the composition of his army, overwhelmingly Welsh and French, could scarcely add to the appeal of his cause in England. To strike rapidly south-east along Watling Street to London, though possible in logistic terms, would clearly be unwise. Instead Henry Tudor determined on a more easterly tack, hoping to draw in the Stanleys and other allies, and probably at the same time keeping his line of retreat back to Wales open. At Newport he was joined by Talbot with a company of five hundred men,

House in Wyle Cop, Shrewsbury, where Henry Tudor is reputed to have stayed.

the first significant commitment from an English well-wisher. As uncle of the young earl of Shrewsbury as well as a magnate in his own right, Talbot had considerable influence with the gentry of Shropshire and the High Peak district. Since he seems to have been operating in concert with the Stanleys, he might also have brought news of their dispositions. Indeed the following evening Sir William Stanley rode across from Stone for consultations with Henry Tudor, who was now camped at Stafford. At this meeting the pretender must have agreed to slow down his advance while the Stanleys pushed on ahead into the midlands. As well as providing much needed rest for the rebel troops, such a strategy would create more time and space to gather in supporters. It is otherwise hard to explain the slow pace from this point onwards. It had taken a bare week to traverse a hundred and fifty miles of harsh terrain from Dale to Shrewsbury, but most of the following week, throughout which time the king was massing his troops, to move the fifty miles on good roads through Stafford to Lichfield.[19]

The Stanleys had heard news of the landing of Henry Tudor as early if not earlier than Richard III, and had begun to marshal their forces in response to the pretender's appeals even before the king's summons. If the chronology of *Lady Bessy* is reliable, they stole another march on the king by setting out on Monday 15 August. Riding out from Lathom, with retainers and levies falling in at Warrington and other centres, Lord Stanley headed for Newcastle under Lyme. More closely shadowing the invading army Sir William Stanley moved from Holt on the Welsh border to Nantwich were he spent the night. Presumably an opportunity was found for discussions between the two brothers. Their subsequent movements certainly seem to have been co-ordinated. Keeping their two armies separate, they maintained independent courses and speeds. Lord Stanley pressed ahead on a more easterly tack, with the objective of striking as far as possible into the midlands and protecting the front against the king. He seems to have reached Lichfield by 17 August. Moving more slowly from Nantwich to Stone, whence he rode across to meet Henry Tudor, the younger Stanley gave more open encouragement to the rebel army. On 20 August he stage-managed the pretender's entry into Lichfield, organising a reception with cannonade and other military honours. Meanwhile Lord Stanley, who had withdrawn from Lichfield some days earlier, as if retreating before the rebel advance, maintained an effective smokescreen behind which the rebels consolidated their forces. By 19 August he was in the vicinity of Atherstone, apparently blocking the road to London but also covering Watling Street at the point at which the king, moving down from Nottingham, would seek to intercept the rebels' progress.[20]

The fanfare and festivities at Lichfield smack of bravado. The pretender's army could scarcely have looked impressive, after one week at sea and two weeks on the road. It is hard to know how many Englishmen had joined the cause. Presumably Gilbert Talbot drew in some of the Shropshire gentry. Certainly John Mynde of Little Sutton led ten men 'defensibly arrayed' into the rebel camp, and other local captains might have brought in their levies. In Staffordshire old retainers of the duke of Buckingham and friends of James Blount would have been willing recruits: Hugh Pershal, Humphrey Stanley, Reginald Hassall, Hugh Eardswick, who all fought at Bosworth, presumably joined the rebel host at Stafford or Lichfield. Quite possibly sections of the Staffordshire muster and other counties were diverted to the rebel cause. A contingent from the city of Chester fought for Henry Tudor, though doubtless under Stanleyite leadership.[21] All in all, the Stanleys' determination to retain their independent commands, for all its strategic sense, must have been demoralising. With at least a thousand men in arms, Sir William Stanley could have powerfully reinforced the gallant rebel army, but after briefly conducting joint exercises at Lichfield he precipitately left to join his brother beyond Tamworth. Meanwhile Lord Stanley with an even larger force was establishing

Blue Boar Inn, Leicester, known as the White Boar when Richard stayed there in 1485; from an engraving by John Flower, 1826.

himself somewhere around Hinckley, where Fosse Way intersected with Watling Street, perhaps throwing up earth ramparts at Stapleton.

By this stage Richard III himself had good reason to feel anxious. Receiving intelligence of Henry Tudor's encampment near Lichfield and Lord Stanley's 'retreat' towards Atherstone, he could still get no proper impression of what was happening. Clearly the Stanleys were playing for time, and some at least were

King Richard's Chamber at the Blue Boar Inn, Leicester, from an engraving by Thomas Featherstone, 1838.

proving false. Lord Strange had been caught trying to escape, and while under pressure he divulged that Sir William Stanley and Sir John Savage were involved in the conspiracy he stoutly affirmed that his father would rally to the royal standard. Meanwhile, in his communications with the king, Lord Stanley was doubtless able to defend his movements in sound strategic terms: he was after all blocking the road to London to the rebel advance. Obviously the king had delayed too long in Nottingham, and needed to move his headquarters south to Leicester. Unfortunately his mobilisation of the north was far from complete. There was still no sign of Northumberland, and the citizens of York did not dispatch their contingent until 19 August. Nevertheless during the night and the following morning more troops arrived, and on Saturday 20 August the king arrayed his army and led them in battle formation to Leicester, which might well have been the intended rendezvous with the Stanleys as well as with Norfolk, Brackenbury and other units from the south.[22]

The royal host reached Leicester by sunset. According to local tradition the king took up quarters in the inn which bore his badge, the White Boar.[23] In all likelihood Norfolk and his contingent were already quartered in the town and surrounding villages, and Brackenbury arrived soon afterwards. On the following day Northumberland likewise appeared, with many other northern lords and knights. Gradually there was assembled what the Crowland chronicler thought was the largest army ever mustered on one man's behalf in England. In addition to the duke of Norfolk, the earls of Northumberland, Surrey, Lincoln and Shrewsbury were present. It is certain that Lords Ferrers and Zouche were in the royal host, and there are strong grounds for believing that Lords Scrope of Bolton, Fitzhugh, Scrope of Masham, Ogle and Greystoke gave their support. *The Ballad of Bosworth Field* records the presence of all these peers, and in addition the earls of Kent and Westmorland, Lords Dudley, Maltravers, Grey of Codnor and Welles, and numerous others, all of whom might have been present, even if not as active combatants. Since the ballad provides the most complete list of lords and knights whose presence at Bosworth is documented in other sources, and since it names so many men who are known to have been supporters of the Ricardian regime, it seems reasonable to accept it as an authentic, if slightly garbled and by no means infallible, source. What cannot be contested is that the royal army was both large and distinguished, and included many more lords and knights than the two dozen men who were subsequently attainted.[24]

*   *   *

The king's main concern at this stage must have been Lord Stanley. It was far easier to face the threat from Henry Tudor than to deal with an undeclared enemy, who had under his command several thousand men and had established himself in a strong defensive position. The large-scale earthworks at Stapleton, which the early antiquarians believed dated from 1485, might well have been the Stanleyite camp.[25] Messages passed back and forth as the wily lord evaded the king's direct requests to join the royal host. A quarter of a century earlier Stanley had played a similar game. Prior to the battle of Blore heath, he had countered royal orders to bring his troops in with a request to be allowed to command the vanguard. It might well be that on this occasion as well Stanley claimed to be operating as the king's advance guard. It is perhaps significant that one chronicler at least thought that he was in charge of the royal vanguard. How committed Lord Stanley was to Henry Tudor is hard to establish. Given the predicament of Lord Strange, as well as the tactical advantages to be derived from not declaring his hand, it would have been foolish to declare openly for the pretender. Yet there can be no doubt that he was deliberately undermining the king's strategic planning, and it seems likely that his manœuvres were securing political and military objectives vital to the rebel cause. Besides maintaining a screen behind which Henry Tudor could draw breath and rally support, he had also pushed a wedge between the king and southern England, making it possible to disrupt the official musters and give heart to would-be rebels. There might even have been some skirmishing: the ballads in fact record an incident a day or two before the battle in which Sir William Stanley thought that his brother had come under attack. If Richard Boughton, sheriff of Leicestershire and Warwickshire, who died on 20 August, was killed while raising royal levies, it might well have been the work of the Stanleys. At the same time Sir Thomas Bourchier and Sir Walter Hungerford, who deserted from Brackenbury's

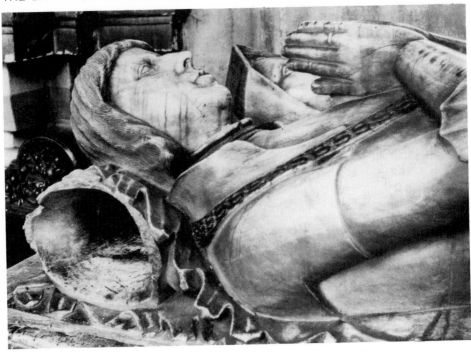

Simon Digby (died 1519); effigy at Coleshill, Warwickshire.

company at Stony Stratford, would have passed through Stanley lines to reach Henry Tudor.[26]

Still Richard III was not alone in his frustration with the house of Stanley. The young pretender likewise had good reason to despair of their temporising. The darkest moment came during the move from Lichfield to Tamworth apparently on the evening of 20 August. It had probably been assumed that Sir William Stanley and his company would have remained with the rebel army after their joint exercises in the city, but instead the sound of gunfire from afar had prompted their sudden departure, allegedly to aid Lord Stanley. Then to add to his misery, on the road south Henry became detached from his host and had to spend a desolate night with only a few companions in a potentially hostile countryside. Not surprisingly his army was on the point of breaking up, when he rode into camp the next morning. He managed to put a brave face on the scrape by telling his men that he had been making contact with potential supporters. The arrival of Bourchier and Hungerford at this time was doubtless an opportune boost to his soldiers' morale.

Henry Tudor spent Sunday 21 August near Atherstone, perhaps attending services and receiving hospitality at Merevale abbey. His troops were foraging throughout the district: three months later he would repay the villages of Atherstone, Witherley, Mancetter and Fenny Drayton for corn taken by his soldiers.[27] At some stage in the day he finally secured a meeting with his stepfather to seal their alliance and make plans for the coming battle. Doubtless Lord Stanley was promised high advancement: Robert Lindsay later alleged that

Bow Bridge, Leicester, across which Richard III led out his troops; engraving from Throsby's History of Leicester, *1791.*

he was actually bribed. What agreements were made about strategy remain a mystery, but apparently Henry Tudor believed that the Stanleyite forces would fight as part of his army. Soon after nightfall there were further recruits. Sir John Savage, Sir Simon Digby, Sir Brian Sandford, all men of standing and experience, had defected with their companies from the royal host. Meanwhile John Hardwick, a gentleman from the district, offered his services as a local guide, and probably suggested an encampment on Whitemoors a few miles to the north.[28]

On the same day Richard III led his vast host out of Leicester in the direction of Atherstone. Learning from spies that Henry Tudor was moving towards Whitemoors, and that the Stanleys were positioned a few miles directly to the south, the king established his camp in the neighbourhood of Sutton Cheney. In the darkness of the evening the villagers of Market Bosworth must have seen the lights of camp-fires like a string of glowing beads hanging from the hills which framed their southern pastures. There can have been few who slept soundly: in addition to the distinguished knights who defected to the rebels under cover of darkness, there must have been many common soldiers who scampered back to their homes to avoid the fighting. By all reports the king passed a terrible night, tormented by dreams or apparitions, and observers predictably pointed to the workings of a deeply troubled conscience. On the other hand it seems most unlikely that the young Henry Tudor, camped on the windswept Whitemoors on the eve of his first battle, and a battle for the highest possible stakes, slept any easier.

Bosworth Field, 22 August 1485

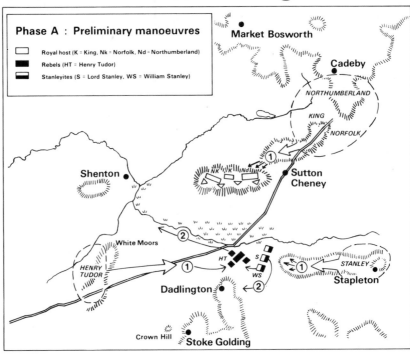

Phase A : Preliminary manoeuvres

Royal host (K = King, Nk = Norfolk, Nd = Northumberland)

Rebels (HT = Henry Tudor)

Stanleyites (S = Lord Stanley, WS = William Stanley)

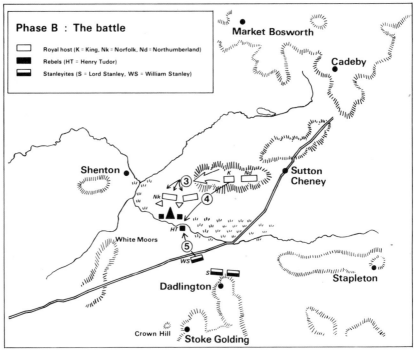

Phase B : The battle

Royal host (K = King, Nk = Norfolk, Nd = Northumberland)

Rebels (HT = Henry Tudor)

Stanleyites (S = Lord Stanley, WS = William Stanley)

6 Ordeal by Battle

It was late August, and dawn still came early. Even so there can have been few encamped in the neighbourhood of Bosworth still asleep at first light. Throughout the night sentries had kept watch while spies sallied forth. From the king and pretender downwards, the soldiers in the two armies could have hoped for no more than a few hours' fretful sleep, and a good hour before dawn the two camps must have come alive with preparations for the day. The hammering of steel, the clanking of armour, the neighing of horses, all disturbed the peace of this quiet countryside. The chief protagonists prepared themselves spiritually as well as mentally. The forthcoming battle was to be no ordinary passage of arms. For all the hard-fought engagements of the previous thirty years, or for that matter the previous centuries, not once had a king and a would-be king confronted each other personally on the field. It would be an old-style 'ordeal by battle' between two claimants to the crown, and it was firmly believed that God would be on hand to give final judgement on the title of Richard III and the claims of Henry Tudor.

Rising behind the royal camp around Sutton Cheney, the sun revealed the lie of the land and the dispositions of the various armies.[1] In the fresh early morning air the king probably rode out with his scouts to the top of Ambion hill to consider the battle-site. Ambion hill was a tongue of high ground jutting westwards from Sutton Cheney, and doubtless it had been decided the day before to occupy this commanding eminence. He looked down from the hill: its southern escarpment fell away quite steeply to marshy ground below, while the western slope down to the river would also be easily defensible. Beneath the grass, still green in high summer, he could see the clay soil which gave the rough pasture the name of Redmoor. Across the intervening lowland, still perhaps enveloped in mist, he could see the uplands which formed a ridge framing the site. In this part of the country settlements were made on the hills rather than in the badly-drained valleys. On his right hand side, looking north, was the village of Market Bosworth, with its square church tower. Directly ahead of him was the village of Shenton and to the south he could see the spire of Stoke Golding. It was in this sector that he would have seen the lights from the camps of his enemies the previous evening. To the south-west he could see the host of Henry Tudor out on Whitemoors and to the south he could see the army of Lord Stanley. He would have been gratified to note the strength of his own chosen

Sutton Cheney Church, where Richard traditionally heard his last Mass.

position, the still modest size of the pretender's army, and the distance maintained by the Stanleyites. He might well have been concerned, however, by signs that his chief protagonist had ordered an early start and seemed bent on seizing the initiative.

If he had a brief moment of equanimity surveying the scene with the shrewd eye of an experienced strategist, he was far from composed on his return to camp. According to all reports he had slept poorly, and was more than usually grim, ashen faced and given to blustering rage. According to the Crowland chronicle, the camp was a scene of great confusion, with no chaplains to perform divine service for him, and no breakfast prepared for him. Since this source was not generally known in Tudor times, it is interesting that two early oral traditions record similar tales. Lord Morley who compiled a book of miracles associated with the eucharist remembered a story told by a man called Bigod who served Richard III as carver and fought for him at Bosworth. Allegedly the king 'called in the morning for to have mass said before him, but when his chaplain had one thing ready, evermore they wanted another, when they had wine they lacked bread'. At last, with the enemy advancing, he was constrained to go out to do battle without the benefit of hearing mass. If this story is reliable, it would indicate that the king missed his breakfast, which he would have postponed until after divine service. In the *Ballad of Bosworth Field* Sir William Stanley grimly promised to give him a 'breakfast' he would not forget. Perhaps the king simply drank fresh water from the spring later called King Richard's well.[2]

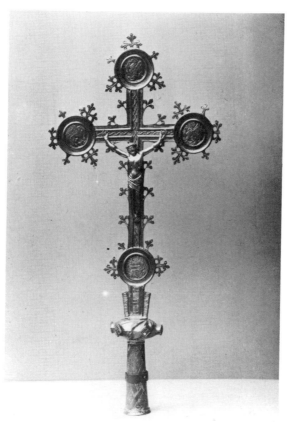

Processional cross, found at Bosworth in 1778, the roundels have symbols on the reverse which may represent Yorkist sun-bursts.

All the evidence points to the king being caught on the wrong foot on the morning of the battle. It might well be that he had intended first of all to draw up his army on the hill-top in an impressive show of strength. The assembly of so many lords and men-at-arms under the royal banner, established in a strong defensive position, could be depended upon to terrify all but the most fool-hardy opponent. The king might reasonably have expected that his enemies would attempt a hurried juncture and huddled defence, which could then be broken by systematic attack, or even that they would break and run, in which case they could be picked off at leisure. What he did not allow for was the determination of Henry Tudor and his captains, who seemed resolved on a direct assault on the king's position. Their bravado might well have immediately increased fears of treachery in the royal camp. The duke of Norfolk had received an anonymous piece of doggerel warning him to be 'not too bold' because the king had been 'bought and sold';[3] there had been defections from the royal host during the night; and the loyalty of Northumberland seems to have been in doubt. To compound his difficulties, the king had to get his troops into position more quickly than he expected. The shape of the hill gave him little room for

King Richard's Well, a cairn marking the spring from which Richard is traditionally said to have drunk during the Battle; it was erected in 1813.

manœuvre, and the immense size of his army probably made it unwieldy.

Nevertheless Richard III, as rapidly as possible, marshalled his troops. It was customary to divide a large army into three 'battles', and the royal host fell naturally into three main commands. For the most part historians have talked about a 'vanguard' under Norfolk, a main body under the king, and a 'rearguard' under Northumberland, but this formulation ought not be taken too literally or accepted too uncritically. The limited space available on the hill would have led to drastic modifications of any classical battle-plan, and the use of the conventional terminology inevitably gives a far too orderly impression. Moreover the sources themselves are far less clear on the matter than is often supposed. Polydore Vergil referred solely to a long battle-line with Norfolk commanding the archers at the front: it is his English translators who introduced the firm tripartite structure. A number of the foreign sources also assumed this pattern, but their testimony only adds to the confusion. De Valera has a vanguard under the 'grand chamberlain' but also a left wing under 'Tamerlant'; Molinet, the most reliable, has a vanguard under the joint command of Norfolk and Brackenbury; Lindsay has a vanguard under Stanley and Brackenbury.[4] Of course, a great deal depends on the particular perspective taken, whether, for example, the 'front' of the royal army is taken as facing south or west, or whether the Stanleyites are regarded as a part of the royal host, either as an advance guard or as a left wing.

What can be claimed is that in deploying his forces on Ambion hill the king aimed for maximum visual effect. According to Vergil the king drew out his forces at fearsome length. To their enemies to the south-west and the potential traitors to the south the whole crest must have bristled with standards, lances, and bills. He placed Norfolk, his most experienced and reliable commander, in charge of a thick front-line, possibly stretching right round the southern and western rims of the hill. It was tightly packed with both men-at-arms and archers, for the most part companies from the southern counties, and there were cannons chained together at strategic points. The king kept under his command an impressive company of lords and retainers, predominantly mounted knights. Presumably it included his nephew the earl of Lincoln, such close friends as Viscount Lovell and the Lords Scrope, and the hostage Lord Strange. According to tradition, he sent an illegitimate son, Richard 'Plantagenet' to watch out the battle from a safe distance, perhaps in the company of churchmen and other non-combatants. The earl of Northumberland and his company, along with a number of other lords and the northern levies, brought up the rear, doubtless with the responsibility of protecting the eastern approach to Sutton Cheney. All in all the royal host must have comprised at least 10,000, and possibly over 15,000 men.[5]

*   *   *

Henry Tudor awoke before dawn, heard mass and took refreshment, and by daybreak was ready for action. In contrast to the unwieldy royal host on the tight ledge of Ambion hill, he had a small, mobile army, with all the room in the world to deploy itself. He had only about 5,000 men, scarcely sufficient for more than

Standard of Richard III, flying on Ambion Hill.

one full battalion. He and his advisers resolved to commit the bulk of the army as a vanguard under the experienced leadership of the earl of Oxford. With units of French and Scottish mercenaries and divisions of Welsh archers under his command, Oxford was presumably assisted by captains such as Philbert de Chandée, Bernard Stuart and Rhys ap Thomas. The majority of English men-at-arms probably fought in the wings under Gilbert Talbot and John Savage, two expert cavalrymen. Henry Tudor followed with a small, but distinguished company including the earl of Pembroke, the fighting bishop of Exeter, and other well-born exiles, as well as his standard-bearer William Brandon, the giant John Cheney and an elite corps of guardsmen. In leaving himself such a slender battalion, the pretender was clearly depending on reinforcement from the Stanleys, but what undertakings had been given are obscure. According to Polydore Vergil, Henry Tudor expected Lord Stanley to bring his troops to form a single fighting force, and was alarmed when the wary lord replied that he would commit his men at an opportune time. Putting a brave face on another set-back, the young pretender could only hope that fortune would favour the bold.⁶

The position of the Stanleys, who together had at least 5,000 men in arms, cannot be described with any confidence.⁷ The Crowland chronicler, Molinet and Commines say that they were firmly on the side of the rebels. On the other hand, De Valera and Lindsay imply that they were actually part of the royal army. Polydore Vergil, generally the most authoritative of sources, and the balladeers, surely the most knowledgeable on the Stanleys, offer more complex accounts. Both affirm that the Stanleys approached the battle as if uncommitted, that during the battle their forces were divided, and that Sir William Stanley played a more active role than his brother.⁸ The most likely reconstruction is that after leaving their base at Stapleton at dawn they set out on a course which would keep them roughly equidistant from the royal host and the rebel army. Their position to the south of Ambion hill could be, indeed was, interpreted in a number of ways: they were maintaining a common front with Richard III against Henry Tudor; they were waiting to effect a juncture with their rebel allies; or they were intending to sit on the side-lines to come in on the winning side. To add to their options, they could even divide their forces and pursue several strategies at once. There seems to have been little doubt that Lord Stanley wanted to see his stepson triumph, but naturally wished to minimise the risks to his own following, not least his own son, who was a hostage of the king. Meanwhile there were urgent appeals from Henry Tudor, who had begun to lead his army down from Whitemoors, and ugly threats from the king, possibly communicated by Sir Robert Brackenbury.

*   *   *

Though both Richard III and Henry Tudor doubtless found words of encouragement for their men, it seems highly unlikely that either of the two protagonists had the inclination, still less the time, for long perorations. According to the Crowland chronicler, the king in a rather weary fashion told his men that whichever side won the victory it would prove the utter destruction of England: he was determined to crush his opponents once and for all, while his enemies for their part doubtless planned to wreak vengeance on his own men. Even Polydore Vergil, who in true Renaissance style generally larded his narrative with invented speeches, put no words into the mouths of the combatants at Bosworth. In such circumstances little credence can be placed in the verbose oratory recorded by Edward Hall, writing a generation later and with Vergil his main source for the events of 1485.⁹ Nevertheless there is some interest in this material beyond the fact that it was developed further by Shakespeare. Most basically, it shows how people in Hall's lifetime imagined Richard III and Henry VII, and what they thought the two leaders might have said to their troops. Since memories of the two kings were still quite strong, it might even be possible to tease out of the preposterous rhetoric some prosaic insights into the atmosphere of the time.

In the speech attributed to Richard III, Hall had ample scope to add substantially to the 'black legend' of the misshapen tyrant, but what is most

Standard of Richard III; drawn by Julian Rowe.

Standard of Henry Tudor; drawn by Julian Rowe.

remarkable is the degree to which he has presented a sympathetic figure. The king began by stressing the quality of his government, and commending the commitment of his chief subjects, 'by whose prudent and politic counsel I have so governed my realm, people and subjects, that I have omitted nothing appertaining to the office of a just prince'. There is plenty of evidence that Richard did like to present himelf in this fashion, and this line is not wholly alien to the Tudor tradition. Rather more curious is the author's lack of interest in exploiting its potential for irony. Hall's king is no hypocrite, but is disarmingly candid in addressing the weaknesses of his position. He admitted that in gaining the crown he was 'seduced and provoked by sinister counsel and diabolical temptation' to commit 'a facinorous and detestable act', but he begged his men to forget his abominable crime, as he daily remembered to lament it and expiate it through 'strait penance and salt tears'. In a tone more appropriate to a battlefield address, he continued by castigating his rival as an unknown adventurer inspired by the devil 'to covet our realm, crown and dignity', and mocking him as a 'Welsh milksop', who never saw army, nor was exercised in martial affairs, by reason whereof he neither can nor is able on his own wit or experience to guide or rule an host'. He pointed to the 'company of traitors, thieves, outlaws and renegades of our nation' who were his supporters, and the 'beggarly Bretons and fainthearted Frenchmen' who had come to despoil the realm. Such men were unworthy adversaries. The English traitors and renegades, once they see the royal standard and the might of the realm displayed against them, 'will either shamefully fly or humbly submit themselves to our grace and mercy'. As for the French, 'their valiantness is such that our noble progenitors and your valiant parents have them oftener vanquished and overcome in a month' than they thought possible in a year. Still more the inspiring commander than the braying bully, Hall's king ended by calling on his troops to cast away their doubts and fears and 'like valiant champions advance forth your standards' and to test whether 'your enemies can . . . try the title of battle by dint of sword'.

Needless to say, Henry Tudor is also endowed by Hall with considerable powers of oratory, though again a serious attempt is made at imaginative reconstruction. The young pretender is presented as laying firm claim to the moral high ground. He affirmed his strong belief that God would aid his enterprise, because there can be no more just cause, no 'more honest, goodly or Godly quarrel than to fight against a captain, being an homicide and murderer of his own blood and progeny, an extreme destroyer of his nobility, and to his and our country . . . a fiery brand and a burden intolerable'. Like the king, he sought to stress the community of interest between himself and his men, pointing out that just as his chief adversary 'keepeth me from the crown and regiment of this noble realm' so his partisans 'occupy your lands, cut down your woods and destroy your manors, letting your wives and children range abroad for their living'. Of course, in pressing the justice of his cause, Henry did not elaborate on his own title, but rather expatiated on the tyranny of his opponent, whom he compared to Tarquin and Nero. More effectively perhaps, he rehearsed the great dangers through which they had successfully come as evidence that God had already blessed their enterprise. It was this assurance of divine favour, along with their own prospects for material reward, that they must bear in mind as they stand 'like sheep in a fold circumcepted and compassed between our enemies and our doubtful friends'. This latter statement is the only evidence for the theory that the Stanleys positioned themselves on both the northern and southern sides of the field, but even if it was meant to be taken literally, which is doubtful, it could be taken to apply just as well to Northumberland or the other units in the royal army which the pretender claimed were sympathetic to him. Whatever the case, Hall's young hero is depicted as ending his speech with a fine call for his men to advance in the name of God and St George, as 'true men against traitors . . . true inheritors against usurpers, the scourges of God against tyrants', and to display his banner 'with a good courage, march forth like strong and rombustious champions, and begin the battle like hardy conquerors'.

*   *   *

As Richard III arranged his vast host on Ambion hill, Henry Tudor and the earl of Oxford led their gallant army down from Whitemoors probably aiming to follow for a while the road to Sutton Cheney which passed to the south of the hill and close to the point at which Lord Stanley was assembling his men. Of course,

Standard of Henry Tudor, flying from the position occupied by his troops during the Battle.

the evidence available to reconstruct their approach and subsequent manœuvres is extremely limited. Apart from Ambion hill itself, the only other topographical reference point is the marsh mentioned by both Polydore Vergil and Jean Molinet. Although the area was drained in the sixteenth century, it almost certainly lay at the foot of the southern slopes of the hill, but how extensive it was is open to debate. According to Vergil Henry Tudor and his army approached the enemy with the marsh on their right hand, and in so doing had the sun behind them. Such a scenario, implying that the rebels were attacking from an easterly direction, has left a number of historians incredulous.[10] Yet it is a possible manœuvre. They might have followed an easterly course to confront the full length of the royal army, and then changed tack to make an assault on the western slopes of Ambion hill. In fact both Jean Molinet and the author of *The Rose of England* imply that the rebel commanders first drew in front of the king's line, and then decided to aim for the flank, in order to put the sun and wind behind them and avoid the king's cannons.[11] The strategy might have made sense from other points of view. The easterly path took them close to the position of the Stanleyites, and Henry Tudor might well have determined upon trying to hustle them into a full commitment. Perhaps he even hoped to draw the king's cavalry down into the marsh. Far from a direct assault on the western slope of Ambion hill being the natural opening gambit, the initial push eastwards had much to commend it.

Although Polydore Vergil does not describe a meeting between Henry Tudor and the Stanleyites on the field, his narrative implies that the rebel army aimed for such a juncture. The pretender left a gap in his formation to be filled by his allies, who were positioned midway between him and the enemy, and almost certainly his path was chosen to allow a union. What happened as they drew close is left obscure. In his redaction of Vergil's account, Hall recognised the difficulty, and described Lord Stanley's committing his troops at this stage. Judging from the confusion of the other sources the manœuvres were far more complex. The ballad tradition offers the most clues, and carries the more conviction in that it assigns a rather inglorious role to Lord Stanley. It records that Henry Tudor requested the vanguard of Stanley's army, but was given only a handful of brave young cavalrymen. Since Sir William Stanley commanded the Stanleyite rearguard, it can be assumed that its involvement had been agreed upon. What seems to have happened is that at the approach of Henry Tudor, the main body of the Stanleyite army withdrew, and Lord Stanley watched out the battle from the top of a nearby hill. Under cover of the manœuvre, however, a select company of Stanleyites reinforced the pretender's retinue, while, maintaining a little distance, Sir William Stanley also brought his battalion in behind the rebels. Such a sequence of events might explain some of the confusion apparent in the report of De Valera who claimed that the king's left wing under 'Lord Tamerlant', possibly a conflation of Northumberland and Stanley, swept across the front of the king's line to join the rebel assault, and in the later account of Lindsay who maintained that the king's vanguard under Lord Stanley, far from blocking the approach of Henry Tudor, turned and fought alongside him.[12]

*   *   *

From the top of Ambion hill the king watched the movements on the heath below him. He saw Henry Tudor and his army advance steadily across Redmoor plain. He strained his eyes to identify his chief adversaries, and acknowledged the pretender's wisdom in allowing the earl of Oxford to command in the field.

As the rebels approached the Stanleys, he tried to make sense of the manœuvres. Nothing could conceal the fact that Lord Stanley was making no resistance, and among the king's captains there were murmurs against the all too evident treachery. There might have been some relief in Stanley's apparent withdrawal from the field, but the king's rage knew no bounds. He swore vengeance on the house of Stanley, and on all the gentry between Shrewsbury and Lancaster. For the moment Lord Strange alone bore the brunt of his wrath, and his immediate execution was ordered. According to the ballad tradition, the popular young lord mournfully farewelled his kinsmen, friends and country, and instructed his servant to take a ring to his wife with the message that she should escape the country with their child. Happily the execution was not carried out. The Crowland chronicler believed that certain counsellors, fearful of the outcome of the battle, persuaded the king to delay proceedings, while the balladeer wrote that punishment was deferred until all three Stanleys were in the king's power.[13] Perhaps in the excitement and confusion of the battle the orders were simply overlooked.

The king's attention was again focused on the small rebel army which paused in front of his battle-line, doubtless hoping for reinforcement but almost inviting attack. He ordered his gunners to fire, more to undermine their morale than to do serious damage from such a range.[14] Then he noticed purposeful movements among their ranks, as the whole force began to shift to a north-easterly tack. Obviously Oxford was intent on an assault on the western slope, and for the moment the rebels had the marsh on their right as protection. Meanwhile a battalion of Stanleyites had remained in place, perhaps with the intention of lending support, or even threatening the king's eastern side, where the unreliable Northumberland was positioned. The king and the duke of Norfolk quickly strengthened the most immediately threatened south-western quadrant. Already lines of archers were maintaining a withering fire on the troops below. It was arranged that, as soon as the rebels moved beyond the cover of the marsh, Norfolk would lead the front-line, composed of knots of men-at-arms with units of archers and billmen, against them. Kneeling down, making the sign of the cross, and kissing the ground, the old campaigners observed the age-old ritual,[15] and then encouraged their less experienced comrades in the push down the hill. There were wild shouts and loud clashes of steel as the king's front line smashed into the rebel vanguard, and for a while it was total pandemonium. All parties knew that a great deal depended on the results of this initial encounter. The massed attack was a determined attempt by the king and Norfolk to snatch back the initiative. There was every likelihood that it would completely skittle the central phalanx of the pretender's army.

The earl of Oxford's adroit leadership and the valour of the troops under his command prevented an early rout. Planting his standards firmly in the ground, he ordered the men to draw in around them, organising them into a dense wedge formation.[16] Raw levies would have lacked both the nerves and the discipline for such a manœuvre, and he doubtless banked on the professionalism of his French and Scottish brigades. He was not disappointed by them, and must have been further gratified by the effect of the movement on his opponents. Genuinely surprised to meet such cool and determined resistance, and perhaps sensing

Standards used by Henry Tudor at Bosworth, the Dun Cow of Warwick, and St George; drawn by Oliver Harris.

some sort of trap, the royal forces drew back in disarray. Perhaps the king's formidable front-line was already a spent force: in the stampede down the hill it must have been difficult for the troops to bring their force to bear on the rebel vanguard, and the sharp incline doubtless carried many of the less seasoned or less committed foot-soldiers far off target. At a most dangerous moment the pretender's army had been able to convert near disaster into a huge psychological lift.

There was little time for self-congratulation. With Oxford's vanguard in a tight defensive bloc, the rebels were still pinned down by numerically superior forces. The cavalry wings under Savage and Talbot were able to relieve the pressure to a degree. Jabbing and hacking from their saddles, they wreaked havoc among Norfolk's foot-soldiers. There was fierce fighting on both sides, but gradually the rebels were able to create space for themselves, as groups of their opponents began to take to their heels. Yet, despite their gallant efforts, the odds against them remained formidable. Even if the king's whole front-line could be driven from the field, there seemed little prospect of being able to claw their way up the slope. Meanwhile on the crest of the hill the great warrior-king himself along with a powerful body of armoured knights awaited them, to say nothing of Northumberland's battalion further to the rear. For the first long hour of the battle it must have seemed that all that heroism could accomplish would be to stave off defeat rather than to achieve victory.

There is no doubt that most of the fighting took place on the borders of the marsh on the south-west slopes of Ambion hill, and it was in this sector that most of the carnage was perpetrated. Rather surprisingly the pretender's army suffered few casualties, certainly not among men of note, though the lightly armed Welsh foot-soldiers might have taken quite a beating. On the other hand the king's front-line seems to have borne heavy losses, including many of its captains and its chief commander. Such a pattern confirms the impression that the massed assault began to break early, and that the men were cut down in a rout. It might well be that lack of commitment was a factor in this failure. Norfolk's divisions were composed for the most part of men from the southern and eastern counties, men whose loyalty to the Ricardian regime must have been questionable. Even if Norfolk had the respect of his troops, many of the other captains, especially northerners like Sir Robert Brackenbury, Sir John Huddleston and Edward Frank, would not have had the confidence of the men they were leading. The chroniclers certainly claim that a large proportion of the royal army fought under compulsion and without conviction. A few might have turned and fought for Henry Tudor. Most simply threw down their arms and fled at the first opportunity, leaving their captains to be hacked down as they struggled in their armour back to the horse-pack.[17]

In all likelihood it was in this part of the field as well that there took place several passages of arms which were to pass into legend. Sir Gervase Clifton and John Byron were friends and neighbours who found themselves on opposite sides of the field. A prominent royal retainer and Nottinghamshire landowner, Clifton must have found it impossible, even if he had so desired, to avoid committing himself to the royal host. Byron, on the other hand, a man with interests in the north-west as well as Nottinghamshire, had thrown in his lot with the pretender. Tradition has it that they made a battlefield pact according to which whoever survived would protect the interests of his fellow. In the heat of the battle, however, there were also opportunities to settle private scores. Another north midlands squire, John Babington of Dethick, was allegedly slain by James Blount, who was in this instance more motivated by the prospect of an inheritance than zeal for the Tudor cause. In the event he slew the wrong man. It was John Babington of Chilwell who was his intended target. Personal

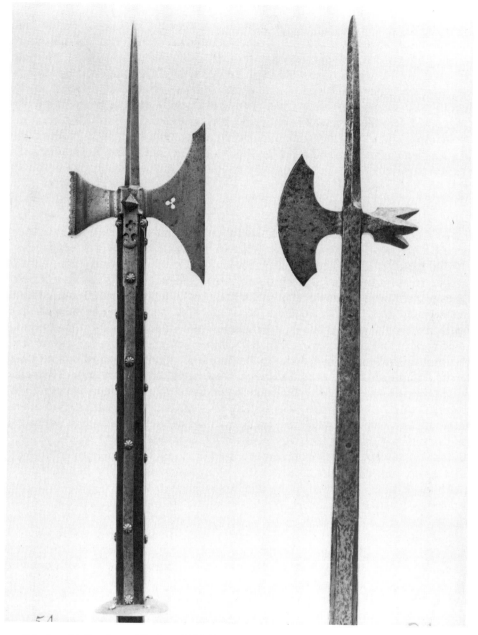

Pole Axes: (a) French, possibly about 1450, blade is 6 inches long; (b) French, about 1470, blade is $7\frac{1}{2}$ inches long.

animosity doubtless played its part among the higher ranks as well. The earl of Oxford might not have been inclined to be merciful to Lord Ferrers, who occupied some of his ancestral lands, most immediately the Leicestershire manor of Wigston. His grievances against the duke of Norfolk were even more substantial. Old rivals for leadership of East Anglian society, the pair had fought against each other at Barnet, when Oxford had worsted his opponent in the battle, only to be robbed of victory by the failure of his allies. While he languished in jail, it was Norfolk who was granted the lion's share of his patrimony. It was certainly time to turn the tables, and both Jean Molinet, the Burgundian chronicler, and John Beaumont, the Jacobean poet, depict Oxford's slaying of Norfolk.[18]

* * *

While the grim encounter between the two vanguards still hung in the balance, King Richard resolved to throw himself into the fray. By temperament a soldier, he doubtless had watched the action with mounting frustration. The earl of Oxford's bold advance and stout defence would have won his respect, but the lacklustre showing and general half-heartedness of his own vanguard must have been all the more galling. He smelt treachery in the wind. The unspeakable Lord Stanley had proved false as he expected, while to his rear Northumberland remained sullen and unco-operative. Neither of the two power-brokers had committed themselves fully to Henry Tudor, but as the prospect of a rapid royal triumph diminished they would surely become bolder in their defiance. Even his chief counsellors and close friends were becoming dispirited and anxious. The experienced Spanish captain Juan de Salazar, among others, openly advised him to flee.[19] The king was resolute. For over two years he had waited to prove his title in a show of arms. He would live or die a king.

In so great a cause Richard knew that he must be his own champion. Only by bold action himself could he arrest the rot in his army, and he determined to strike directly at the soft centre of the enemy forces, the 'Welsh milksop' himself. Scanning the mêlée below for signs of Henry Tudor, he at last sighted him with a small entourage at some distance from the rest of his army and from the immobile battalion of Sir William Stanley. He drew together a select company of lords and knights for a cavalry charge. Presumably it included a number of peers who were closest to him, though some of the more illustrious, like the earl of Lincoln and Viscount Lovell, might have been left to hold the hill. For the most part it was composed of household men and retainers, men like Sir Robert Percy, controller of the household, Sir Percival Thirlwall, his standard-bearer, and such 'knights of the body' as Sir Richard Radcliffe, Sir Ralph Ashton, Sir Marmaduke Constable, Sir Thomas Markenfield, Sir John Neville, Sir Thomas Pilkington, Sir Thomas Broughton, Sir James Harrington and Sir John Grey. He donned his helmet girt with a thin golden crown, and with banners unfurled led the breakneck, blood-curdling charge down the hillside.

The thunderous charge of a crowned king with his leading paladins must have been an awesome spectacle.[20] Knots of men-at-arms and pikemen locked in mortal combat must have paused in their trading of blows to take in what has

German Gothic war harness for man and horse, of the last quarter of the fifteenth century; the weight of the man's plate armour is just over 59 lbs.

been termed 'the swan-song of medieval English chivalry'. Henry Tudor and his companions had to bear the brunt of this powerful assault, and there must have been many among his supporters who doubted the capacity of their young leader, a novice in arms, to hold his own. Probably at the very moment of impact the king skewered the gallant standard-bearer, William Brandon, and the standard fell into the press. With his sword or perhaps an axe he continued to hack his way towards the upstart who dared claim his crown. Strong Sir John Cheney blocked his way, and the rebels rallied. Rhys Fawr ap Maredudd, a Welshman of immense stature, recovered the Red Dragon standard, and defended it with fierce resolve. Above all, Henry Tudor himself held firm, fighting far more stoutly than even his growing band of admirers had dared hope.[21]

For a few more minutes the issue hung in balance. The king and his stalwart retainers pressed perilously close, perhaps only a matter of feet from piercing the very heart of the rebel host. The king's knights were thrown on the defensive. Some were cut off and slain. Some made good their escape. Others formed a tight knot around their lord. Like a drowning man trying to keep the shore in sight, the king felt himself being swept away from his quarry by a strong tide. In the press around him life-long friends like Sir Robert Percy and trusted retainers like Sir Richard Charlton and Sir Thomas Gower were being picked off one by one. Most would have been dragged from their horses and butchered by foot-soldiers. Sir Percival Thirlwall, as he gallantly sought to hold the royal standard aloft, had his legs hewn from under him.[22] In vain the king called for support from other units of the royal army, and in vain his few remaining comrades urged him to escape the field. Richard determined to fight on, in defiance of fortune.

Shaking himself free from the stalwart men-at-arms who had huddled round to defend him, and still reeling from the terrible onslaught, Henry Tudor saw hundreds of red-coated soldiers swarming around his increasingly beleaguered assailants. He knew that he owed his deliverance to Sir William Stanley, who had at long last committed his troops to the fray. While it has often been assumed that they rode in to succour the pretender from a position on the north side of the field, it seems far more probable that they were foot-soldiers who had been arrayed with the rest of the Stanleyite army to the south of Ambion hill. In all likelihood they had fallen in behind the rebels as a sort of rearguard. The speed with which they moved to rescue the pretender indicates that they were not too far away. Sir William Stanley had not been involved in the fighting until this point, and presumably his company looked sufficiently uncommitted for the king to risk the threat it posed to his cavalry charge. However it might have been, there is no doubt that the intervention of the younger Stanley was fatal for Richard III and proved the salvation of Henry Tudor.

With grim determination King Richard fought on, crying out against the traitors who had conspired against him and the fair-weather friends who were deserting him. All the sources testify to his bravery in the end. Rather curiously there are no English descriptions of the manner of his death. Shakespeare had access to a tradition that his horse was taken from under him, and he cried out for a replacement, but apparently no knowledge of how and by whom he was slain. With dramatic licence he has Henry Tudor dealing the fatal stroke, but only in a laconic stage direction. Writing in Burgundy a few years after the event, Jean Molinet's account deserves to be better known, especially as it finds partial corroboration in a tradition current in the neighbourhood in the eighteenth century.[23] First of all he describes the king's horse becoming stuck in the mire. If it is the same mire which Vergil referred to later, the statement would imply that

Memorial to Richard III, erected in 1973 at the spot where he is said to have been killed.

the cavalry charge had taken place to the south of the struggle between the vanguards. Since there is no suggestion that the king was trying to escape, quite the reverse, it can be assumed that he had been pushed back into the treacherous swamp. Molinet then records that, unhorsed and overpowered, he was hacked to death by Welsh pikemen. Again this information accords with probability. Sir William Stanley was chamberlain of north Wales, and there were many Welsh foot-soldiers in his company. Moreover if the king had been vanquished in honourable combat by an English gentleman, as opposed to being butchered by low-born Welshmen, the event would have been well documented.

The king fell in the mud, and his assailants continued to hack and jab at the writhing body. To kill God's anointed took a special sort of resolve, which transcended normal thresholds of human decency. The tyrant must be unkinged by desecration, and all the chroniclers testify to the indignities to which his corpse was subjected. Probably even before Henry Tudor and his companions forced a path through to the site of the last stand, there was no longer any trace of humanity, let alone majesty, in his once handsome face. Besmirched by the mud and dirt, lacerated and mangled in the press, the barely recognisable body was being stripped of its armour and raiment. Naked he would be slung over a horse, his hair hanging down, his shame evident to all.

*   *   *

Shouts of jubilation echoed round the field, where only the most desultory skirmishing continued. In many parts of the battle there had been no action at all, and even in the fiercest sector it is probable that the fighting became less animated after King Richard's charge. It must have been recognised on both sides that the trial of combat would be finally determined in the fierce encounter between the two chief adversaries. There were the ambiguous manœuvres of the Stanleys: the rank-and-file of both armies had presumably been assured of their commitment. There was the strange inactivity of the large battalion under Northumberland: both sides must have been perplexed to observe it sitting out the battle. There were the numerous other lords and gentlemen who had sworn to fight for the king but who showed themselves to be half-hearted. Obviously a few must have sympathised with the rebels; others cared nothing for Henry Tudor, but cared less for Richard III. Such men deserted at the first opportunity, and as the smell of betrayal and defeat spread abroad even committed Ricardians took to their heels. With considerable relish, the Crowland chronicler observed that prominent among the deserters were many of the northerners who had so much enjoyed the king's favour and trust.[24]

The battle had been short, sharp and decisive. After as little as two hours of fighting, Richard III had been slain and his vast army broken and routed. Obviously the death of the king himself was an enormous stroke of good fortune for Henry Tudor. Few monarchs at this time jeopardised their persons in battle. The king might well have watched the outcome of the contest from the relative safety of Ambion hill, and retreated to fight another day. Yet the spectacular cavalry charge must not be dismissed as sheer impetuosity. As the ruler of the realm, the king had had the power and prestige to assemble a formidable army. Once driven from the field, there was no chance that such a force could be reconstituted. At this critical juncture he knew that his position was being undermined by diffidence and treachery, and that his only chance lay in taking the supreme gamble. To stiffen the resolve of his own supporters and to strike fear in the hearts of potential defectors, he had to bring the battle to a rapid climax. Above all he knew that the whole kingdom expected him to enter the lists personally in this judgement of arms. He had sworn that he would live or die as king of England.

Banner of Richard III, flying over the modern memorial stone.

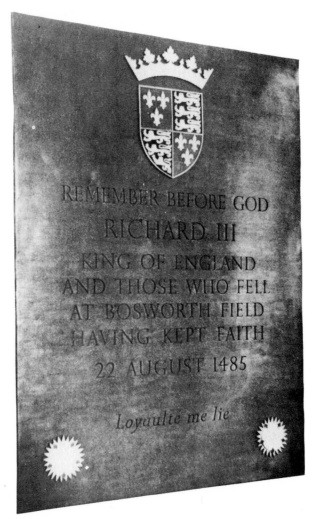

REMEMBER BEFORE GOD
RICHARD III
KING OF ENGLAND
AND THOSE WHO FELL
AT BOSWORTH FIELD
HAVING KEPT FAITH
22 AUGUST 1485

Loyaulté me lie

Memorial brass to Richard III and those who fell at Bosworth, in Sutton Cheney Church, erected in 1967.

It was all over by mid-morning. The king was a wretched corpse, and his most loyal lieutenant, the duke of Norfolk, also lay dead. The casualties were not high, perhaps no more than a thousand all told, but included some distinguished names: Lord Ferrers, Sir Richard Radcliffe, Sir Robert Percy, Sir Robert Brackenbury, Sir Richard Charlton, Sir John Ferrers and others. There were few pockets of resistance. There is a tradition that the earl of Surrey held his own for a time, but along with many other lords and gentlemen he was soon taken into captivity. Throughout the battle there had been flights from the field. Viscount Lovell, the Stafford brothers and numerous others made good their escapes at some stage, but Lord Stanley and his company bestirred themselves to round up some of the gentry who took to horse. Now the conquering army had the chance to attend to its own dead and wounded, and to reap the fruits of victory. Though there must have been many foreign mercenaries and Welsh foot-soldiers left dead on the field, William Brandon was the only notable casualty on the winning side. For the survivors there was plunder aplenty amid the carnage, and among the deserted pavilions of the royal host. A great many choice items were gathered up by agents of Sir William Stanley and found a home at Holt castle. A great deal of quality silverware appeared in the markets of London in the following months.[25]

Finally Henry Tudor and his captains, now including Lord Stanley, for-gathered on the summit of a small hill, later called Crown hill, to the south of the battlefield. The young pretender was acclaimed king by the jubilant throng, and he in turn thanked his comrades-in-arms for their loyalty and valour. Meanwhile the coronet of the dead king was retrieved from the carnage on Redmoor plain. Perhaps, as a venerable tradition relates, it had been found under a thorn-bush, where, it has been surmised, it might have been concealed for future retrieval by a dishonest soldier. While the crowd shouted 'God save King Henry! God save King Henry!', Lord Stanley or his brother, both of whom always had an eye for the main chance, placed the crown on the brow of the triumphant Henry Tudor.[26]

7 The Tudor Triumph

The first weeks of the Tudor age are quite as mysterious as the last days of Richard III. Poor though the chronicle sources are for the battle itself, they become even more exiguous for the crucial time in which the victors at Bosworth transformed themselves into an effective government. Polydore Vergil, the best source, offers no more than an outline narrative, with a few points of detail and interesting comments. Rather more disappointingly there is little official documentation for a full month. A royal proclamation made in the aftermath of the battle has survived, but there are no other records of royal business until late in September. Thenceforward a steady stream of grants to the king's supporters, both grand and humble, provides useful information about the composition of his army at Bosworth and the nature of the new political establishment. For details of the lords and gentlemen who were to be punished for their adherence to Richard III, however, it is necessary to wait until the acts of attainder in early November. Obviously the battle of Bosworth cast a long shadow, but some reconstruction of actions and attitudes in the intervening time must be attempted. For all its obscurity the first month or so was crucial in determining the character of the early Tudor regime, and indeed for shaping the views of posterity towards the preceding reign. Most of what can be known about Bosworth Field is either derived from men's words or inferred from men's actions after the event. Unfortunately for the historian, it might well have been that one important early decision made by the king and his advisers was to draw a discreet veil over some of the less than honourable dealings associated with the Tudor triumph.

The royal progress from Bosworth on 22 August to the triumphal entry into London on 3rd September can be imagined well enough. After the battlefield celebrations, the jubilant victors formed themselves into a cavalcade, and with banners flying and trumpets blowing rode at a stately pace into Leicester. For the townsmen who greeted them in the streets, there were two focuses of attention: the grisly carcase, thrown over a humble steed, of the monarch who had left town amid such regal pomp the previous day, and the young man, riding high in the saddle, who was being hailed by his soldiers as King Henry VII. Presumably the new king and his captains were well received. The worthy burghers of Leicester were doubtless quick to repudiate their Ricardian connections. The inn-keeper who had provided accommodation for the late king

Plaque near the modern Bow Bridge, Leicester.

had the easiest task: a coat of paint converted the sign of the White Boar to a Blue Boar, the badge of the earl of Oxford. The ordinary townsmen proved their loyalty by jeering at the corpse which had been unceremoniously dumped in a trough in the Newarke, and which was to be kept on public display until the Franciscan convent gave it decent burial.[1] After so long on the road, Henry Tudor and his men must have relished the hospitality afforded them. The main party stayed on in the town for several days, and it was perhaps as late as Friday 26 August before it took the road south. Even then the new king made slow progress, presumably pausing at such centres as Northampton and St Albans. According to Polydore Vergil he made his way like a victorious general, and was greeted with great joy in all the places en route. The countryfolk flocked to the roadside to hail him as king and throughout the length of the journey there were laden tables and overflowing goblets to refresh the weary champions. Finally, twelve days after his victory, he was admitted into the capital.[2]

*   *   *

Henry Tudor and his entourage did not linger in Leicester for recreation alone. In between the rejoicing and the receptions, there were a great many urgent matters which had to be resolved before he progressed south. His triumph on the battlefield had to be consolidated in the realm at large, and the lands to the north of the Trent could be expected to show some resistance. The new monarch would have been foolish to press south until more reassuring intelligence was gained from this quarter. One of his earliest moves had been to send Robert Willoughby to Sheriff Hutton castle to secure the person of the earl of Warwick. It was with some relief that the young man, the last of the Plantagenets and a natural focus for Yorkist opposition, was brought into custody. Welcome tidings of the Princess Elizabeth were also received. She was unharmed, and accompanied by chaperones had been sent on to await her all-conquering hero in London. Gradually positive reports must have come in from other parts of the kingdom. Individual lords and gentlemen, perhaps including some who had escaped capture at Bosworth, rode in to pay homage to the new king. Deputations from the towns and communities of southern England must also have beaten a path towards the prince, perhaps bringing gifts of money and much needed clothes and finery.

After the trauma of Bosworth, the new king saw as his first task the establishment of his authority, and the restoration of law and order in the realm. In a proclamation issued soon after the battle, 'Henry by the grace of God, King of England and of France, prince of Wales and lord of Ireland', informed his subjects that 'Richard, duke of Gloucester, lately called King Richard' had been slain 'at a place called Sandeford', along with a number of other named lords and gentlemen, and that his body had been put on public display. Specific orders for an immediate return to normalcy were then given. The king's subjects were charged, on pain of death, not to rob or despoil any of the soldiers returning from the battlefield, but to allow them to return to their homes unmolested. Furthermore, there was to be no private vengeance taken on the houses of gentlefolk, and there must be a complete end to feuding 'for old or for new matters'.[3] Both measures seem statesmanlike and, in so far as they were deigned to protect the people who had fought against him, genuinely conciliatory. The instructions also indicate the general strategy with regard to the defeated army. The ordinary levies assembled in the late king's name were sent back to their homes, but the lords and gentlemen were to be detained at the royal pleasure a little while longer. The proclamation also contained the, probably deliberate, misinformation that, along with the duke of Norfolk and Lord Ferrers, the earls of Lincoln and Surrey and Viscount Lovell were among the slain. In its public pronouncements the new regime certainly would have been well advised to stress the completeness of its victory. Even if Ricardian loyalists accepted the death of the king with resignation, news of the survival of Lincoln and the others could have made for a heady brew in some areas. What Henry Tudor must have feared was that all the inevitable discontents and fears might find a focus in one of the old king's lieutenants and fuse into a single resistance movement.

Henry VII was to find that more was required in the winning of a kingdom than the defeat and the death of Richard III, especially when his triumph had more to do with the lack of support for the man on the throne than with the merits of his supplanter. In fact, even in the first flush of victory, the Tudor regime might well have found the path to political acceptance harder than has sometimes been imagined. Its power-base was extremely narrow at the start. The earls of Pembroke and Oxford, for all their loyalty, bravery and indeed

Elizabeth of York (1465–1503), eldest daughter of Edward IV and Elizabeth Woodville, and wife of Henry VII.

talent, had no recent political experience. The marquis of Dorset lacked credibility, while two other prospective peers, Edward Courtenay and John Welles, were lightweights. Of course, the regime included several eminent churchmen and experienced bureaucrats, and had the support of an impressive group of knights and gentlemen, like Giles Daubeney, Edward Poynings, Robert Willoughby, Richard Edgecombe and Reginald Bray, many of whom were men of influence in their counties. Certainly there were the makings of an inner cabinet and a new elite, but such a government could not but appear fragile, makeshift, and unrepresentative. If it were to survive at all, the regime had to establish confidence in its ability to offer the realm peace and stability. Fine-sounding proclamations were well and good, but in the provinces more attention was paid to the mouthpiece than the message. In the circumstances of 1485 this meant winning over as many of the magnates and local notables who had worked with the old regime as was seemly, and securing their active collaboration in the establishment of orderly government.

It is difficult to reconstruct the political horse-trading at this time. In the days after the battle Leicester must have witnessed many extraordinary scenes. Henry Tudor had won his crown, and his friends and supporters expected their due reward, or at the very least the restoration of their rights. Jasper Tudor, who was to be made duke of Bedford, must be found appropriate endowment. The earl of Oxford naturally anticipated high advancement. In the mean time he, like many of the other exiles, was impatient to be restored to his patrimony. The claimants to the earldom of Devon and the barony of Welles, not to mention other hopefuls, wanted past grievances redressed. In addition to all the king's companions in exile seeking to cash in their credit, there were many more recent supporters who anticipated a share in the spoils. The most notable were the Stanleys. Lord Stanley, the new king's stepfather, would become earl of Derby, and Sir William Stanley would be appointed chamberlain of the royal household. There was also Rhys ap Thomas and other Welsh captains, and the valiant Gilbert Talbot and John Savage. Yet it was necessary to move with great caution. The gradual restoration of old rights was politically feasible, though not without occasional embarrassment. Since the new regime had no wish to alienate Richard Hastings, for example, there were two peers with the title of Lord Welles in early Tudor times.[4] The granting of additional rewards, however, had necessarily to be at the expense of the dead and defeated, and too many forfeitures could only compound the difficulties of reconciling the realm to the new regime.

Seeking to heal the wounds of the last days, years, even decades, and also to build a sound foundation for the future, the king and his counsellors had to spend much time determining a policy towards the notables killed fighting for Richard III and interviewing the large number of lords and gentlemen who had been rounded up after the battle. It is necessary to imagine some sort of informal tribunal, which heard petitions and responses, denunciations and excuses, threats and promises traded back and forth. It had to balance its own estimation of guilt and desire for revenge against the potential gain to be derived from overlooking past faults and offering honourable means of redemption. The death of the duke of Norfolk simplified the problem of the Howards, whose

Sir Robert Willoughby, later Lord Willoughby de Broke (died 1501); effigy at Callington, Cornwall.

close identification with the regime and great wealth in any case singled them out for exemplary punishment. A number of the prominent Ricardians were likewise to be attainted, but this step was not taken automatically. Viscount Lovell, who as the old king's close friend might not have expected mercy, sealed his fate by taking to his heels. Lord Ferrers of Chartley was among the slain, and since he had enriched himself at the expense of Oxford and other exiles there was no one to speak against his attainder. Young Lord Zouche was also for some reason treated with severity: he was imprisoned and attainted, though later pardoned. Only three men seem to have been put to death after the battle. William Bracher and his son were relatively humble royal agents from the West Country. The only notable victim was William Catesby. His last will and testament dated 25 August provides a rare sense of the atmosphere at Leicester at this time. After a poignant tribute to his 'dear and well beloved wife', he expressed his belief that the king who 'is called a good and gracious prince' will be a 'good and gracious lord' to his children, and affirmed that he had never willingly offended him and, as God was his judge, had always loved him. In a codicil he requested that Lovell, if ever he should come to grace, be asked to pray for him, and with wry humour also appealed to Stanley, Strange 'and all that blood' to 'pray for my soul, for ye have not for my body, as I trusted in you'.[5]

The major chroniclers rightly insist that Henry VII showed considerable clemency. There was justifiable concern at the strategem by which the king dated his reign from the day before Bosworth, thus laying all his opponents open

William Catesby (died 1485) and Margaret Zouche his wife; brass at Ashby St Ledgers, Northamptonshire.

to treason charges. Yet the number of attainders decided upon was remarkably small, and for the most part restricted to men who were already dead, like Norfolk and Ferrers, or had remained defiant, like Lovell and Humphrey Stafford. Some historians have regarded this list as a more or less complete roll-call of the lords and knights who fought for Richard III at Bosworth. This assumption is patently absurd. In the first place the majority of men attainted were southerners, whereas there is every reason to suppose that northerners predominated in the royal army. Even without calling on the testimony of *The Ballad of Bosworth Field*, it is possible to document many notables who were present at the field but were not subsequently attainted. Thus early chronicles and other records indicate that the earl of Lincoln, the earl of Shrewsbury, Sir Robert Percy, Sir Ralph Ashton, Sir Humphrey Beaufort, Sir Thomas Gower and William Allington were at Bosworth on the king's side. None suffered forfeiture, and fortunately in two cases there is interesting circumstantial detail. For all the notoriety of Sir Ralph Ashton, for example, his Lancashire patrimony was allowed to pass to his son, Richard Ashton, who had had the foresight to fight on the side of the rebels, in all probability under Stanley leadership. Meanwhile the interests of the heir of William Allington were protected, though not disinterestedly, by the intervention of the earl of Oxford.[6]

Just as the number of lords and gentlemen in Richard III's army has been consistently under-estimated, so the full dimensions of Henry Tudor's early attempts at reconciliation have not been properly appreciated. The peers who sought the king's grace had many avenues open to them. The duke of Suffolk and the earl of Arundel, neither of whom were at Bosworth, could have spoken for their sons, the earl of Lincoln and Lord Maltravers, who were probably among the captives. The new king's willingness to pardon Lincoln seems particularly magnanimous. Some of the older peers at Bosworth, like the shrewd earl of Kent and the innocuous earl of Nottingham, might not have taken part in the fighting, and readily exonerated themselves in terms of their allegiance to the crown, doubtless making assurances of a similarly unquestioning loyalty to their new sovereign. The younger lords could be even more readily excused for becoming implicated in the Ricardian regime. The earl of Shrewsbury seems to have been in a roughly equivalent position to Lord Strange. With Gilbert Talbot to speak for him, he was doubtless treated with kindness. The young earl of Westmorland and Lord Lumley likewise could have been credibly presented as political innocents. The sources indicate that large numbers of other notables simply pleaded that they had been at the battle under duress, and the new regime must have been constrained by its own rhetoric to accept this plea. In all likelihood the king's acts of mercy were fuelled by the payment of fines, which went some way towards reimbursing the costs sustained by the exiles. Unfortunately some of the men actually killed in the fighting lacked advocates and financial agents. Geoffrey St German, a Northamptonshire squire, was included in the act of attainder, until his daughter successfully appealed on the grounds that, threatened with the loss of 'life, land and goods', he had been in the field from fear alone and 'full sore against his will'.[7]

For the moment Henry VII was in no position to strike too hard a bargain. In order to make himself effective ruler of the kingdom he had to give strikingly generous terms to many lords in the hope of winning their loyalty and co-operation. His position was weakest in northern England, a turbulent region at the best of times. There were few prominent lineages north of the Trent which had not been implicated in the Ricardian regime, but to move against all of them would be to court disaster. Even if the fledgling regime had the military muscle to break a general northern rising, the resultant power vacuum would leave the realm open to Scots invasion. Policies of general conciliation and then 'divide and rule' had most to commend them. A proclamation of 11 October which publicised the availability of pardons to the knights and gentry of Nottinghamshire, Yorkshire, Durham, Westmorland, Cumberland and Northumberland who had taken the field against him almost certainly reflects policies decided upon some weeks earlier. As regards the rule and governance of the north, however, suitable candidates for royal backing were hard to find. The earl of Northumberland might have seemed the natural counter-balance to Ricardian loyalism. Yet while his neutrality at Bosworth had played its part in undermining the late king's position, Henry Tudor did not feel inclined to gratitude. According to Jean Molinet, it was believed that Northumberland was angling to play king-maker and to raise the young earl of Warwick to the throne. It might also have been recognised that through its betrayal of Richard III, the house of Percy had put in grave jeopardy its standing and reputation in many parts of the north. For the moment at least the new regime moved in quite

Gold seal ring with a boar enamelled in white on the bezel, found at Bosworth, now in the Devonshire Collection at Chatsworth.

another direction in its search for a chief lieutenant in the north, and picked the old king's cousin Lord Fitzhugh. Probably following up agreements made in the aftermath of the battle, he was granted the stewardships of Middleham, Richmond and Barnard Castle, the heartland of Ricardian power, on 24 September, and on the following day he was put at the head of the commissions of array in all the northern counties, and given the responsibility of receiving oaths of allegiance from the knights and commons in those parts.[8]

Though a surprising choice at first glance, it seems that the re-appointment of a man used by Richard III was not so untypical of the new regime's dealings in sensitive regions. Of course, Lord Fitzhugh was possibly a less committed Ricardian than has been supposed. A nephew of the Kingmaker and self-appointed guardian of the Neville interest, he could well have been the leader of the northerners whose loyalty was put under strain by the king's alleged desire to be rid of Queen Anne. Yet *The Ballad of Bosworth Field* is probably correct in including him, along with the Lords Scrope and others from this connection, among the royal stalwarts at the battle. Once the king was dead, however, there was much to be said for collaborating with his supplanter, especially if Fitzhugh did not relish the ascendancy of Northumberland or some other northern rival. Indeed there is reason to suppose that many, if not most, of the men appointed to represent the new government in the north had also been at Bosworth.[9] Thus Sir Thomas Markenfield and Sir Christopher Moresby, both prominent retainers of the former king and, according to the ballad tradition, with him in the battlefield, were nominated as sheriffs of Yorkshire and Cumberland respectively. Richard III's office-holders in the southern counties were not so fortunate. The local communities were far more likely to be braying for their blood than rallying behind them, and Henry Tudor had many suitable candidates from among his entourage. Even so, it is possible that some of the new sheriffs appointed in other regions had been in arms against him at Bosworth. It is generally assumed, for example, that because Sir John Paston was appointed sheriff of Norfolk and Suffolk soon after the battle he must therefore have disobeyed the summons to arms. This assumption can now be questioned. Even if among the vanquished, Paston would have been vouched for by the earl of Oxford, and been commended as a man who could assist the new regime in areas of old Howard influence in East Anglia.

*   *   *

The five weeks between the battle of Bosworth and Michaelmas, the end of the accounting year, were anxious times for both victors and vanquished. The highways must have buzzed with wild rumour and false report, and none of the participants in high politics, from the new king downwards, could have gained a clear view of the whole chess-board. The first week, perhaps even longer, Henry Tudor had remained at Leicester, maintaining a large number of men in arms and keeping under house-arrest the more prominent Ricardian supporters who had fallen into his hands. There was time for messengers to ride to the most distant parts with tidings of the victory and firm intelligence of the demise of Richard III, and then to return with reports of the reactions in the provinces. Although the names of the new sheriffs were not recorded in chancery until the 12 September, it must have been in the first week or so that the new regime had found the men they could work with, both from their own company and more importantly from the shattered remnants of the royal army. The petition of Robert Throckmorton, the new sheriff of Warwick and Leicester, certainly implies that the sheriffs were appointed very soon after Bosworth: he complained that the disturbed conditions in his bailiwick made it impossible for him to raise the sums for which he was responsible before Michaelmas.[10] Conversely, even before the royal host arrived in London it had probably become evident which men were to remain out in the cold. Northumberland, Surrey and Zouche were to remain in custody, but could hope for the chance to work their way back into royal favour. Stubbornly remaining in sanctuary, Lovell and the Stafford brothers were putting themselves beyond the pale, though posing no immediate threat. Only in the far north-west was there open defiance. Sir James Harrington and his brother, Sir Thomas Pilkington, Sir Thomas Broughton, Sir Robert Middleton, and Thomas Metcalfe and his brother had taken to the hills, and threatened to raise the north and perhaps draw in the Scots to reverse the decision at Bosworth. Along with Sir Richard Radcliffe, they were the only northerners who were exempted from the general pardon and duly attainted. Yet it might well be that the opposition of most of them had as much to do with their long-standing feud with the house of Stanley as any diehard Ricardian commitment.[11]

As the tentative advance southwards turned into a triumphal progress, the

Cannon ball found at Bosworth, 2 inches in diameter.

Tudor regime grew in assurance. On 3 September Henry VII consummated his victory with a ceremonial entry into London. The mayor and aldermen had paid their respects to the new king at the first opportunity, and in the previous week there must have been a great many comings and goings between the royal camp and city hall. A number of the king's party, probably including the blind poet Bernard André, had been sent ahead to make preparations. Once admitted into the city, Henry was formally received at Shoreditch, and the city-fathers inaugurated a whole round of festivities and banqueting. André recited the first of a whole series of Latin poems he would compose to celebrate the great occasions of the king's life, and the populace was entertained with musical and dramatic interludes. In splendid array, the king and his fellow exiles processed through the streets to St Paul's cathedral, where he piously placed the three banners under which his army had fought: one displaying the arms of St George, another the famous Red Dragon, and a third the Tartaron and Duncow. After prayers of thanksgiving and the offering of a *Te Deum*, the king retired, apparently taking up residence at the palace of Thomas Kemp, bishop of London.[12]

The young king must have felt as if he was riding on air, as he basked in the joyous acclaim of the London crowds. A bare month ago he was in the wilds of Wales with a derisory force and his royal adversary with the armed might of the entire kingdom massed against him, and less than a fortnight previously, blood-stained from the battle, he must still have doubted the completeness of his triumph. For the first time he could feel himself to be truly king, as make-shift camps gave place to palatial residences, and as the camaraderie of fellow-exiles gave place to the company of counsellors and courtiers, as the rough world of soldiering was transformed into milieux more comfortable, domestic and feminine. Indeed to add immeasurably to the headiness of the time, the young man must have been reeling from his encounter with two ladies who were henceforward to play major parts in his life. The first was Lady Margaret Beaufort, his mother, with whom he was reunited after fourteen years, to say nothing of earlier separations. As the king's mother this remarkable lady was a major force in the new Tudor order, putting her considerable qualities and her religious and educational ideals to the service of the English church and people. The second lady was Elizabeth of York, Henry Tudor's promised bride, whom he had never met before at all. She was an attractive girl and it was a fitting match, but the daughter of Edward IV and Elizabeth Woodville was never to command the respect and honour accorded to the king's mother.

Even so there was precious little time for sentimental reunion and languid courtship. From Michaelmas onwards the new government had to deal with a mountain of business, including some which had piled up during the strange inactivity of Richard III's last quarter. The Tudor court sought to establish relations with foreign powers. Charles VIII of France had already recognised the new regime, and on 12 October a firm truce between the two countries was announced.[13] Meanwhile the chancery worked overtime committing to parchment and paper some of the more important decisions made in the heady weeks after Bosworth. It was a time for Henry Tudor to repay the loyalty of his friends with formal grants of office and lands. There were extensive rewards to the earl of Oxford, Sir Edward Woodville, Sir Richard Edgecombe, Sir John Risley and others 'for service overseas and at our late victorious field' to their 'great charge, labour and jeopardy'. Perhaps less deserved was the bounty lavished on 'the king's right entirely beloved father' Lord Stanley 'in consideration of the good and praiseworthy services performed by him before now with great personal exertions and costs, . . . now lately in the king's conflict within the realm of England'. There were other last-minute recruits among the beneficiaries: Sir William Stanley, Sir John Savage and his kinsmen, the Digby brothers, six of whom allegedly fought at Bosworth, and John Byron. Quite a number of Welshmen found themselves in favour with their 'kinsman king', including churchmen like Dr John Morgan as well as old servitors like Piers Lloyd.[14] Above all, the king and his counsellors had to set in train preparations for the coronation and the first parliament, scheduled for the 30 October and 7 November respectively. It would be through the ritual theatre of the crowning and consecration and in the public forum of a parliamentary assembly that the legitimacy of the new regime would be made explicit and the nature of the new dispensation revealed.

Earthenware costrel (water bottle) found at Bosworth, diameter 8½ inches.

The coronation was stage-managed brilliantly, and it was a remarkable display of pageantry and solidarity.[15] Many of the participants, and presumably most of the organisers, were able to draw on the experience of another coronation a little more than two years earlier, and indeed the form of ceremony from Richard III's time was only slightly adapted to omit the parts referring to the queen. Elizabeth of York would have to wait her turn: a dispensation for their marriage had to be obtained from the pope, and in any case there must be no implication that Henry

Tudor was king by courtesy of his wife. The archbishop of Canterbury was performing his third coronation, having presided at both Yorkist ceremonies as well as having witnessed in his thirty years in the see the 're-adeption' of Henry VI and the brief reign of Edward V. There was even more irony in the occasion for the king's champion, Sir Robert Dymmock, who issued a challenge to anyone denying Henry Tudor's right just as he had done at the coronation of Richard III. Many of the other participants had also attended the previous ceremony, not least the new king's mother, but the new regime was concerned to present the most impressive show of solidarity possible. The king's uncle Jasper was created duke of Bedford to take his place along with the duke of Suffolk, Richard III's brother-in-law, while Thomas Stanley was made earl of Derby and Edward Courtenay given his due as earl of Devon to add to the otherwise rather thin showing of earls. With Surrey, Northumberland and Warwick in detention, the stout Oxford would otherwise have only the disgruntled Lincoln and the time-serving Nottingham as his peers.

A week later the newly anointed king presided in majesty at the opening of parliament. With his title to the throne implicitly accepted by the very existence of the parliament, and tersely asserted by the new speaker, Henry Tudor chose merely to remind the assembled lords and common in general terms of his hereditary right, and more especially his title 'by the true judgement of God'. The king had already chosen his chief officers of state and appointed judges, and the personnel of the new government could now be revealed to public scrutiny. On the whole it was an impressive affirmation of continuity with the regime of Edward IV. Bishops Alcock and Morton, both of whom were prominent ministers prior to the usurpation of 1483, were chancellor and keeper of the privy seal. The more important lay counsellors and household officials were drawn from the knights and gentlemen who had formed his entourage in exile or who had joined his cause in England, but it was not novel to appoint to such positions talented men from respectable landed families rather than young aristocrats. Indeed one of the most urgent requirements of the parliament was to reverse the acts of attainder that had been passed against so many prominent members of the new ruling elite. At the same time the government pushed forward with the indictment of the Ricardian regime and the destruction of its chief supporters. The late king 'by usurpation and not by right' was indicted on general charges of tyranny and 'the murder of innocents', and the late duke of Norfolk, the earl of Surrey, Lords Lovell, Ferrers and Zouche, along with some twenty-odd other knights and gentlemen were attainted for high treason. There was some consternation at the charge that the accused committed treason through assembling at Leicester on 21 August. It was specious of Henry Tudor to claim that he was truly king on the day before the battle. Nevertheless the acts were passed, and the faithful commons granted the new king financial aid. Some provisions were made for the restoration of public order, and a petition that the king should take Elizabeth of York as his wife concluded the proceedings on a positive note.[16]

Over Christmas 1485 Henry VII allowed himself to relax, and to look forward to the promise of the New Year. His courtship proceeded apace, and the papal dispensation for him to marry his distant cousin was on its way. A splendid

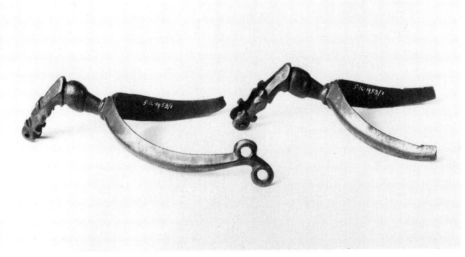

Spurs traditionally from the battlefield at Bosworth, but probably seventeenth century rather than medieval.

wedding was celebrated, and a great deal was made in words and images of the union of the houses of Lancaster and York. A child was soon conceived, perhaps on the very wedding night, and by spring, when Henry Tudor set off to tour his realm, and in particular to visit the potentially disaffected north, he had reason to hope that the Tudor dynasty had been established. A great deal had been made in court pageantry and propaganda of Henry VII's descent from Cadwaladr, the last British prince to rule in England, and the old prophecies associated with Merlin regarding the re-establishment of this blood line. Exhilarated by the prospect of new beginnings, he doubtless already had in mind a name for his first child. If God vouchsafed a male heir, he would be named Arthur.

*   *   *

In truth the blithe young man who set out to see his kingdom in the spring of 1486 was soon to be disabused of the optimism which he, after so many years of disappointments, had briefly allowed himself to feel. The appearance of the 'sweating sickness' in England at the time of his accession seemed a bad omen. The superstitious felt that it betokened a harsh regime, while the best that was said was that the king would have to hold his kingdom by the sweat of his brow. For all the apparent relief at the defeat of Richard III, there were still signs that sections of the political nation, typically willing the ends of good government without accepting the means, were loathe to allow the Tudor regime all the power and resources it considered it needed. There was no doubt that Henry Tudor would have to work at the business of government, and he was soon committing himself to the unsparing regimen of paper-work, which would characterise his rule. In the decade that followed Henry VII would have to

Sir Robert Harcourt (died 1503), possibly one of Henry Tudor's standard bearers at Bosworth; effigy at Stanton Harcourt, Oxfordshire.

labour in other ways as well as to make his line secure, ways which would convert him into a suspicious, ruthless and mean old man. It would take many years of alarms and incursions before the people at large reconciled themselves to the necessities of the state.

As he proceeded northwards, Henry Tudor was warned about the plot of Viscount Lovell, who had escaped from sanctuary to raise a rebellion in the north. It is an interesting reflection on the man and the times that he would not believe the tale, feeling that his informants were simply trying to ingratiate themselves at the accused's expense. At York he was surprised by the seriousness of the movement: Lovell had raised a sizeable company in and around Richard III's old lordships of Middleham and Richmond, while Stafford, his ally, was fomenting rebellion in Worcestershire. It had been a wise move on the king's part to retain in his household a force of two hundred retainers, because it was this force, supplemented by other retinues, which put the rebels to flight. It was doubtless with some relief that he returned to the safety of southern England, but the abortive rising was merely the foretaste of unrest to come. In the following year the earl of Lincoln showed his true colours and threw in his lot with Lovell and other disaffected Yorkists, who had the backing of Margaret of York, the dowager duchess of Burgundy. To lend a spurious dignity to their cause they groomed a boy called Lambert Simnel to impersonate the captive earl of Warwick. More menacingly, they were able to establish a secure base for their operations in Ireland, where there were old loyalties to the house of York as well as long-standing grievances to exploit. With the pretender crowned in Dublin, a substantial force landed in north-west England, and pushed across the Pennines, attracting disaffected lords and gentry on its way. In many respects it was a repeat of the Bosworth campaign: the rebel host on both occasions was predominantly non-English, and the royal mobilisation again seems to have encountered a great deal of apathy and defeatism if not treachery. At the battle of Stoke in 1487, as at Bosworth two years earlier, Henry Tudor owed his victory to the boldness and commitment of his own and his friends' troops, and to the military resources of the house of Stanley, who committed a 'great host' under Lord Strange.[17]

The Tudor regime could now hope to put down firm roots. The rebellion of 1487 had brought out of the woodwork the chief enemies of the regime, and the triumph at Stoke had eliminated them. Lincoln was killed in the fighting, and Lovell disappeared without trace. A whole new round of attainders exacted just retribution on the main protagonists, while a whole series of fines and bonds were inflicted on other malcontents. Lord Scrope of Masham, for example, had to enter a massive bond not to leave the environs of London. Gradually the old Ricardian connection was broken. Edward Frank intrigued with Lovell, and spent several terms in prison, and was advised by an astrologer to give up the struggle. Thomas Metcalfe apparently committed suicide. Meanwhile the womenfolk sought lives of decent obscurity. The queen's mother, Elizabeth Woodville, who seems to have been involved in the intrigue, was kept under close watch at Bermondsey nunnery. The duchess of Norfolk and Lady Lovell were given modest pensions. The wife of Sir Richard Radcliffe took the veil. The daughter of Sir Robert Brackenbury was perhaps taken in by the Howards, themselves living in much straitened circumstances.[18]

Henry VII and Elizabeth of York were blessed with a male heir, and Prince Arthur was soon followed by other children. Yet dynastic stability remained illusive. The north was still restive, not least the city of York, where the late king's name was still revered in some quarters. Northumberland was murdered while collecting royal taxes in 1489 allegedly because of the commons' anger at 'his disappointing of King Richard at Bosworth'. Another Yorkist pretender appeared in the person of Perkin Warbeck, and with foreign backing he was able to cause the English government much anxiety throughout most of the 1490s. Intrigue was even rife at court. The chamberlain of the household, Sir William Stanley, confessed to treasonable talk and was executed in 1495. The tragic death of Prince Arthur in 1502 fuelled further speculation about the succession, at least for prominent members of the Calais garrison. There was talk of the candidature of the duke of Buckingham and the De La Pole brothers, but none of the merits of Prince Henry. Arrested at this time was Sir James Tyrell, a veteran of many intrigues. Before his execution he allegedly confessed to the murders of the princes on the orders of Richard III. Henry Tudor finally needed to lay some ghosts to rest.

For Henry VII the battle of Bosworth had brought a life-time of trials and tribulations. Though still in his forties, he aged dramatically in the last decade of his reign. Over the years he had lost most of his soul-mates and friends. His wife died in childbirth in early 1503, while his uncle the duke of Bedford passed away in 1495. Steadily most of his old comrades-in-arms at Bosworth Field died: John Savage in action at Boulogne in 1492, Richard Guildford on pilgrimage in the Holy Land in 1506, Giles Daubeney in his bed in 1508.[19] Memories of the 'victorious journey' of 1485 disappeared with them. Unless he had the chance to meet the earl of Derby before his death in 1504, Polydore Vergil could have interviewed only the earls of Oxford and Surrey among the chief commanders. The king himself seems to have been disinclined to have the event commemorated. Bernard André was kept in the dark about the encounter, and no funds were set aside for a battlefield chapel. The cool and cautious Henry Tudor had no mind to look back.

Signature of Henry VII.

8 1485 in English History

It began on an August morning with a brutal encounter in the Leicestershire countryside. Within hours the news of the battle was being spread in all directions, and within days reports of the victory of Henry Tudor had been carried to the border of the realm. It was a matter of all-consuming interest. Many inhabitants of England and Wales had relatives and friends at the field, whose fates would have been uncertain for days, and whose adventures would enliven conversations for weeks. More important the crown had passed to a largely unknown pretender, and right across the realm hopes and fears were intermingled, as the significance of the battle was pondered in both general and particular terms. Yet it is hard to know what more general meaning contemporaries might have found in the news. Doubtless a fairly constant refrain in discussions would have been the workings of Providence. God had made His judgement in a trial of arms. The continuator of the Crowland chronicle wrote that Henry Tudor was universally praised, as if he had been sent by God to deliver His people from their afflictions. Looking back on English history, he was struck by the parallels with 1066, when another usurper of the throne had been killed in battle by an invader from Normandy, and by the strangely unfortunate fates of the three Kings Richard.[1]

A major difficulty in assessing the contemporary significance of the battle of Bosworth is its remarkably slow birth as a historical event. Like the dog which did not bark in the night, the failure of the battle to establish itself as a major landmark in men's perceptions of time is an important fact well worth pondering. Only gradually did the battle acquire a name, still less an agreed name. Henry Tudor granted rewards to his followers for distinguished services in his 'late victorious journey' and official reports talked of men assembled in warlike array at Leicester or being killed at 'Sandeford', but not of the battle of Bosworth. It is true enough that events take time to acquire sufficient significance to be honoured with a clear appellation. Perhaps it was widely felt that the victory which brought Henry Tudor to power could well be soon overshadowed by the triumph of a new claimant to the throne. What is worth stressing, however, is that, contrary to common assumption, Henry VII did not immediately set to work to give an official, propagandist view of the battle. Rather the reverse might have been true, that there was a concerted attempt by the court and many participants in the battle to damp down idle tale-telling and vain speculation.

Most of the earliest accounts of Bosworth Field, recording little more than the basic facts derived from the first royal proclamation, are inserted in town chronicles indiscriminately amidst the ephemera of local news. In the second continuation of the Crowland chronicle one Englishman at least presented an informed and intelligent account, but it seems not to have been widely read in Tudor England. The thoughtful, though occasionally muddled, narratives produced on the continent were likewise ignored. It is not until Robert Fabian and others expanded the range of the London chronicle tradition to give a full account of English history around the end of the fifteenth century, and Polydore Vergil began work on his ambitious *Anglica Historia* in the second decade of the sixteenth century that the battle of Bosworth can be seen as a landmark of sorts in English history. Even then the event is simply the occasion of the overthrow of Richard III and the victory of Henry Tudor. Nevertheless, since both histories organised their material by reigns, 1485 was inevitably presented as opening a new chapter in the history of England.

As the Tudor dynasty established itself, the nation was encouraged to think in terms of new beginnings. For the government it was important to portray the old times as characterised by civil war and dynastic strife. This view of the recent past was neither wholly propagandist nor particularly novel. Throughout the Yorkist age there had been continuous laments about the 'savage beast' within the English polity. In 1461 George Neville, bishop of Exeter, had written to an Italian colleague that his people were 'a race deserving pity even from the French' because of their 'intestine' wars. Consciousness of England's shameful reputation as a country of regicides and parricides, as well as a concern not to re-open too many recent wounds in England itself, might well acount for the evident reluctance of Henry Tudor and his counsellors to be specific in their charges against Richard III. For similar reasons Bosworth Field would not have been seen as a particularly positive symbol. Far more appealing were images of renewal and reconciliation, the idea of an English polity restored and harmonised under a new monarchy. While Henry VII had no wish to appear to owe his throne to his wife, from the first great store was set by the symbolism of the union of the Red and White Roses. Since the Red Rose was not a particularly important Lancastrian badge, its employment by Henry Tudor must have been a deliberate ploy, and the appearance of the theme of intermingled roses in the Crowland chronicle and other early sources suggested that it might have made some headway in England even before Bosworth. After Henry and Elizabeth produced male heirs, and even more after their son succeeded to the throne, this image became even more strongly entrenched and reverently elaborated. It found its most enterprising exponent in Edward Hall, who wrote a vernacular history whose theme was 'the union of the two noble and illustrious families of Lancaster and York, being long in continual dissension for the crown of this noble realm, with all the acts done in both the times of the princes, both of the one lineage and of the other, beginning at the time of Henry IV, the first author of this division, and so successively proceeding to the reign of the high and prudent prince King Henry VIII, the indubitable flower and very heir of both the said lineages'. This drama of English kingship was incorporated by Raphael Holinshed into his larger-scale history of England, and thence was reworked in

German sallet of about 1450–60.

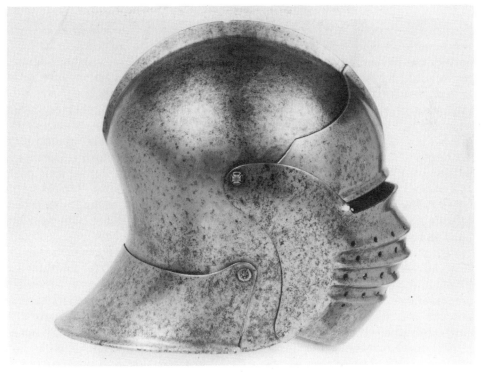

North Italian sallet of the last quarter of the fifteenth century.

blank verse by William Shakespeare in his cycle of history plays. Its power was such as to entrench for many generations a dynastic view of the civil wars of the fifteenth century, and to inspire Sir Walter Scott to designate them the Wars of the Roses'.[2]

As the Tudor age began to take on a character of its own, it was tempting to contrast it in more general terms with the fifteenth-century past. In this manner English writers began to accord a larger significance to the new dispensation vouchsafed them in 1485. Most essentially the triumph of Henry Tudor had restored peace and order to the realm, and the re-establishment of a strong monarchy had made possible the advancement of the 'common weal'. The splendour of Henry VIII's court, his wars and vigorous diplomacy, and above all the break with Rome, harnessed new currents of nationalism in support of a resurgent monarchy. The establishment of the Church of England, the dissolution of the monasteries and the progress of Protestantism, all served to heighten the consciousness of living in a new era. Population growth, economic expansion, inflation and social dislocation likewise served to distance men from the old world. Above all the achievements of the Elizabethan world entrenched the consciousness of the Tudor age as a new and glorious epoch. Inevitably Tudor England depicted its past as a foil to set off its own achievements. The fifteenth century was a time of national humiliation. It was a bellicose, lawless and factious age when 'overmighty subjects' had made and unmade kings, terrorised the countryside and feuded among themselves. It was the darkest hour of papistry and superstition before the dawn of humanism and reform. Of course, central to all the problems, it was a time of monarchical weakness. English history between 1399 and 1485 was seen as a cautionary tale as to what happened when the hereditary principle was challenged, and when the crown became the focus of aristocratic ambitions. Given the dynastic instability which persisted throughout the Tudor age, belief in the vision became a shibboleth among all right-thinking Englishmen. The reputation of Richard III was the great casualty of this process. Since he was an anointed king of the blood royal, who had been overthrown to make way for the Tudors, it was necessary to present him not only as a usurper and a tyrant, but also an unnatural monster.

During the course of the sixteenth and seventeenth centuries European writers were also seeing their own age as representing a break with past centuries. The intellectual and cultural movement known as the Renaissance, which self-consciously sought to restore the literary and æsthetic ideals of Greece and Rome, inevitably adopted a tripartite view of history. On the one hand there was classical antiquity whose world was brought to an end by the barbarian invasions. At the other end there was the 'modern' age which sought to restore the classical heritage and build on its foundations. The centuries in between, quite literally the middle ages, were centuries of darkness, barbarism and ignorance, whose scholastic philosophy and Gothic style had straitjacketed thought and debased expression. For the humanists of Renaissance Italy the slow dawn of modern times was apparent soon after 1400: subsequently some significance attached itself to the fall of Constantinople in 1453. Of course, the progress of the Renaissance in northern Europe was slow and uneven, and a movement which was far from homogeneous in Italy assumed a variety of forms

Battle axe, possibly German, dating from the end of the fifteenth century.

elsewhere. Nevertheless in all the countries north of the Alps, humanism and other classicising impulses became apparent over the course of the late fifteenth and early sixteenth centuries. Early historians of the Renaissance could not resist trying to pinpoint when the old values began to be displaced by the new. In France the first expedition to Italy of 1494, which brought many Frenchmen face to face with Renaissance art for this time, was treated as an important turning-point. In England the beginning of the Tudor dynasty in 1485 seemed equal portentous. It is appropriate that Francis Bacon, one of the most self-consciously 'modern' of the men born in the Elizabethan age, should apply himself to a history of the reign of Henry VII.[3]

Nevertheless it took time for the notion that 1485 marked a clear watershed between two wholly different ages to establish itself. Bacon is for the most part innocent of this sort of theorising. He was most interested in Henry VII as an exemplum of sound statecraft. Yet an implicit assumption of his work is that his reign did institute the sound political framework for the material prosperity and cultural achievement of his own times. He also felt that the period 'from the union of the Roses to the union of the kingdoms' had a coherence of its own. From the late seventeenth century onwards the idea that the modern age began in 1485 became a commonplace of English history. The Enlightenment *philosophe* was even less tolerant of the institutions of the middle ages than the

Renaissance humanist had been of Gothic literature and art. He tended to see English life before 1485 as characterised by noble power, priestly privilege and peasant ignorance, and only to consider the Tudor age, with its strengthening of monarchy, church reform and material progress, as laying the foundations for his own world. This view is best expressed in David Humes's *History of England*. At the end of his account of the reign of Richard III, he paused to remark that he had brought the reader 'through a series of many barbarous ages' to 'the dawn of civility and science', and would thenceforward be able to present him 'a spectacle more worthy of his attention'.[4] Over the course of the nineteenth and early twentieth centuries, slowly and almost imperceptibly this firm periodisation became a fixed habit of mind. Even if most serious historians used the date 1485 more out of convenience than absolute conviction, the division entrenched itself in the world of scholarship, becoming enshrined in textbooks, syllabuses, schools of history, even styles of research. Countless generations of schoolchildren can certainly be forgiven for believing that their counterparts in 1485 found that over their summer vacation the middle ages had given way to modern times.

*   *   *

Strange to say, the view that 1485 constituted the major divide in English history seems never to have been fully argued. For the most part it was simply assumed. While old habits of thought die hard in many quarters, the traditional periodisation has been increasingly jettisoned by recent generations of historians. Even in the late nineteenth century individual works of scholarship deliberately cut across the divide, but since the Second World War what used to be daring forays across a well-guarded border have become large-scale incursions into a de-militarised zone. 'Modernists' have sought to colonise the second half of the fifteenth century, while 'medievalists' have tried to annex early Tudor England, though curiously without really coming to terms with each other, still less abandoning their own distinctive identities. In this new no-man's-land 1485 is fast becoming no more than a convenient landmark.[5]

Of course, the most basic challenge to the idea of 1485 as a watershed in English history is the clear evidence that men at the time did not feel that their world had been transformed by the victory of Henry Tudor at Bosworth. Richard III had been overthrown, but whatever the character of his rule it had been short-lived. The new king was an unknown quantity, but there was no thought that he would be other than a more or less worthy monarch in the traditional style. Still less was it possible to see in him the future course of sixteenth-century history. Indeed it would have been a brave man in 1485 who would have forecast a Tudor dynasty. The battle of Stoke came close to reversing the decision of Bosworth Field. Furthermore uncertainties about the succession continued until within a few years of the king's death. Even in the cut-and-dried field of dynastic history it is hard to date the point at which men would have felt sure that a Tudor age had begun.[6]

Henry Tudor brought to the tasks of kingship his own distinctive style, and there is some contemporary warrant for the view that his rule was recognisably different from his Yorkist predecessors. The idea of Henry VII as the archetypical 'new monarch' has had a long run. Yet there is no break in the history of the English constitution in 1485, and the habit of ascribing to him specifically new governmental institutions and initiatives has been roundly challenged. The first Tudor inherited a constitution and an administrative system many centuries old, and his use of the household as the mainspring of executive action was anticipated by the Yorkists as well as earlier kings. Similarly his institutional strategies for the enforcement of monarchical authority and the maintenance of law and order had been developed by his immediate predecessors: a committee of the king's council had exercised judicial authority over serious breaches of the peace long before it became known as the court of star chamber, and regional councils for the marches of Wales and for the north had been pioneered in the decade before Bosworth. Obviously, if there is any sense at all in the concept of a 'new monarchy', it is necessary to adopt a periodisation which embraces Edward IV as well as Henry Tudor. Even then the really important division in the constitutional and administrative history of England would seem to occur in the third and fourth decades of the sixteenth century, during the rule of Cardinal Wolsey, and, even more impressively, during the time of the Reformation parliament.[7]

The advent of the Tudors was seen as laying the foundations for a new national unity, and as transforming in other respects the political and social life of the nation. His strengthening of the crown, his firm dealing with the feudal aristocracy, his development of a new office-holding elite and alliance with the 'middle classes', his breaking of regional power-bases, and his beneficence towards Wales, all served to integrate the realm into a single commonwealth. Here again it is the case that long-term developments, traceable over many centuries, have been attached, for convenience, to 1485. Needless to say, the monarchy had long been a focus of national unity, and indeed the civil wars of the fifteenth century testify to its vital importance in English life. It is true that Henry VII proved unusually severe in his dealings with sections of the peerage, particularly in terms of financial actions, but he started his reign with conciliatory gestures. Lord Mountjoy's advice to his son in 1485 'not to desire to be great about princes, for it is dangerous' reflected a growing tendency among peers to adopt a low profile, but such self-effacement was more a result of the vicissitudes of the previous years than a fear of the Tudors. It must be stressed as well that the new king's firmest measures against the nobles came late in his reign. His act against the abuses of 'livery and maintenance' had to wait until 1504, and then largely repeated provisions enacted in 1468. In truth the secular shift in the balance of power away from the old aristocracy towards a new 'service' nobility and a career-minded gentry was scarcely a result of Tudor policy. The political establishments of the 1470s and 1490s were in any case remarkably similar in composition. Even in terms of the Welsh connection, the house of York with their Mortimer ancestry had blazed the trail which the house of Tudor followed.[8]

If the establishment of the new dynasty did not transform politics, it can hardly be expected to have revolutionised other fields of English life. Long-term demographic movements had a major, almost determinant, impact on the

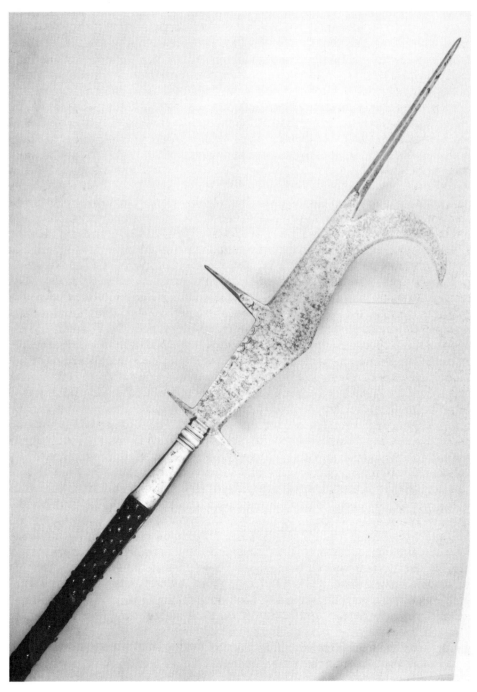

Italian bill, dating from the sixteenth century.

economic and social structure of fifteenth-century England, and were for the most part only marginally affected by the comings and goings of kings. The numbers of lives lost in the civil war was minimal compared with plague mortalities, and indeed the thousand or so killed at Bosworth was rapidly overshadowed by the heavy losses in the sweating sickness which ravaged England through the late summer and autumn of 1485. Of course, the campaigning and insecurity of life at various stages of the Wars of the Roses doubtless adversely affected the economy, but destruction and disruption seem to have been localised, and restricted to particular phases like 1469–71, and, for that matter, 1485–7. In any case, if it is a question of tracing the beginnings of the long expansionary cycle which, with occasional crises and troughs, would continue through until the late sixteenth century, it is more appropriate to make a start in the last half of Edward IV's reign than at the beginning of Tudor times. The crude data available for charting population movements indicates that a demographic recovery began in the 1470s, and the figures available for cloth exports show an even more dramatic upsurge in this decade, in large measure in response to a general revival of the European economy. While the capacity of the crown to intervene constructively in commerce might well have been over-estimated, there can be no doubt that in the promotion of the nation's trading interests and in the involvement of the crown in profitable business ventures the easy-going Edward IV had little to learn from his calculating son-in-law.[9]

The significance of 1485 in other aspects of life is similarly open to dispute. The accession of Henry Tudor had no discernible impact on the church, still less on the age-old religious traditions of the country. The episcopate was largely unaffected. Almost all the churchmen who appear to have been associated with the Ricardian regime, like Bishops Russell, Langton and Shirwood, continued in the royal service after 1485. For understandable reasons, Bishop Stillington was somewhat under a cloud, but he seems to have been in semi-retirement. It needs little stressing that the crucial transformations which separate modern times from former centuries took place with the break with Rome, the dissolution of the monasteries and the spread of Protestantism from the 1530s onwards. As regards culture and the arts it is hard to be as categorical. The new ideals of learning and fashions in art associated with Renaissance Italy do seem to make more headway in England in the early Tudor era, and their success had not a little to do with court sponsorship. Henry VII patronised a large number of humanists from the continent, not least Bernard André and Polydore Vergil, and gave important commissions to the Florentine sculptor Torrigiano. On the other hand, the seeds of English humanism were sown in the 1460s and 1470s. Two prominent Yorkist lords, John Tiptoft, earl of Worcester and Anthony Woodville, Earl Rivers, were active sponsors and fair exemplars of Renaissance ideals. Richard III himself patronised churchmen who were at the forefront of the new learning, and received his greatest tribute in a private letter from Bishop Russell to William Selling, prior of Christ Church, the foremost Greek scholar in the realm. On the other side of the divide, it can be plausibly argued that whatever further progress was made in the reign of Henry VII, Renaissance humanism did not take firm root in England until the

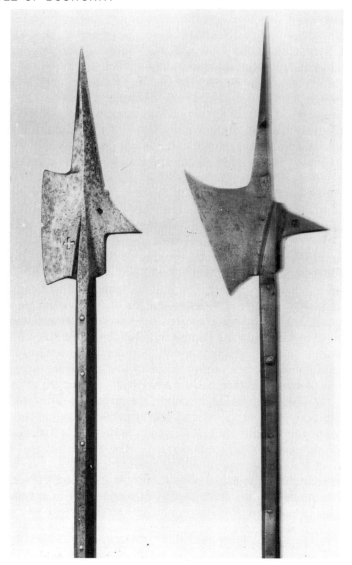

Halberds of the fifteenth century: (a) Swiss, early fifteenth century; (b) German, of about 1500.

second decade of the sixteenth century, and remained a fragile flower for another two generations.[10]

Given the very real continuities through the late fifteenth and early sixteenth centuries, it is patently absurd to make a hard and fast division at 1485 between 'medieval' and 'modern' times. It is interesting to note that the three great 'discoveries' associated by Francis Bacon with the making of the modern world all, in a sense, straddle this periodisation. Gunpowder had been in use throughout the Wars of the Roses. Cannons and fire-arms might appear to represent a challenge to aristocratic military power, but in England there was no sudden shift in the strategic balance in favour of the crown. The compass had likewise been in use for some time, and certainly had begun to play its part in European maritime expansion long before 1485. Though the Portuguese made the running for most of the fifteenth century, English merchant adventurers had similar aspirations. It is true that Henry VII gave cautious approval to the voyages of the Cabot brothers, but Bristol merchants had fitted out several, possibly successful, expeditions to 'Brasil' in the last years of Edward IV's reign.[11] Printing through moveable type was likewise a European innovation of the fifteenth century. Even more clearly its introduction into England did not have to await the 'Tudor peace'. Caxton's establishment of a printing press was rather a tribute to the confidence inspired by the Yorkist regime in the 1470s. Obviously there are grounds for viewing the whole era of the late fifteenth and sixteenth centuries as a transitional age of great creativity and constructive energy.

*   *   *

The battle of Bosworth did not transform English life in 1485, but it is not the case that the event has only a spurious importance. Even though the reign of Henry VII witnessed the continuation of trends already apparent in the 1470s, it must not be concluded that within the late fifteenth century itself there were not phases of accelerated change, shifts of gear, points of crisis and arrested development. In many spheres of national life indeed the period between, say, 1483 and 1487 can be seen as one of crisis. Even with the limited data available, there are indications that the demographic recovery evident in the last third of the fifteenth century temporarily faltered in the mid-1480s. More striking is the brief downturn in cloth exports in the quinquennium 1482–7.[12] Of course such patterns cannot be connected more than tenuously with the circumstances of Richard III's reign and the battle of Bosworth, but they provide some slight support for the traditional periodisation. Similarly in the realm of culture there is a sense in which England's openness to new cultural influences from the continent, so marked in the reign of Edward IV, and given further stimulus by the court of Henry VII, is less evident in the intervening years.

Needless to say, the idea that the period 1483–7 represented a time of crisis is most easily sustained in the political arena. The work of Edward IV in reviving a strong, personal monarchy was inevitably jeopardised by the succession in April 1483 of Edward V. The usurpation of his uncle Richard III less than three months later, the political executions associated with the coup, and the major rising against the new regime all made 1483 a dangerous year. Even in this deeply disturbed time, however, it would have been impossible to imagine the bizarre political scenario of 1487. The new king had been largely unknown four years earlier. Even more remarkable, he was about to be confronted by a military challenge quite as formidable as his own in 1485, mounted on behalf of the son of an Oxford tailor masquerading as the imprisoned son of the duke of Clarence. Needless to say, men who lived through such 'whirling times' must have felt that their realm was going through a series of feverish convulsions. The battle of

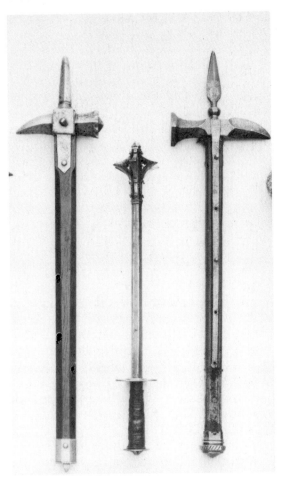

War hammers and maces: (a) French war hammer, for breaking open plate armour, about 1450, weighs nearly 3 lbs; (b) South German Gothic mace, about 1470, weighs nearly 3 lbs; (c) Italian war hammer, about 1490, weighs nearly 3½ lbs.

Bosworth has a cardinal significance in what was a protracted crisis of the English monarchy. In its harsh judgement of the Ricardian regime it drew to a close one phase of the crisis, but the manner of Henry Tudor's victory inaugurated another.

It is seldom appreciated how traumatic Richard III and his reign were for the English polity. It would have been far easier if the man had been a savage monster and his rule an unmitigated tyranny. Unhappily he came close to the model of English kingship. He had the makings of a great soldier-king, a generous patron of the church, a fearless champion of justice and a far-sighted advocate of the 'common weal'. His preference for the old warrior nobility, and for virtuous and learned churchmen, harked back to the best traditions of the Christian kingship. Beneath the expedients and compromises evident in his policies it is possible to see a noble vision of a national monarchy, pursued by the most thoroughly English of kings. Yet his failure was total. Most obviously he failed to win the co-operation of the new elites of late fifteenth century England, the ruling circle of courtiers and bureaucrats at Westminster, the 'service' gentry of the Home Counties, and the merchants of London. Perhaps more significantly he failed to hold the loyalty of the nobles and churchmen who were his natural supporters and seem to have acquiesced in his usurpation. Even major office-holders seem to have been disaffected: it is more than a coincidence that Chancellor Russell had to be relieved of a great seal both at the time of Buckingham's revolt and shortly before Henry Tudor's invasion.[13] It took a great deal to drive the civilian gentry of southern England to rebellion and exile, to alienate so many richly-rewarded aristocratic allies, and to prompt so many churchmen and office-holders to desert their natural obedience to the established king. For all its qualities, the regime of Richard III was felt to be doomed. The king himself increasingly looked like a man marked down for divine retribution. There is no doubt that contemporaries in some wise held him responsible for the murder of the princes, and the imputed crime poisoned irremediably Ricardian politics.

The battle of Bosworth was more a condemnation of Richard III than an endorsement of his supplanter. A number of the magnates involved in the power-play might even have had other candidates in mind for the throne. Despite his professed role as deliverer of the English people from a wicked tyrant, Henry Tudor was a usurper with only the narrowest of power-bases. In the early years he had to rely on the military muscle of the Stanleys and other prominent supporters, and had to make deals with a great many lords and gentry who had served the previous regime. The battle of Bosworth bore bitter fruit in other respects. The sheer adventurism and general preposterousness of the dynastic challenges to Henry VII speak for themselves. If an unknown pretender, supported largely by foreign mercenaries, could advance to the heart of the realm, and challenge the king with the armed might of the kingdom, it could be done again. The affairs of Lambert Simnel and Perkin Warbeck would be incomprehensible were it not for the bizarre career of Henry Tudor.

Nevertheless the scale of this double crisis to the English monarchy presented Henry Tudor with opportunities as well. The evident repugnance felt in many circles against the Ricardian regime provided Henry Tudor with a windfall of committed supporters. Despite Richard III's efforts to be conciliatory, so many members of the Yorkist elite joined the Lancastrian pretender in exile that the victory of 1485 can almost be regarded as a Yorkist restoration. Particularly significant was the commitment of the prosperous and influential southern counties. The political settlement afterwards, in which many magnates were presumably willing to compound heavily for their association with a parricide and tyrant, set a pattern of royal relations with his lords which would reappear over the course of the reign.

The Tudor regime was thus particularly well placed to capitalise ideologically on the background to 1485. From the earliest times great stress was laid on the trials and tribulations of Richard III's reign, and the deliverance secured by Henry Tudor. Pietro Carmeliano devised an epic poem in which God viewed with piteous eye the spectacle of Ricardian England, and called upon a council of saints for a solution. The spirit of the blessed Henry VI proposed his nephew as the agent of deliverance, and his marriage to Elizabeth of York as a means of national reconciliation. The Tudor 'myth' was in the making even before the crises of the 1480s were fully resolved.[14] Nevertheless it served no ideological purpose to dwell on the actual details of the battle of Bosworth, on the squalid slaying of a valiant warrior-king. It is ironic that the event about which Henry VII's court historiographer could find next to nothing to say should have been regarded for most of the last half millenium as marking the major divide in English history.

APPENDIX

I. Government Sources and Common Intelligence

(a) *Proclamation of Henry Tudor*

DATE: 22–3 August 1485. AUTHOR: King and council. TEXT: *Tudor Royal Proclamations*, Vol. I. The Early Tudors (1485–1553), ed. P.L. Hughes and J.P. Larkin (New Haven, 1964), p. 3. (English; spelling modernised.)

'And moreover, the king ascertaineth you that Richard duke of Gloucester, late called King Richard, was slain at a place called Sandeford, within the shire of Leicester, and brought dead off the field unto the town of Leicester, and there was laid openly, that every man might see and look upon him. And also there was slain upon the same field, John late duke of Norfolk, John late earl of Lincoln, Thomas late earl of Surrey, Francis Viscount Lovell, Sir Walter Devereux, Lord Ferrers, Richard Radcliffe, knight, Robert Brackenbury, knight, with many other knights, squires and gentlemen, of whose souls God have mercy.'

(b) *York Memoranda*

DATE: 23 August. AUTHOR: Mayor and aldermen of York. TEXT: York City Archives, House Book, B2–4, f.169v. (Also printed in *Extracts from the Municipal Records of the City of York during the Reigns of Edward IV, Edward V and Richard III*, ed. R. Davies (London, 1843), pp. 218, 217. (English; spelling modernised.)

Memorandum of meeting in council chamber on the Vigil of St Bartholomew, 'where it was shown by divers persons, and especially by John Sponer, sent unto the field of Redemore to bring tidings from the same to the city, that King Richard, late mercifully reigning upon us, was through great treason of the duke of Norfolk and many others that turned against him, with many other lords and nobles of this north parts, was piteously slain and murdered, to the great heaviness of this city'.

There is also a summary record of the battle at 'Rodemore near Leicester'. It is followed by information obviously derived from the king's proclamation, though a clerk has later crossed through the names of the three lords (Lincoln, Surrey and Lovell) who had been wrongly reported as slain.

(c) *Parliamentary Record*

> DATE: November 1485. AUTHOR: King and council. TEXT: *Rotuli Parliamentorum*, ed. J. Strachey, 6 vols. (London, 1767–83), VI, p. 276. (English; spelling modernised.)

The act of attainder records that 'Richard, late duke of Gloucester, calling and naming himself, by usurpation, King Richard the Third'. John late duke of Norfolk, Thomas earl of Surrey, Francis Viscount Lovell, Walter Devereux late Lord Ferrers, John Lord Zouche, Robert Harrington, Richard Charlton, Richard Radcliffe, William Berkeley of Weobley, Robert Brackenbury, Thomas Pilkington, Robert Middleton, James Harrington knights, Walter Hopton, William Catesby, Roger Wake, William Sapcote, Humphrey Stafford, William Clerk of Wenlock, Geoffrey St German, Richard Watkins, Herald of Arms, Richard Revel of Derbyshire, Thomas Poulter junior of Kent, John Walsh alias Hastings, John Kendal, secretary, John Buck, Andrew Ratt, and William Bramton of Burford, on 21 August in 'the first year of the reign of our sovereign lord, assembled to them at Leicester . . . a great host, traitorously intending, imagining and conspiring the destruction of the king's royal person, our sovereign liege lord. And they, with the same host, with banners spread, mightily armed and defenced with all manner [of] arms, as guns, bows, arrows, spears, 'glaives', axes, and all other manner [of] articles apt or needful to give and cause mighty battle against our sovereign lord'. Keeping the host together, they led them on 22 August to a field in Leicestershire, and 'there by great and continued deliberation, traitorously levied war against our said sovereign lord and his true subjects there being in his service and assistance under a banner of our said sovereign lord, to the subversion of this realm, and common weal of the same.'

(d) *Historical Notes of Londoner*

> DATE: Probably 1485–6, though later copy. AUTHOR: Londoner, using civic records. TEXT: R.F. Green, 'Historical notes of a London citizen, 1483–1488, *E.H.R.* 96 (1981), 589 (English; spelling modernised.)

'This year the earl of Richmond and Jasper, earl of Pembroke . . . came forth into England and met with King Richard III at Redesmore, and there was King Richard slain and the duke of Norfolk and Lord Ferrers and Brackenbury, with many other. This battle was the 22 August, 1485. Likewise, in this year the earl of Northumberland and the earl of Surrey were taken and brought into the Fleet of London, and there they were nine days, and then they were led into the Tower of London, and there they were two days, and after had to the castle of Queenborough in Kent.'

(e) *Miscellaneous Town Chronicles*

> DATE: Probably compiled annually, but recopied and updated in early 16th century. AUTHORS: Citizens of London and Calais. TEXTS: London 'Vitellius A XVI': C.L. Kingsford (ed.), *Chronicles of London* (Oxford, 1905), p. 193; Calais Chronicle: *The Chronicle of Calais in the*

Reigns of Henry VII and Henry VIII to the Year 1540, ed. J.G. Nichols (Camden Society 35, 1846), p. 1. (English; spelling modernised.)

The London chronicle 'Vitellius A XVI' records that on 22 August 'this year . . . was the field of Bosworth' at which King Richard, the duke of Norfolk, Brackenbury and many others were slain, and the earl of Surrey taken prisoner, 'by the power of King Henry the Seventh'. The Calais chronicle dates the battle to St Bartholomew's eve and locates it at 'Bosworth heath', but otherwise follows the same pattern. In addition, it records the death of Sir William Brandon as well as the slaying of Radcliffe, Catesby and the 'gentle' Brackenbury; it includes the earl of Northumberland, the earl of Shrewsbury and Lord Zouche among the prisoners; and it documents the escape of Lord Lovell.

II. Independent English Reporters

(a) *Continuation of the Crowland Chronicle*

> DATE: 1486. AUTHOR: Possibly John Russell, or other ex-civil servant in his entourage. TEXT: *'Historiae Croylandensis,'* in W. Fulman (ed.), *Rerum Anglicarum Scriptorum Veterum*, Vol. I (Oxford, 1684), pp. 573–5. Emendation from A. Hanham, *Richard III and the Early Historians 1483–1535* (Oxford, 1975), p. 100. (Latin; own translation; see translation in *Ingulph's Chronicles*, ed. H.T. Riley (London, 1893), pp. 501–5.)

With Henry Tudor and his men advancing towards him, King Richard felt it necessary 'to move the army, though its numbers were not yet fully made up, from Nottingham, and to come to Leicester. Here was found ready to fight for the king a greater number of soldiers than had ever been seen before in England assembled on one side. On the Sunday before the feast of Bartholomew the Apostle, the king proceeded on his way, amid the greatest pomp, and wearing the crown on his head; being attended by John Howard, duke of Norfolk, and Henry Percy, earl of Northumberland, and other mighty lords, knights and esquires, together with a countless multitude of the common people. On leaving Leicester, he was informed by scouts where the enemy most probably intended to spend the next night; upon which, he encamped near the abbey of Merevale, at a distance of about eight miles from town.

'The chief men of the opposing army were: in the first place, Henry, earl of Richmond, whom they called their King Henry VII; John Vere, earl of Oxford; John, Lord Welles, of Welles, uncle to Henry VII; Thomas, Lord Stanley and William his brother; Edward Woodville, brother of Queen Elizabeth, a most valiant knight; John Cheney, John Savage, Robert Willoughby, William Berkeley, James Blount, Thomas Arundel, Richard Edgecombe, Edward Poynings, Richard Guildford, and many others who had been raised to knighthood, both before the present troubles and at the beginning of this campaign. Of churchmen present as counsellors, who likewise had suffered exile, there were the venerable father, Peter, bishop of Exeter, the flower of the knighthood of his country, Master Robert Morton, clerk of the rolls of chancery,

Christopher Urswick, and Richard Fox, who were subsequently appointed almoner and secretary respectively, together with many others.

'At day-break on Monday morning there were no chaplains on King Richard's side ready to celebrate mass, nor any breakfast prepared to restore his flagging spirits. For he had seen dreadful visions in the night, in which he was surrounded by a multitude of demons, as he himself testified in the morning. He consequently presented a countenance which, always drawn, was on this occasion more livid and ghastly than usual, and asserted that the issue of this day's battle, to whichever side the victory was granted, would be the utter destruction of the kingdom of England. He declared that it was his intention, if he proved the victor, to crush all the traitors on the opposing side; and at the same time he predicted that his adversary would do the same to the supporters of his party, if victory should fall to him. At length with the enemy commander and his soldiers approaching at a fair pace, the king ordered that Lord Strange should be instantly beheaded. The persons to whom this duty was entrusted, however, seeing that the issue was doubtful in the extreme, and that a matter of more weight than the destruction of one man was in hand, deferred the performance of the king's cruel order, left the man to his own disposal and returned to the thickest of the fight.

'A most fierce battle thus began between the two sides. The earl of Richmond with his men proceeded directly against King Richard. For his part, the earl of Oxford, the next in rank in the army and a most valiant soldier, drew up of his forces, consisting of a large body of French and English troops, opposite the wing in which the duke of Norfolk had taken up his position. In the place where the earl of Northumberland was posted, with a large company of reasonably good men, no engagement could be discerned, and no battle blows given or received. In the end a glorious victory was given by heaven to the earl of Richmond, now sole king, along with a most precious crown, which King Richard had previously worn on his head. For in the thick of the fight, and not in the act of flight, King Richard fell in the field, struck by many mortal wounds, as a bold and most valiant prince. Then the duke of Norfolk, Sir Richard Radcliffe, Sir Robert Brackenbury, keeper of the Tower of London, John Kendal, secretary, Sir Robert Percy, controller of the king's household, Walter Devereux, Lord Ferrers, and many others were slain in this fierce battle, and many, especially northerners, in whom the king so greatly trusted, took to flight without engaging; and there was left no part of the opposing army of sufficient significance or substance for the glorious victor Henry VII to engage, and so add to his experience in battle.

'Thus through this battle peace was obtained for the whole realm. King Richard's body was found among the other slain. * * * Many other insults were heaped on it, and, not very humanely, a halter was thrown round the neck, and it was carried to Leicester. The new king, graced with the crown he won with such distinction, proceeded to the same place. Meanwhile, many nobles and others were taken into captivity, most notably Henry, earl of Northumberland, and Thomas Howard, earl of Surrey, first-born of the deceased duke of Norfolk. There was also taken prisoner William Catesby, who was pre-eminent among all the counsellors of the late king, and whose head was cut off at Leicester, as a last reward for his excellent service. Also two yeomen from the West Country, named Bracher, who fell into the hands of the victors, were hanged. Moreover there has been no word, nor has it been written or remembered, that any other persons, after the end of the fighting, were dealt with in this fashion, but that, on the contrary, the new prince showed mercy to all. He began to receive the praises of all, as if he were an angel sent from heaven, through whom God had deigned to visit His people, and to deliver them from the evils with which it had been previously and immoderately afflicted.

'And thus concluding this history . . . (we) have brought the narrative down to this battle, which was fought near Merevale, and which took place on 22 August, 1485.'

(b) *John Rous of Warwick*

> DATE: c. 1490. AUTHOR: John Rous (d. 1492), a Warwickshire priest. TEXT: *Historia Johannis Rossi Warwicensis de Regibus Anglie*, ed. T. Hearne (London, 1716), p. 218. (Latin; own translation; see also version in Hanham, *Early Historians*, pp. 123–4.)

'At length, as the life of King Richard neared its evening, many secretly left him and joining the exiled southerners became adherents of Henry, earl of Richmond, nephew of Henry VI, by his uterine brother. Landing at Milford Haven in Wales on the Feast of the Transfiguration with a relatively small band, Henry gained many followers on the road. When finally he met King Richard and his great army on the eighth day of the feast of the Assumption A.D. 1485, on the border of Warwickshire and Leicestershire, he slew him in the field of battle.

'This King Richard, who in his time was cruel beyond measure, reigned for three years and a little more, in the way that Antichrist is to reign, and like him, he was confounded at the peak of his fortunes. For having with him the crown itself, together with a great mass of treasure, he was suddenly cut down like a wretch in the thick of his army by a comparatively small force of armed men. But yet, if I may say the truth to his credit, though small in body and feeble of limb, he bore himself like a gallant knight and acted with distinction as his own champion until his last breath, shouting oftentimes that he was betrayed, and crying "Treason! Treason! Treason!" So, tasting what he had often served to others, he ended his life most miserably, and finally was buried in the choir of the Friars Minor at Leicester.'

III. Foreign Reporters and Chroniclers

(a) *A Castilian Report*

> DATE: Early 1486. AUTHOR: Diego de Valera, Castilian courtier. TEXT: E.M. Nokes and G. Wheeler, 'A Spanish account of the battle of Bosworth', *The Ricardian*, 2, no. 36 (1972), 2. (Spanish; in translation.)

Entering England by way of Wales, and conquering all before him, Henry Tudor 'crossed as far as a town called Coventry, near which King Richard stood in the field with as many as 70,000 combatants. But . . . previous to his entry into England, he had the assurance that my Lord "Tamerlant", one of the principal nobles of England, and sundry other leading men, who had given him their oath and seals, would give him assistance when they came to battle and would fight against King Richard, and so they did. Though his people came with faint heart, as not knowing the secret but fully aware of the multitude of King Richard's army, he greatly heartened them to come to the battlefield.

'When King Richard was certified of the near approach of Earl Henry in battle array, he ordered his lines and entrusted the van to his grand chamberlain with 7,000 fighting men. My Lord "Tamerlant" with King Richard's left wing left his position and passed in front of the king's vanguard with 10,000 men, then, turning his back on Earl Henry, he began to fight fiercely against the king's van, and so did all the others who had plighted their faith to Earl Henry. Now when Salazar, your little vassal, who was there in King Richard's service, saw the treason of the king's people, he went up to him and said: "Sire, take steps to put your person in safety, without expecting to have the victory in today's battle, owing to the manifest treason in your following". But the king replied: "Salazar, God forbid I yield one step. This day I will die as a king or win". Then he placed over his head-armour the crown royal, which they declare to be worth 120,000 crowns, and having donned his coat-of-arms began to fight with much vigour, putting heart into those that remained loyal, so that by his sole effort he upheld the battle for a long time. But in the end the king's army was beaten and he himself killed, and in this battle above 10,000 are said to have perished on both sides. Salazar fought bravely, but for all this was able to escape. There died most of those who loyally served the king, and there was lost all the king's treasure, which he brought with him into the field. After winning this victory Earl Henry was at once acclaimed king by all parties. He ordered the dead king to be placed in a little hermitage near the place of battle, and had him covered from the waist downward with a black rag of poor quality, ordering him to be exposed there three days to the universal gaze.'

(b) *Memoirs of Philippe de Commines*

> DATE: c. 1490. AUTHOR: Philippe de Commines, French-Burgundian chronicler. TEXT: *Memoires de Philippe de Commynes*, ed. L.M.E. Dupont, 3 vols. (Paris, 1840, 1843, 1847), II, pp. 159–60. (French; own translation; see translation in P. de Commynes, *Memoirs. The Reign of Louis XI, 1461–1483*, ed. M. Jones (Harmondsworth, 1972), p. 355).

Assisted by the king of France, Henry Tudor, earl of Richmond launches an expedition from Normandy and lands in Wales. 'King Richard marched against him, but Lord Stanley, an English knight and husband of the earl's mother, brought him 26,000 men. They fought a battle. King Richard was slain in the fighting, and the earl of Richmond was crowned king of England on the field with his crown. Was this mere chance? It was truly the judgement of Almighty God!'

(c) *Chronicles of Jean Molinet*

DATE: c. 1490. AUTHOR: Jean Molinet, historiographer to Burgundian court. TEXT: *Chroniques de Jean Molinet (1474–1506)*, ed. G. Doutrepont and O. Jodogne, 3 vols. (Academie Royale de Belgique. Classe des Lettres et des Sciences Morales et Politiques. Collection des Anciens Auteurs Belges, Brussels, 1935–7), I, pp. 434–6. (French; own translation, with assistance from Professor I.H. Smith, Department of Modern Languages, University of Tasmania).

When the armies came together, 'King Richard prepared his "battles", where there was a vanguard and a rearguard; he had around 60,000 combatants and a great number of cannons. The leader of the vanguard was Lord John Howard, whom King Richard had made duke of Norfolk, granting him lands and lordships confiscated from the earl of Oxford. Another lord, Brackenbury, captain of the Tower of London, was also in command of the van, which had 11,000 or 12,000 men altogether. The place was chosen and the day assigned for the eighth day of the Assumption of the Blessed Virgin Mary, to battle power against power. The French also made their preparations marching against the English, being in the field a quarter of a league away.

'The king had the artillery of his army fire on the earl of Richmond, and so the French, knowing by the king's shot the lie of the land and the order of his battle, resolved, in order to avoid the fire, to mass their troops against the flank rather than the front of the king's battle. Thus they obtained the mastery of his vanguard, which after several feats of arms on both sides was dispersed. In this conflict was taken the duke of Norfolk with his son. The former was taken to the earl of Richmond, who sent him on to the earl of Oxford who had him dispatched.

'The vanguard of King Richard, which was put to flight, was picked off by Lord Stanley who with all of 20,000 combatants came at a good pace to the aid of the earl. The earl of Northumberland, who was on the king's side with 10,000 men, ought to have charged the French, but did nothing except to flee, both he and his company, and to abandon his King Richard, for he had an undertaking with the earl of Richmond, as had some others who deserted him in his need. The king bore himself valiantly according to his destiny, and wore the crown on his head; but when he saw this discomfiture and found himself alone on the field he thought to run after the others. His horse leapt into a marsh from which it could not retrieve itself. One of the Welshmen then came after him, and struck him dead with a halberd, and another took his body and put it before him on his horse and carried it, hair hanging as one would bear a sheep.

'And so he who had miserably killed numerous people, ended his days iniquitously and filthily in the dirt and the mire, and he who had despoiled churches was displayed to the people naked and without any clothing, and without royal solemnity was buried at the entrance to a village church.

'The vanguard [or in one text 'rearguard'] which the grand chamberlain of England led, seeing King Richard dead, turned in flight; and there were in this battle only 300 slain on either side.'

(d) *John Major's Latin History*

> DATE: Before 1521. AUTHOR: John Major, (d. 1550), Scots theologian and historian. TEXT: J. Major. *A History of Greater Britain*, ed. A. Constable (Scottish Historical Society, 1892), p. 393. (Latin; in translation.)

This chronicle relates that the king of France supplied Henry Tudor with 5,000 men, including 1,000 Scots, for the invasion of England, and that 'John son of Robert Haddington was chief and leader of the Scots.'

(e) *Pittscottie's Chronicles*

> DATE: 1570s, but drawing on oral tradition. AUTHOR: Robert Lindsay of Pittscottie. TEXT: *The Historie and Cronicles of Scotland from the Slauchter of King James the First to the Ane Thousande Fyve Hundreith Thrie Scoir Fyftein Yeir, written and collected by Robert Lindesay of Pittscottie*, ed. A.J.G. Mackay, 3 vols. (Scottish Text Society, 1899–1911), I, pp. 190–9. (Middle Scots; slightly modernised.)

Henry Tudor arrives in England with 10,000 men, including 3,000 Englishmen, 6,000 Frenchmen and 1,000 Scots, namely the Scots company under Sir Alexander Bruce of Earlshall. Richard raises a vast army to resist him, numbering 100,000. Henry secretly tries to win over key nobles, most especially Lord Stanley who was 'captain of 1,000 bows of ordinance which was a great part of King Richard's vanguard', promising to make him the greatest lord in the land, and Sir 'Edward' Brackenbury, lieutenant of the Tower of London, captain of the ordnance in the royal vanguard. The two lords first demand of King Richard that he restore the lands of certain friends, formerly in the service of Edward IV. When he refuses, telling them to ask for rewards when they have performed service, they offer their support to Henry Tudor and promise to 'set the crown upon his head'. Henry is pleased and arrays his men, now 30,000 strong, with the vanguard of 10,000 men under the command of Alexander Bruce. Richard has to give battle, and determines to wear his crown. While in a tent, it is stolen for a short while by a Highlander called MacGregor.

The next day the two armies meet. Richard positions his vanguard with his great artillery. Henry marches forward first, but the royal vanguard 'that should have opposed them gave them place and let them go by, themselves turned around and faced King Richard as if they had been his enemies'. The two battle lines fight 'stoutly for a long while with uncertain victory, but at last many of King Richard's battle fled from him and passed to Prince Henry dreading that victory should fall to him at length. Some others of King Richard's army stood and looked on while they saw who had the victory. But this King Richard fought so cruelly that he was slain, for he would not be taken, and there was slain on his party with him the duke of Norfolk with many other lords and gentlemen and in like manner was taken alive his son the earl of Surrey and had to the Tower of London and put in prison where he remained a long time ever he was relieved. By this King Henry passed over this battle and won the victory thereof, and that by the Scots' and Frenchmen's support.'

IV. The Mainstream of Tudor Historiography

(a) *Bernard André Court Historian*

DATE: c. 1500. AUTHOR: Bernard André, French humanist in service of Henry VII. TEXT: B. André, *'Vita Henrici Septimi'* in *Memorials of King Henry VII*, ed. J. Gairdner (London, Roll Series, 1858), p. 32. (Latin; own translation.)

After gaining military assistance from the king of France, Henry Tudor lands in Wales, with the earl of Oxford and Lord Chandée as his commanders. King Richard reacts furiously, ordering his retainers to destroy the rebels with fire and sword. He summons the armed might of the kingdom, but Lord Stanley and his kinsmen go over to the pretender. On the battle itself, André simply notes:

'I have learned somewhat of this battle from oral sources, but in this matter the eye is a more reliable witness than the ear. Rather than affirm anything rashly, therefore, I pass over the date, place and order of battle, for as I have said I lack the illumination of eye-witnesses. Until I am more fully instructed, for this field of battle I shall leave blank a space as broad *   *   *   *   *   * '

He then records the celebrations and speech of thanksgiving, noting the presence among the victorious troops of his clerical colleagues the bishop of Winchester, the bishop of St Asaph and the dean of Windsor, namely Richard Fox, Michael Deacon and Christopher Urswick. More gaps are left for details of the burial of Richard III and the names of the captives. Saturday is given as the day of the battle.

(b) *Robert Fabian and the Great Chronicle*

DATE: 1500–13. AUTHOR: Robert Fabian (d. 1513), citizen of London. TEXTS: *The Chronicle of Fabian, which he nameth the Concordaunce of Histories newly perused and continued from the beginnyng of Kyng Henry the Seventh to th'Ende of Queene Mary* (London, 1559), pp. 519–20; *The Great Chronicle of London*, ed. A.H. Thomas and I.D. Thornley (London, 1938), pp. 237–8. (English; spelling modernised.)

Fabian's Chronicle reports in a few sentences the landing of Henry Tudor, his growing number of supporters, including 'such as were in sundry sanctuaries', and the king's rapid mobilisation. The armies meet at 'a village in Leicestershire named Bosworth'. A 'sharp battle' is fought, 'and sharper it should have been, if the king's party had been fast to him. But many toward the field refused him, and went unto that other party. And some stood hoving afar off till they saw to which party the victory fell'. The *Great Chronicle of London* is more wordy:

'Then King Richard in all haste arrayed his people and made quick provision for to meet his enemies which at the beginning were but of small strength. But as soon as his landing was known to many of the knights and squires of this land, they gathered much people in the king's name and straight sped them unto that other party, by means whereof his power hugely increased. Then King Richard being well accompanied sped him towards his said enemies till he came to Leicester, and that other party which in this while had proclaimed himself King

Henry VII drew fast thitherward. But that night King Richard lost much of his people, for many gentlemen that held good countenance with master Brackenbury then lieutenant of the Tower, and had for many of them done right kindly, took their leave of him, in giving to him thanks for his kindness before showed, and exhorted him to go with them, for they feared not to show unto him that they would go unto that other party, and so departed, leaving him almost alone. In this while the earl of Derby and the earl of Northumberland which had each of them great company made slow speed toward King Richard, so that he with the duke of Norfolk and the earl of Surrey, the Lord Lovell and others departed from Leicester with great triumph and pomp upon the morn being the 22 August, and after continued his journey till he came unto a village called Bosworth where in the fields adjoining both hosts met, and fought a sharp and long fight whereof in the end, the victory fell unto King Henry. In this battle was slain King Richard, the duke of Norfolk, the Lord Lovell with Brackenbury and many others. And incontinently, as it was said, Sir William Stanley which won the possession of King Richard's helmet with the crown being upon it came straight to King Henry and set it upon his head saying, "Sir, here I make you King of England". In this field was taken the earl of Surrey with others.

'And thus by great fortune and grace upon the 22 August won this noble prince possession of this land, and then was he conveyed to Leicester the same night, and there received with all honour and gladness. And Richard late King as gloriously as he by the morning departed from that town, so as irreverently was he that afternoon brought into that town, for his body despoiled to the skin, and nought being left about him, so much as would cover his privy member, he was trussed behind a pursuivant called Norroy as an hog or another vile beast, and so all besprung with mire and filth was brought to a church in Leicester for all men to wonder upon, and there lastly irreverently buried.'

(c) *Polydore Vergil*

DATE: Composed c. 1503–13, though not published until 1534. AUTHOR: Polydore Vergil of Urbino, in England from 1502, wrote at request of Henry VII. TEXT: *Polydori Vergilii Urbinatis Anglicæ Historiæ Libri Vigintiseptem* (Basel, 1555), pp. 562–4 (Latin; own translation, with assistance of Dr R. Develin, Classics Department, University of Tasmania; see also the sixteenth-century English translation published as *Three Books of Polydore Vergil's 'English History', comprising the Reigns of Henry VI, Edward IV and Richard III, from an Early Translation, preserved among the Manuscripts of the Old Royal Library in the British Museum*, ed. H. Ellis (Camden Society, old series 29, 1844), pp. 221–6.)

Polydore Vergil recounts in some detail the progress of Henry Tudor from Milford Haven and the preparations by King Richard to resist him. He describes a meeting between the pretender and the Stanleys at Atherstone, at which a common strategy is agreed upon. In the mean time the royal army moves out from Leicester, and camps near Bosworth. During the night the king has terrible visions, which in the chronicler's opinion were not dreams but the workings of a guilty conscience:

'The day after King Richard, well furnished in all things, drew his whole army out of their encampments, and arrayed his battle-line, extended at such a wonderful length, and composed of footmen and horsemen packed together in such a way that the mass of armed men struck terror in the hearts of the distant onlookers. In the front he placed the archers, like a most strong bulwark, appointing as their leader John, duke of Norfolk. To the rear of this long battle-line followed the king himself, with a select force of soldiers.

'Meanwhile . . . early in the morning [Henry Tudor] commanded his soldiery to set to arms, and at the same time sent to Thomas Stanley, who now approached the place of the fight, midway between the two armies, to come in with his forces, so that the men could be put in formation. He answered that Henry should set his own men in line, while he would be at hand with his army in proper array. Since this reply was given contrary to what was expected, and to what the opportunity of the time and the greatness of the cause demanded, Henry became rather anxious and began to lose heart. Nevertheless without delay he arranged his men, from necessity, in this fashion. He drew up a simple battle-line on account of the fewness of his men. In front of the line he placed archers, putting the earl of Oxford in command; to defend it on the right wing he positioned Gilbert Talbot, and on the left wing in truth he placed John Savage. He himself, relying on the aid of Thomas Stanley, followed with one company of horsemen and a few foot-soldiers. For all in all the number of soldiers was scarcely 5,000, not counting the Stanleyites of whom about 3,000 were in the battle under the leadership of William Stanley. The king's forces were at least twice as many.

'Thus the battle-line on each side was arrayed. As soon as the two armies came within sight of each other, the soldiers donned their helms and prepared for the battle, waiting for the signal to attack with attentive ears. There was a marsh between them, which Henry deliberately left on his right, to serve his men as a defensive wall. In doing this he simultaneously put the sun behind him. The king, as soon as he saw the enemy advance past the marsh, ordered his men to charge. Suddenly raising a great shout they attacked first with arrows, and their opponents, in no wise holding back from the fight, returned the fire fiercely. When it came to close quarters, however, the dealing was done with swords.

'In the mean time the earl of Oxford, afraid that in the fighting his men would be surrounded by the multitude, gave out the order through the ranks that no soldier should go more than ten feet from the standards. When in response to the command all the men massed together and drew back a little from the fray, their opponents, suspecting a trick, took fright and broke off from fighting for a while. In truth many, who wished the king damned rather than saved, were not reluctant to do so, and for that reason fought less stoutly. Then the earl of Oxford in the one part, with tightly grouped units, attacked the enemy afresh, and the others in the other part pressing together in wedge formation renewed the battle.

'While the battle thus raged between the front lines in both sectors, Richard learnt, first from spies, that Henry was some way off with a few armed men as his retinue, and then, as the latter drew nearer, recognised him more certainly from his standards. Inflamed with anger, he spurred his horse, and rode against him from the other side, beyond the battle-line. Henry saw Richard come upon him, and since all hope of safety lay in arms, he eagerly offered himself for the contest. In the first charge Richard killed several men; toppled Henry's standard, along with the standard-bearer William Brandon; contended with John Cheney, a man of surpassing bravery, who stood in his way, and thrust him to the ground with great force; and made a path for himself through the press of steel.

'Nevertheless Henry held out against the attack longer than his troops, who now almost despaired of victory, had thought likely. Then, behold, William Stanley came in support with 3,000 men.. Indeed it was at this point that, with the rest of his men taking to their heels, Richard was slain fighting in the thickest of the press. Meanwhile the earl of Oxford, after a brief struggle, likewise quickly put to flight the remainder of the troops who fought in the front line, a great number of whom were killed in the rout. Yet many more, who supported Richard out of fear and not of their own will, purposely held off from the battle, and departed unharmed, as men who desired not the safety but the destruction of the prince whom they detested. About 1,000 men were slain, including from the nobility John duke of Norfolk, Walter Lord Ferrers, Robert Brackenbury, Richard Radcliffe and several others. Two days after at Leicester, William Catesby, lawyer, with a few associates, was executed. Among those that took to their heels, Francis Lord Lovell, Humphrey Stafford, with Thomas his brother, and many companions, fled into the sanctuary of St. John which is near Colchester, a town on the Essex coast. There was a huge number of captives, for when Richard was killed, all men threw down their weapons, and freely submitted themselves to Henry's obedience, which the majority would have done at the outset, if with Richard's scouts rushing back and forth it had been possible. Amongst them the chief were Henry earl of Northumberland and Thomas earl of Surrey. The latter was put in prison, where he remained for a long time, the former was received in favour as a friend at heart. Henry lost in the battle scarcely a hundred soldiers, amongst whom one notable was William Brandon, who bore Henry's battle standard. The battle was fought on the 11th day before the kalends of September, in the year of man's salvation 1486 [sic], and the struggle lasted more than two hours.

'The report is that Richard could have saved himself by flight. His companions, seeing from the very outset of the battle that the soldiers were wielding their arms feebly and sluggishly, and that some were secretly deserting, suspected treason, and urged him to fly. When his cause obviously began to falter, they brought him a swift horse. Yet he, who was not unaware that the people hated him, setting aside hope of all future success, allegedly replied, such was the great fierceness and force of his mind, that that very day he would make an end either of war or life. Knowing for certain that that day would either deliver him a pacified realm thenceforward or else take it away forever, he went into the fray wearing the royal crown, so that he might thereby make either a beginning or an end of his reign. Thus the miserable man suddenly had such an end as customarily befalls them that for justice, divine law and virtue substitute wilfulness, impiety and depravity. To be sure, these are far more forcible object-lessons than the voices of men to deter those persons who allow no time to pass free from some wickedness, cruelty, or mischief.

'Immediately after gaining victory, Henry gave thanks to Almighty God with many prayers. Then filled with unbelievable happiness, he took himself to the nearest hill, where after he had congratulated his soldiers and ordered them to care for the wounded and to bury the slain, he gave eternal thanks to his captains, promising that he would remember their good services. In the mean time the soldiers saluted him as king with a great shout, applauding him with most willing hearts. Seeing this, Thomas Stanley immediately placed Richard's crown, found among the spoil, on his head, as though he had become king by command of the people, acclaimed in the ancestral manner; and that was the first omen of his felicity.'

(d) *Hall's Chronicle*

DATE: c. 1540. AUTHOR: Edward Hall (d. 1547), lawyer of London. TEXT: Edward Halle, *The Union of the Two Noble Families of Lancaster and York* (London, 1550) (Facsimile, 1970), 'The Tragical Doings of King Richard the Third', fos. 29d–35. (English; spelling modernised.)

In his account of the campaigning and deployment of troops, Hall mainly follows Vergil's *Anglica Historia*, but at the appropriate point he inserts set-speeches by the two captains:

'When both these armies were thus ordered and all men ready to set forward, King Richard called his chieftains together and to them said:

"Most faithful and assured fellows, most trusty and well beloved friends and elected captains by whose wisdom and policy I have obtained the crown ... by whose prudent and politic counsel I have so governed my realm ... that I have omitted nothing appertaining to the office of a just prince ... And although in the ... obtaining of the garland I being seduced and provoked by sinister counsel and diabolical temptation did commit a facinorous and detestable act ... I have with strait penance and salt tears (as I trust) expiated and clearly purged the same offence, which abominable crime I require you of friendship as clearly to forget, as I daily remember to deplore and lament ... I doubt not but you know how the devil, continual enemy to human nature ... hath entered into the heart of an unknown Welshman (whose father I never knew, nor him personally saw) exciting him to aspire and covet our realm, crown and dignity, and thereof clearly to deprive and spoil us and our posterity: ye see further how a company of traitors, thieves, outlaws and renegades of our own nation be aiders and partakers of his feat and enterprise, ready at hand to overcome and oppress us: you see also what a number of beggarly Bretons and fainthearted Frenchmen be with him arrived to destroy us, our wives and children ... [You will] perceive that we have manifest causes, and apparent tokens of triumph and victory. And to begin with the earl of Richmond, captain of this rebellion, he is a Welsh milksop, a man of small courage and of less experience of martial acts and feats of war, brought up by my brother's means and mine like a captive in a close cage in the court of Francis duke of Brittany, and never saw army, nor was exercised in martial affairs, by reason whereof he neither can nor is able of his own wit or experience to guide or rule an host ... Secondarily, fear not ... for when the traitors ... shall see us with banner displayed come against them, remembering their oath ... will either shamefully fly or humbly submit themselves to our grace and mercy. And as for the Frenchmen and Bretons, their valiantness is such that our noble progenitors and your valiant parents have them oftener vanquished and overcome in one month than they ... imagined possible ... in a whole year.... Wherefore, considering all these advantages, expel out of your thoughts all doubts and avoid out of your minds all fear, and like valiant champions advance forth your standards and essay whether your enemies can decide and try the title of battle by dint of sword.... And as for me, I assure you, this day I will triumph by glorious victory, or suffer death for immortal fame...."

'This exhortation encouraged all such as favoured him, but such as were present more for dread than love kissed them openly whom they inwardly hated. . . . So was his people to him unsure and unfaithful at his end, as he was to his nephews untrue and unnatural in his beginning.

'When the earl of Richmond knew by his foreriders that the king was so near embattled, he rode about his army, from rank to rank from wing to wing, giving comfortable words to all men, and that finished (being armed in all pieces saving his helmet) mounted on a little hill, so that all his people might see and behold him perfectly to their great rejoicing; for he was a man of no great stature, but so formed and decorated with all gifts and lineaments of nature that he seemed more an angelical creature than a terrestrial personage, his countenance and aspect was cheerful and courageous, his hair yellow like the burnished gold, his eyes grey shining and quick, prompt and ready in answering, but of such sobriety that it could never be judged whether he were more dull than quick in speaking (such was his temperance). And when he had overlooked his army over every side, he paused a while, and after with a loud voice and bold spirit spake to his companions these or like words following:

"If ever God gave victory to men fighting in a just quarrel. . . . I doubt not but God will rather aid us (yea and fight for us) than see us vanquished . . . Our cause is so just that no enterprise can be of more virtue, both by the laws divine and civil, for what can be more honest, goodly or Godly quarrel than to fight against a captain, being an homicide and murderer of his own blood or progeny, an extreme destroyer of his nobility, and to his and our country and the poor subjects of the same a deadly mallet, a fiery brand and a burden intolerable. Beside him consider who be of his band and company, such as by murder and untruth . . . have disinherited me and you . . . For he that calleth himself king, keepeth me from the crown and regiment of this noble realm and country contrary to all justice and equity. Likewise his mates and friends occupy your lands, cut down your woods and destroy your manors, letting your wives and children range abroad for their living; which persons for their penance and punishment I doubt but not God of His goodness will either deliver into our hands . . . or cause them . . . to fly and not abide the battle: beside this I assure you that there be yonder in the great battle men brought thither for fear and not for love, soldiers by force compelled and not with good will assembled, persons which desire rather the destruction than salvation of their master and captain . . . Behold your Richard which is both Tarquin and Nero; yea, a tyrant more than Nero, for he hath not only murdered his nephew being his king and sovereign lord, bastarded his noble brethren and defamed the womb of his virtuous and womanly mother, but also compassed all the means and ways that he could invent how to stup'rate and carnally know his own niece under the pretence of a cloaked matrimony, which lady I have sworn and promised to take to my mate and wife. . . . If this cause be not just, and this quarrel Godly, let God the giver of victory judge and determine. . . . And this remember . . . that before us be our enemies, and on either side of us such as I neither surely trust nor greatly believe. Backward we cannot fly: so that here we stand like sheep in a fold circumcepted and compassed between our enemies and our doubtful friends. Therefore let all fear be set aside, and like sworn brethren let us join in one, for this day shall be the end of our travail and the gain of our labour, either by honourable death or famous victory: and as I trust the battle shall not be so sore as the profit shall be sweet. Remember the victory is not gotten with the multitude of men, but with the courage of hearts and valiantness of minds. The smaller that our number is the more glory is to us if we vanquish, if we be overcome, yet no laud is to be attributed to the victors, considering that ten men fought against one . . . And now advance forward . . . true inheritors against usurpers, the scourges of God against tyrants, display my banner with a good courage, march forth like strong and robustious champions, and begin the battle like hardy conquerors, the battle is at hand, and the victory approacheth, and if we shamefully recoil or cowardly fly, we and all our sequel be destroyed and dishonoured forever. . . ."

'These cheerful words he set forth with such gesture of his body and smiling countenance, as though already he had vanquished his enemies and gotten the spoil.

'He had scantly finished his saying, but the one army espied the other. Lord, how hastily the soldiers buckled their helms, how quickly the archers bent their bows and frushed their feathers, how readily the billmen shook their bills and proved their staves, ready to approach and join, when the terrible trumpet should sound the bloody blast to victory or death. Between both armies there was a great marsh which the earl of Richmond left on his right hand, for this intent that it should be on that side a defence for his part, and in so doing he had the sun at his back and in the faces of his enemies. When King Richard saw the earl's company was past the marsh he commanded with all haste to set upon them; then the trumpets blew, and the soldiers shouted, and the king's archers courageously let fly their arrows, the earl's bowmen stood not still but paid them home again. The terrible shot once passed, the armies joined and came to hand strokes, where neither sword nor bill was spared, at which encounter the Lord Stanley joined with the earl.'

After this last insertion, Hall continues largely paraphrasing Vergil's account of the Oxford's defensive manouevre, the break-up of the royal vanguard, the king's final charge and death, and the battlefield coronation. In several places additional details are offered. Thus to the record of the death of the duke of Norfolk, he adds that he was warned 'to refrain from the field in so much that the night before he should set forward toward the king, one wrote on his gate:

> "Jack of Norfolk be not too bold
> For Dicken thy master is bought and sold."

'Yet all this notwithstanding he regarded more his oath, his honour and promise made to King Richard; like a gentleman and faithful subject to his prince he absented not himself from his master, but as he faithfully lived under him, so he manfully died with him to his great fame and laud.'

In a similar fashion after rehearsing the predicament of Lord Strange before and during the battle, Hall notes that after the king's death the keepers of his tents submitted themselves as prisoners of their young hostage.

Hall ends his account of Richard III by leaving 'to God which knew his interior cogitations at the hour of his death, I remit the punishment of his offences committed in his life.'

V. The Ballad Tradition

(a) *The Rose of England*

DATE: Earliest of ballads on Bosworth, in all likelihood first composed in 1485, but only extant in mid-17th century manuscript. AUTHOR: Anonymous. TEXT: B.L., Additional MS. 27,879; *The English and Scottish Popular Ballads*, ed. F.J. Child, 5 vols. (New York, 1957), III, pp. 331–3. (English; spelling modernised.)

The ballad begins with an extended allegory on England as a garden with a Rose bush (the house of Lancaster) which is disrupted by a White Boar (Richard III), who drives the last sprig, Henry Tudor (the 'Rose of England') into exile. Henry Tudor lands at Milford Haven to claim his right, bringing with him the earl of Oxford (the 'Blue Boar') to fight against the White Boar. He sends to Lord Stanley (the 'Old Eagle') for assistance, and wins the support of Rhys ap Thomas and other Welshmen. Advancing on Shrewsbury, the town is held against him by its bailiff, Mitton, who finally opens the gates on receipt of a letter from Sir William Stanley. Promising steadfast loyalty to the new king, Mitton is pardoned. Henry Tudor proceeds to Newport, and then to Atherstone, where he meets the Stanleys and the forces from Cheshire and Lancashire. Unfortunately Lord Strange (the 'Young Eagle') is a hostage of Richard III and causes Lord Stanley much anxiety. The battle, however, is joined:

> Then the Blue Boar (Oxford) the vanguard had;
> He was both wary and wise of wit;
> The right hand of them (the enemy) he took,
> The sun and wind of them to get.
>
> Then the Eagle (Stanley) followed fast upon his prey,
> With sore dints he did them smite;
> The Talbot (Gilbert Talbot), he bit wondrous sore,
> So well the Unicorn (John Savage) did him acquit.
>
> And then came in the Hart's Head (William Stanley);
> A worthy sight it was to see,
> The jackets that were of white and red,
> How they laid about them lustily.
>
> But now is the fierce field foughten and ended,
> And the White Boar (Richard III) there lieth slain,
> And the Young Eagle (Strange) is preserved,
> And come to his nest again.
>
> But now this garden (England) flourishes freshly and gay,
> With fragrant flowers comely of hue,
> And gardeners it doth maintain;
> I hope they will prove just and true.
>
> Our King (Henry VII), he is the Rose so Red,
> That now does flourish fresh and gay;
> Confound his foes, Lord, we beseech,
> And love His Grace both night and day!

(b)   *The Ballad of Bosworth Field*

DATE: Earliest surviving copy mid-17th century, but prose summary of earlier version late 16th century; form and content indicate initial composition within living memory of battle. AUTHOR: Anonymous member of Stanley entourage, probably eye-witness. TEXT: B.L., Additional MS. 27,879, fos. 434–43; *Bishop Percy's Folio Manuscript. Ballads and Romances*, ed. J.W. Hales and F.J. Furnivall, 3 vols. (London, 1868), III, pp. 233–59; B.L. Harleian MS. 542, f. 34 (prose summary). (English; spelling modernised; readings from prose summary marked #.)

The ballad begins with an appreciation of the wondrous transformation achieved through the accession of Henry VII, and an appeal to Christ to keep England in 'peace and tranquillity'. The exile of Henry Tudor, his return to claim his heritage, his landing at Milford Haven, his appeal to the Stanleys are all recounted. The scene shifts to the court of Richard III, where the king is being counselled to destroy the overmighty Stanleys. Summoned to court, Lord Stanley falls ill at Manchester, and sends in his place Lord Strange, who on arrival is thrown in prison. Hearing of the king's treachery and Henry Tudor's landing, Lord Stanley and Sir William Stanley repudiate their allegiance: the latter promises to make his former lord 'such a breakfast upon a day as never made knight any king in Christendom'. The king replies that whoever opposes him, be it the Great Turk, Prester John or the Sultan of Syria, he will remain king, and threatens to leave no knight or squire alive between Lancaster and Shrewsbury, and to turn into a park the land between Holyhead and St David's.

Then the king sends messengers to every nobleman and knight in the realm, and assembles a company of unprecedented size:

> Thither came the duke of Norfolk upon a day,
> And the earl of Surrey that was his heir;
> The earl of Kent was not away,
> The earl of Shrewsbury brown as bear.

The ballad continues in similar fashion to list the nobles who swore to support the king; the earls of Lincoln, Northumberland and Westmorland, Lords Zouche, Maltravers, Welles, Grey of Codnor, 'Bowes' [Grey of Powys?], Audley, Berkeley [earl of Nottingham?], Ferrers of Chartley, Lovell#, Fitzhugh, Scrope of Masham, Scrope of Bolton, Dacre, Ogle#, Lumley, and Greystoke. There follows a list of other knights who were in attendance, including the following clearly identifiable persons: Ralph Harbottle, Henry Horsey#, Henry Percy, John Grey, Thomas Montgomery, Robert Brackenbury, Richard Charlton, Thomas Markenfield#, Christopher Ward#, Robert Plumpton#, William Gascoigne#, Marmaduke Constable, Martin of the Sea#, John Melton, Gervase Clifton, Henry Pierpoint, John Babington, Humphrey Stafford, Robert Rither, Brian Stapleton, Richard Radcliffe, John Norton#, Thomas Mauleverer, Christopher Moresby, Thomas Broughton, Richard Tempest, Ralph Ashton, Robert Middleton, John Neville, Roger Heron, James Harrington, Robert Harrington and Thomas Pilkington. A number of hypothetical reconstructions can be made from the two garbled renderings of the same name: Henry Bodrugan alias Bodringham ['Bowdrye', 'Landringham'#], Robert Rither ['Ryder', 'Rydyssh'#], Robert Ughtred ['Utridge', 'Owtrege'#], Alexander Baynham ['Fawne', 'Haymor'#], John Huddleston ['Hurlstean', 'Adlyngton'#].

Against the armed might of all England two shires alone (Lancashire and Cheshire) stand for Henry Tudor. On Monday Lord Stanley leads the Lancashire men from Lathom to Newcastle. Sir William Stanley with troops from Cheshire and North Wales moves first from Holt to Nantwich, then on Tuesday to Stone, whence he rides across to meet Henry Tudor at Stafford. The narrative leaps several days to describe the triumphal entry of the pretender and the younger Stanley into Lichfield on the Saturday morning, but the latter abruptly leaves in the direction of Tamworth, where it is reported that Lord Stanley is about to be attacked by the king. The Stanleys are in position near a place called 'Hattersey': Lord Stanley has the vanguard, and Sir William's company comes in as the rearguard. They remain in defensive formation through Sunday, expecting the royal advance, but Henry Tudor arrives first and finally meets Lord Stanley. Early the next morning the battle begins. Henry Tudor desires the vanguard, and Lord Stanley seeing the small size of his company lends him four of his chief knights, Robert Tunstall, John Savage, Hugh Pershal and Humphrey Stanley:

> The Lord Stanley both stern and stout,
> Two 'battles' that day had he
> Of hardy men, withouten doubt
> Better were not in Christenty.

> Sir William, wise and worthy,
> Was hindmost at the outsetting;
> Men said that day that did him see,
> He came betime unto our King.

Then Lord Stanley withdraws to a hill top whence he sees the enemy troops massing. In a highly condensed and confused verse the two sides angle themselves for combat:

> The duke of Norfolk advanced his banner bright,
> So did the young earl of Shrewsbury,
> To the sun and wind right speedily dight,
> So did Oxford, that earl, in company.

The king's ordnance is described: seven score serpentines chained together in a row, a similar number of bombards that blew 'like blasts of thunder', and ten thousand pikes and harquebusiers.

Meanwhile Richard III seeing Lord Stanley's banner on the hill orders the execution of Lord Strange. The young lord prepares for death and sends a message to his lady to leave the country with their child. With the vanguards engaged, the king is persuaded to delay the execution until after the battle. The fighting proceeds. Henry Tudor, Oxford, Savage, Talbot and Pershal all fight stoutly, but the king has superior forces:

> King Richard did in his army ['in a marsh'#] stand,
> He was numbered to forty ['twenty'#] thousand and three
> Of hardy men of heart and hand,
> That under his banner there did be.

> Sir William Stanley wise and worthy
> Remembered the breakfast he promised to him;
> Down at a back [or 'bank'] then cometh he,
> And shortly set upon the King.

> Then they 'countered together sad and sore;
> Archers they let sharp arrows fly,
> They shot guns both fell and far,
> Bows of yews bended did be,

Springals sped them speedily,
Harquebusiers' pellets throughly did thring;
So many banners began to sway
That was on Richard's party, their king.

Then our archers let their shooting be,
With joined weapons were grounded full right,
Brands rang on basinets high,
Battle-axes fast on helms did light.

There died many a doughty knight,
There under foot can they thring;
Thus they fought with main and might
That was Henry's part, our King.

Then to King Richard there came a knight,
And said, 'I hold it time for to flee;
For yonder Stanleys' dints they be so wight,
Against them no man may dree.

'Here is thy horse at thy hand ready;
Another day thou may worship win,
And for to reign with royalty,
To wear the crown, and be our King.'

He said, 'Give me my battle-axe in my hand,
Set the crown of England on my head so high!
For by Him that shope both sea and land,
King of England this day will I die!

One foot will I never flee
Whilst the breath is my breast within!'
As he said, so did it be;
If he lost his life, if he were King.

About his standard can they light,
The crown of gold they hewed him fro,
With doleful dints his death they dight,
The duke of Norfolk that day they slew.

The ballad then records the deaths of Lord Ferrers, the 'noble' Sir Richard Radcliffe, a close counsellor of the king, the 'wight' Sir William Conyers, the 'full doughty' Sir Robert Brackenbury, the 'good' Sir Richard Charlton, all on Richard's side. It commends in particular the valour of the respective standard-bearers: William Brandon, the only notable casualty on Henry Tudor's side, and Sir Percival Thirlwall who did not let fall the royal standard even when his legs were hewn from under him.

Then they moved to a mountain on height,
With a loud voice they cried 'King Henry!';
The crown of gold that was bright,
To the Lord Stanley delivered it be.

Anon to King Henry delivered it he,
The crown that was so delivered to him,
And said, 'Methink ye are best worthy
To wear the crown and be our King.'

The ballad continues with the victors riding to Leicester 'that night' and laying the late king's naked corpse in the Newarke for all to see. After commenting on the wondrousness of Fortune, it concludes with a prayer that the house of Stanley remain safe, illustrious and influential at the court of James I.

(c)　*The Song of Lady Bessy*

> DATE: Earliest extant text c. 1600, and its romantic frills doubtless Elizabethan, but elements could reach back to early 16th century. AUTHOR: Anonymous, but Humphrey Brereton of Cheshire, a hero of romance, is an obvious candidate. TEXT: B.L., Harleian MS. 367, fos. 89–100; *Bishop Percy's Folio Manuscript*, III, pp. 319–63. (English; spelling modernised.)

This ballad focuses on the plight of Lady Bessy (Elizabeth of York) who is trying to resist the advances of Richard III, to avenge her brothers and promote the cause of Henry Tudor, her sweetheart. She appeals to Lord Stanley, who writes to his brother Sir William Stanley, his sons Lord Strange and Edward Stanley, and Sir John Savage and Sir Gilbert Talbot asking them to come secretly to London on 3 May. The Stanleys fear that the king wishes to destroy them as he destroyed the duke of Buckingham, and Talbot fears for his nephew, the earl of Shrewsbury, a royal ward. They agree to support Henry Tudor, with Lord Stanley and Sir William Stanley promising 20,000 and 10,000 men respectively. Lady Bessy and the others send Humphrey Brereton with money and messages to the pretender, who is found at 'Bigeram' abbey. After purchasing arms in Paris and unsuccessfully appealing for further French aid, Henry Tudor replies that he will come to England about Michaelmas, by way of Milford Haven and Shrewsbury. On receipt of this news Lord Stanley withdraws from London to Lathom, leaving Lady Elizabeth in hiding near Leicester, and sends Lord Strange to the king in his place. At Holt castle Sir William Stanley watches for the southwesterly wind that will signal the invasion. He sends Rowland Warburton to Shrewsbury with orders to admit the pretender.

In turn Richard III summons his 'lords of great renown': 'Lord Percy' with 30,000 men; the duke of Norfolk, the earls of Surrey and Kent, the bishop of Durham, Lord Scrope, Sir William 'Bawmer', Sir William Harrington, some with 20,000 men each. The 'earl of Derby' and his brother are ordered to bring their companies. Despite his nephew's life being in jeopardy, Sir William Stanley openly defies the king. As Henry Tudor proceeds to Stafford, he rides across from Stone to greet him, and promises to help him win the crown and marry Lady Bessy. Early on Sunday morning, he hears that his brother is already engaged in battle; he hastens to Lichfield, where his men acclaim Henry as king; then he presses on to Bosworth. Their forces are considerable: Lord Stanley has 20,000 men, Sir William Stanley 10,000 men in 'red coats', their nephew Sir John Savage 1,500 men, and Rhys ap Thomas 10,000 men.

At the battlefield Henry Tudor requests the vanguard from Lord Stanley, who commits to the royal host the troops of John Savage and Rhys ap Thomas, and promises the assistance of Sir William Stanley. Lord Stanley himself takes up position on a nearby hill. His banner is spotted by the king, who orders the execution of Lord Strange. The young lord sends a man called Lathom with a message to his wife to take his son abroad, whence he might in future return to avenge his lineage. The king rejects an appeal by Harrington that execution be deferred until all the Stanleys are captured, but is distracted by the enemy attack.

The battle now rages, with bugles blowing and guns roaring. Rhys ap Thomas breaks through the enemy line pushing 'Lord Percy' from the field. Norfolk takes refuge with his men on a hill, but is killed by Savage. Lord Dacre and many others flee. Harrington counsels retreat, but Richard replies:

> 'Give me my battle-axe in my hand,
> And set my crown on my head so high!
> For by Him that made both sun and moon,
> King of England this day I will die!'

The king is cut down. The crown is hewn from him and his helmet bashed into his head 'until his brains come out with blood'. He is carried to Leicester, where Lady Bessy rebukes the corpse for the death of her brothers. Her marriage with Henry Tudor is recorded. The Stanleys crown the happy couple, but the subsequent fall from grace of the younger Stanley is also noted. The ballad ends with a prayer to God to 'save and keep our comely Queen and the poor comminalty'.

LIST OF ABBREVIATIONS

B.I.H.R.	*Bulletin of the Institute of Historical Research*
B.L.	British Library
C.C.R.	*Calendar of Close Rolls* (H.M.S.O.)
C.I.P.M.	*Calendar of Inquisitions Post Mortem* (H.M.S.O.)
C.P.R.	*Calendar of Patent Rolls* (H.M.S.O.)
E.H.R.	*English Historical Review*
H.M.S.O.	His/Her Majesty's Stationery Office
P.R.O.	Public Record Office, London
T.R.H.S.	*Transactions of the Royal Historical Society*

NOTES

NOTES

1 News From The Field

C.L. Kingsford, *English Historical Literature in the Fifteenth Century* (Oxford, 1913) and, more recently, A. Gransden, *Historical Writing in England. II. c. 1307 to the Early Sixteenth Century* (London, 1982) introduce the major chronicles and annals. A. Hanham, *Richard III and the Early Historians 1483–1535* (Oxford, 1975) is the most detailed guide to the sources for the events around 1485. J. Potter, *Good King Richard?* (London, 1983) offers many interesting insights.

1. York City Archives, House Book, B2–4, f. 169v. *Extracts from the Municipal Records of the City of York during the Reigns of Edward IV, Edward V and Richard III*, ed. R. Davies (London, 1843), pp. 218–19.
2. *Tudor Royal Proclamations*, Vol. 1. The Early Tudors (1485–1553), ed. P.L. Hughes and J.F. Larkin (New Haven, 1964), p. 3; *Rotuli Parliamentorum*, ed. J. Strachey, 6 vols. (London, 1767–83), VI, p. 276; B. André, '*Vita Henrici Septimi*' in *Memorials of King Henry VII*, ed. J. Gairdner (London, Rolls Series, 1858), p. 32.
3. *Calendar of State Papers and Manuscripts existing in the Archives and Collections of Milan*, Vol. 1. 1385–1618, ed. A.B. Hinds (H.M.S.O., 1912), p. 247; *Calendar of State Papers and Manuscripts relating to English Affairs existing in the Archives and Collections of Venice, and in other Libraries of Northern Italy*, Vol. 1. 1202–1509, ed. R. Brown (H.M.S.O., 1864), p. 156; *Calendar of Letters, Despatches, and State Papers, relating to the Negotiations between England and Spain, preserved in the Archives at Simancas and Elsewhere*, Vol. 1. Henry VII, 1485–1509, ed. G.A. Bergenroth (H.M.S.O., 1862), p. 1.
4. E.M. Nokes and G. Wheeler, 'A Spanish account of the battle of Bosworth', *The Ricardian*, 2, no. 36 (1972), 1–5; A. Goodman and A. MacKay, 'A Castilian report on English affairs, 1486', *E.H.R.* 88 (1973), 92–9.
5. *Memoires de Philippe de Commynes*, ed. L.M.E. Dupont, 3 vols. (Paris, 1840, 1843, 1847), II, pp. 159–60, 246. *Chroniques de Jean Molinet (1474–1506)*, ed. G. Doutrepont and O. Jodogne, 3 vols. (Academie Royale de Belgique. Classe des Lettres et des Sciences Morales et Politiques. Collection des Anciens Auteurs Belges. Brussels, 1935–7), I, pp. 434–6. Because he is sometimes in error on points of detail – e.g. he names Edward IV's second son George (I, pp. 430–1) – Molinet has been largely ignored by English historians. Yet he wrote his account of Bosworth soon after 1485: though his narrative goes into the early 16th century the decade 1483 to 1493 is treated most fully and was clearly the most active period of composition (III, p. 33). He was well-placed to gain information from England, not least from sources hostile to the Tudor regime. He includes many verifiable points of detail: for example, the duke of Norfolk's enrichment at the expense of the earl of Oxford, and Lord Stanley's possesion of a crown (I, pp. 434–5).

6. *Joannis Rossi Antiquarii Warwicensis Historia Regum Angliae* ed. T. Hearne (Oxford, 1716) (hereafter Rous, *Historia*), p. 218. (Translation in Hanham, *Early Historians*, pp. 123–4). For his earlier praise of Richard III, see *The Rous Roll* (Facsimile), reprinted with introduction by C. Ross (Gloucester, 1980), no. 63. It should be noted on Rous's behalf that his praise was directed to Richard III as the husband of Anne Neville, the lady of Warwick. His volte-face after 1485 is readily understandable, since he believed that the king caused her death.

7. R.F. Green, 'Historical notes of a London citizen, 1483–1488', *E.H.R.* 96 (1981), 585–9; *Chronicles of London*, ed. C.L. Kingsford (Oxford, 1905), p. 193; *Records of City of York*, p. 217.

8. *The Chronicle of Fabian, which he nameth the Concordaunce of Histories newly perused and continued from the beginnyng of Kyng Henry the Seventh to th'End of Queene Mary* (London, 1559), (for modern edition, see *The New Chronicles of England and France by Robert Fabyan, named by himself the Concordance of Histories*, ed. H. Ellis (London, 1811)); *The Great Chronicle of London*, ed. A.H. Thomas and I.D. Thornley (London, 1938).

9. 'Historiae Croylandensis Continuatio', in *Rerum Anglicarum Scriptores Veterum*, ed. W. Fulman (Oxford, 1684) (hereafter *H.C.C.*); *Ingulph's Chronicles*, ed. H.T. Riley (London, 1893) (hereafter *Crowland*). For emendation, see Hanham, *Early Historians*, p. 100; on date and authorship, Gransden, *Historical Writing*, II, pp. 265–74, 491–2.

10. B. André, '*Vita Henrici Septimi*', p. 32; *The Complete Works of St. Thomas More*. Vol. 2. The History of King Richard III, ed. R.S. Sylvester (New Haven, 1963).

11. *Polydori Vergilii Urbinatis Anglicae Historiae Libri Vigintiseptem* (Basel, 1555) (hereafter Vergil, *A.H.*); *Three Books of Polydore Vergil's 'English History', comprising the Reigns of Henry VI, Edward IV and Richard III, from an Early Translation, preserved among the Manuscripts of the Old Royal Library in the British Museum*, ed. H. Ellis (Camden Society, old series 29, 1844) (hereafter Vergil, *English History*); *The 'Anglica Historia' of Polydore Vergil, A.D. 1485–1537*, ed. D. Hay (Camden Society, new series 74, 1950) (hereafter Vergil, *A.H., 1485–1537*).

12. Edward Halle, *The Union of the Two Noble Families of Lancaster and York* (London, 1550) (Facsimile, 1970), 'The Tragical Doings of King Richard the Third', fos. 29d–35.

13. Raphael Holinshed, *Chronicles of England, Scotland and Ireland*, ed. H. Ellis, 6 vols. (London, 1807–8), III, pp. 438–46; William Shakespeare, *Richard III*, ed. A. Hammond (The Arden Shakespeare, 1981); Sir John Beaumont 'Bosworth Field: a Poem' in J. Nichols, *The History and Antiquities of the County of Leicester*, 4 vols. in 8 (London, 1795–1815), IV, pp. 559–63.

14. John Major, *A History of Greater Britain*, ed. A. Constable (Scottish Historical Society, 1892), p. 393; *The Historie and Chronicles of Scotland from the Slauchter of King James the First to the Ane Thousands Fyve Hundreith Thrie Scoir Fyftein Yeir, written and collected by Robert Lindesay of Pittscottie*, ed. A.J.G. Mackay, 3 vols. (The Scottish Text Society, 1899–1911) (hereafter Lindsay, *Historie*), I, pp. 190–9. For the tradition that Bernard Stuart was also present see E. Cust, *The Stuarts of Aubigny* (London, 1891), p. 27, The presence of Scots is first acknowledged in England by Beaumont ('Bosworth Field: a Poem' in Nichols, *Leicestershire*, p. 561), a Jacobean courtier (F. Skillington, 'Sir John Beaumont of Gracedieu', *Transactions of the Leicestershire Archaeological and Historical Society* 47 (1971–2), 43–50).

15. B.L., Additional MS. 12,060, ff. 19–20. Henry Parker was the son of Sir William Parker (d. 1510), who was standard-bearer and counsellor to Richard III. See *Forty-Six Lives translated from Boccaccio's 'De Claris Mulieribus' by Henry Parker, Lord*

Morley, ed. H.G. Wright (Early English Text Society, original series 214, 1943 for 1940).

16. J. Leland, *Itinerary*, ed. L.T. Smith, 5 vols. (1906–8), II, p. 18; A.L. Rowse, 'The turbulent career of Sir Henry de Bodrugan', *History* 29 (1944), 24; Beaumont, 'Bosworth Field: a Poem' in Nichols, *Leicestershire*, IV, p. 563; W. Burton, *The Description of Leicester-Shire, containing Matters of Antiquitye, Historye, Armourye and Genealogy* (London, 1622), p. 47.

17. Lindsay, *Historie*, pp. 196–8. James III of Scotland had arranged to send an embassy in May 1485, and Henry VII gave the bishop of Dunkeld and others safe-conducts as early as 22 September: N. Macdougall, *James III. A. Political Study* (Edinburgh, 1982), pp. 214, 217. It is conceivable that Dunkeld had actually arrived in England before the death of Richard III.

18. W. Hutton, *The Battle of Bosworth Field between Richard the Third and Henry Earl of Richmond, August 22, 1485*, 2nd ed. J. Nichols (London, 1813), pp. 47–9.

19. *The History of King Richard the Third (1619) by Sir George Buck, Master of the Revels*, ed. A.N. Kincaid (Gloucester, 1982).

20. Nichols, *Leicestershire*, IV, p. 554. An old woman who had read them recalled that there was something about 'the king being set fast in a bog': *Ibid.*, p. 554n. Compare, Molinet, *Chroniques*, I, p. 435.

21. *The English and Scottish Popular Ballads*, ed. F.J. Child, 5 vols. (New York, 1957), III, pp. 331–3 ('Rose of England'); *Bishop Percy's Folio Manuscript. Ballads and Romances*, ed. J.W. Hales and F.J. Furnivall, 3 vols. (London, 1868), III, pp. 233–59 ('Bosworth Feilde', hereafter 'Bosworth Field'); pp. 319–63 ('Ladye Bessiye', hereafter 'Lady Bessy').

22. C. Ross, *Richard III* (London, 1981), pp. 234–7 mounts a strong case for taking 'Bosworth Field' seriously. His case could be greatly strengthened by drawing in evidence from the earlier prose summary (B.L., Harleian MS. 542). Evidence that ballads or more exactly 'talkings' were major sources of 'news' in early Tudor times is not lacking. Songs about the battles of Stoke and Branston (Flodden) were circulating in Cheshire as early as the 1520s: Bodleian Library, Oxford, MS. Lat. MS. Lat. misc. c. 66, f. 104.

23. André, 'Vita Henrici Septimi' p. 33; *Calendar of Entries in the Papal Registers relating to Great Britain and Ireland. Papal Letters*, Vol. XIV, 1484–1492, ed. J.A. Twemlow (H.M.S.O., 1960), p. 18; Vergil, *A.H.*, p. 564 (*English History*, p. 225).

24. *Tudor Royal Proclamations*, I, p. 3; Green, 'Historical notes', 589; Hanham, *Early Historians*, p. 107; Rous, *Historia*, p. 218; Nokes and Wheeler 'Spanish account', 2; *H.C.C.*, p. 575 (*Crowland*, p. 505); *Chronicle of Fabian*, pp. 519–20; Vergil, *A.H.* p. 562 (*English History*, p. 22).

25. Holinshed, *Chronicles*, III, p. 443; Burton, *Description of Leicester-Shire*, p. 47; Hutton, *Bosworth Field*, pp. 135–7; Nichols, *Leicestershire*, IV, p. 558.

2 Civil War and Common Weal

A.L. Rowse, *Bosworth Field and the Wars of the Roses* (London, 1966) offers a sparkling narrative, and shows that insights can still be derived from the Shakespearian perspective. K.B. McFarlane, 'The Wars of the Roses', *Proceedings of the British Academy* 50 (1964) and R.L. Storey, *The End of the House of Lancaster* (London, 1966) are more reliable and no less stimulating guides. The civil wars are also now well served by three recent studies: C. Ross, *The Wars of the Roses* (London, 1976), is the most straightforward and accessible; J. Gillingham, *The Wars of the Roses. Peace and Conflict in*

Fifteenth-Century England (London, 1981), is written with flair and draws valuable insights from a Europe-wide perspective; A Goodman, *The Wars of the Roses. Military Activity and English Society, 1452–97* (London, 1981) is the most original, probing further into the organisation of war and its impact on society. On the wider front the traditional view of the fifteenth century (economic, political and cultural decline) has been much modified. Indeed revisionism is the new orthodoxy: A.R. Myers, *England in the Late Middle Ages* (Harmondsworth, 1952), J.R. Lander, *Conflict and Stability in Fifteenth-Century England* (London, 1969) and F.R.H. Du Boulay, *An age of Ambition. English Society in the Late Middle Ages* (London, 1970). For two richly textured portraits of late fifteenth century England, see P.M. Kendall, *The Yorkist Age. Daily Life during the Wars of the Roses* (London, 1962), G. Hindley, *England in the Age of Caxton* (London, 1979).

1. Rowse, *Bosworth Field and Wars of Roses*, ch. 14.
2. R.A. Griffiths, *The Reign of King Henry VI. The Exercise of Royal Authority, 1422–1461* (London, 1981), B. Wolffe, *Henry VI* (London, 1981), R.A. Griffiths, 'The sense of dynasty in the reign of Henry VI' in C. Ross (ed.), *Patronage, Pedigree and Power in Later Medieval England* (Gloucester, 1979), pp. 13–36.
3. Storey, *End of the House of Lancaster*.
4. K.B. McFarlane, 'Bastard Feudalism', *Bulletin of the Institute of Historical Research* 20 (1945), 161–80, reprinted in K.B. McFarlane, *England in the Fifteenth Century. Collected Essays*(London, 1981), pp. 23–43. See also K.B. McFarlane, *The Nobility of Later Medieval England* (Oxford, 1973).
5. B. Wilkinson, *Constitutional History of England in the Fifteenth Century (1399–1485) with Illustrative Documents* (London, 1964), pp. 182–4. C. Ross, 'Rumour, propaganda and popular opinion during the Wars of the Roses' in R.A. Griffiths (ed.), *Patronage, the Crown and the Provinces in Later Medieval England* (Gloucester, 1981), pp. 15–32.
6. See Gillingham, *Wars of Roses*, ch. 2 (provocatively entitled 'This seat of peace'). Note also his concern that in their revisionist zeal historians have tended to play down the numbers of nobles killed and to under-estimate the period of active compaigning (p. 14).
7. C. Ross, *Edward IV* (London, 1974), pp. 408–10. R. Somerville, *History of the Duchy of Lancaster*, Part I. 1265–1603 (London, 1953), pp. 224, 252.
8. N. Orme, *English Schools in the Middle Ages* (London, 1973), p. 78.
9. N.F. Blake, *Caxton and his World* (London, 1969), ch. 5.

3 The Year of Three Kings

For the events of 1483, most particularly the usurpation and the rebellion Ross, *Richard III*, chs. 4, 5 & 6, is the most instructive guide. The main narrative sources are Dominic Mancini, *The Usurpation of Richard III*, ed. C.A.J. Armstrong, 2nd ed. (Oxford, 1969) and More, *History of King Richard III. British Library Harleian Manuscript 433*, ed. R. Horrox and P.W. Hammond, 4 vols. (Richard III Society, 1979–83) is an exemplary edition of this important text. On the confused chronology of the three months between the death of Edward IV and the coronation of Richard III, A.F. Sutton and P.W. Hammond (eds.), *The Coronation of Richard III. The Extant Documents* (Gloucester, 1983), pp. 13–46 provides an authoriative reconstruction. G. St Aubyn, *The Year of Three Kings 1483* (London, 1983) is highly readable.

1. Ross, *Edward IV*, esp. chs. 10, 11 & 12; D.A.L. Morgan, 'The king's affinity in the

polity of Yorkist England', *T.R.H.S.* 5th series 24 (1973), 1–25.

2. *The Works of John Metham*, ed. H. Craig (Early English Text Society, original series 132, 1916 for 1906), p. 158; Mancini, *Usurpation of Richard III*, pp. 104–5.

3. M.A. Hicks, 'The changing roles of the Wydevilles in Yorkist politics to 1483' in Ross, *Patronage, Pedigree and Power*, pp. 60–86.

4. For further insights on the relations between Rivers and Hastings, see E.W. Ives, 'Andrew Dymmock and the papers of Anthony, Earl Rivers, 1482–3', *B.I.H.R.* 41 (1968), 216–29.

5. E.g. C.T. Wood, 'The deposition of Edward V', *Traditio*, 31 (1975), 247–86.

6. In seeking to understand why Rivers planned to detour north to meet Richard, historians seem to have overlooked the fact that the Woodvilles had a mansion at Grafton Regis, half way between Northampton and Stony Stratford. (Edward IV had first met Elizabeth Woodville there in May 1464: Kendall, *Yorkist Age*, p. 167.) If his kinsmen had been laying up arms there, Rivers had a strong motive for delaying Richard at Northampton.

7. *Records of York*, pp. 148–50.

8. The conventional dating of Hastings' execution has been re-established despite the inherent plausibility of Hanham's careful revisionism. For the original debate, see A. Hanham, 'Richard III, Lord Hastings and the historians', *E.H.R.*, 87 (1972), 235–48, and B.P. Wolffe, 'When and why did Hastings lose his head?', *E.H.R.*, 89 (1974), 835–44. For the attractions of Hanham's thesis, see Wood, 'Deposition of Edward V'. J.A.F. Thomson, 'Richard III and Lord Hastings – a problematical case reviewed', *B.I.H.R.*, 48 (1975), 22–30, reveal its limitations, and two recently discovered items of evidence also tell against it: C.H.D. Coleman, 'The execution of Hastings: a neglected source', *B.I.H.R.*, 53 (1980), 244–7, and Green, 'Historical notes', 588.

9. More, *History of Richard III*, pp. 46–9; W. Campbell (ed.), *Materials for a History of the Reign of Henry VII*, 2 vols. (Rolls Series, 1873, 1877), I, pp. 148–9. More (p. 46) names the man who wounded Stanley as 'one Middleton' who had a private grievance over land. There is in fact evidence of such a property dispute: P.R.O., E 210/477.

10. The Shaws and Chadderton hailed from the Manchester area. In 1499 Sir John Shaw, nephew of the mayor and the preacher, was executor to Chadderton, then chancellor of Elizabeth of York: P.R.O., PROB 11/11, fos. 305–305d.

11. There is an immense literature seeking to exonerate Richard III from the charge of murdering his nephews. To take only one recent statement, A. Williamson, *The Mystery of the Princes. An Investigation into a Supposed Murder* (Dursley, 1978) is quite right to claim that there would not be enough evidence to convict the king in a modern court, but is disingenous in her dismissal of evidence that people at the time believed in his guilt.

12. For letter from Minster Lovell, P.R.O., C81/1392/1, cited in P. Tudor-Craig, *Richard III* (Ipswich, 1973), p. 98; for implication of Buckingham in princes' murder, see now Green, 'Historical notes', 288; for the king's reaction to betrayal, H. Ellis (ed.), *Original Letters Illustrative of English History*, 2nd series Vol. 1 (London, 1827), pp. 159–60.

13. *Harleian MS. 433*, II, pp. 10–11.

14. Ross, *Richard III*, pp. 104–12.

15. According to the informant Lord Strange was setting out with 10,000 men, but it was not known whether he was responding to the king's summons or the duke's appeals: *Plumpton Correspondence*, ed. T. Stapleton (Camden Society, old series 4, 1839), pp. 44–5.

16. *H.C.C.*, p. 570 (*Crowland*, p. 496); A.J. Pollard, 'The tyranny of Richard III', *Journal of Medieval History* 3 (1977), 147–66. For gifts to Stanley, *C.P.R. 1476–1485*, pp. 367, 376. On division of spoils generally see *Harleian MS. 433*, III, pp. 139–55. For southern associations of Fitzhugh, Huddleston and Mauleverer, *C.P.R. 1476–1485*, pp. 558–9, 314, 201. For grant of Tonbridge to Constable, *Harleian MS. 433*, II, p. 81.
17. Molinet, *Chroniques*, I, p. 433; Commines, *Memoirs*, II, p. 158.

4   Kings, Pretenders and Powerbrokers

There are more books on the short reign of Richard III than on any other comparable period of medieval English history. It makes a fascinating exercise to see how changing fashions over time and the personal prejudices of authors have presented different images of the man and his rule: A.R. Myers, 'Richard III and historical tradition', *History* 53 (1968), 181–202 and Potter, *Good King Richard?*. Ross, *Richard III* is now the obvious startiing-place for serious study, though it is still necessary to go back to older accounts, like C.A. Halsted, *Richard III as Duke of Gloucester and King of England*, 2 vols. (London, 1844) and J. Gairdner, *History of the Life and Reign of Richard III* (Cambridge, 1898) for chronological outline and some points of detail. Among the more popular accounts, P.M. Kendall, *Richard III* (London, 1955) and D. Seward, *Richard III. England's Black Legend* (London, 1983) usefully complement each other: the former sympathetic and imaginative, the latter cool and judicious.

1. A.R. Myers, 'The character of Richard III', *History Today* 4 (1954), 511–21 and J. Richards, 'The riddle of Richard III', *History Today* 33, no. 8 (1983), 18–25. The portraits and other memorabilia of Richard III are reproduced and analysed in P. Tudor-Craig, *Richard III* (London, 1973). The famous description in Vergil, *A.H.*, p. 565 (*English History*, pp. 226–7) seems consistent with the portraits.
2. For his religious interests generally, see Ross, *Richard III*, pp. 128–32. For devotional works in his possession, and a private prayer framed for him, see Tudor-Craig, *Richard III*, pp. 23–9, 96–7. As D. Seward argues, it all smacks of an unusually heightened sense of guilt, and the devotion to the noted parricide St Julian might be significant: *England's Black Legend*, pp. 177–9.
3. Von Poppelau's account of his visit to Middleham in May 1484 (not 1483, as in Ross, *Richard III*, p. 139n) is paraphrased by Armstrong as appendix to Mancini, *Usurpation of Richard III*, pp. 136–8.
4. A. Sutton, 'The administration of justice whereunto we be professed', *The Ricardian* 4, no. 53 (1976), 4–15; H.G. Hanbury, 'The legislation of Richard III', *American Journal of Legal History* 6 (1962), 95–113. Richard's consultations with the judges at Westminster was in 1484 (not 1485, as in E.W. Ives, *The Common Lawyers of Pre-Reformation England. Thomas Kebell: A Case Study* (Cambridge, 1983), pp. 259–60).
5. A. Sutton, 'Richard III's "tytylle & right": a new discovery', *The Ricardian* 4, no. 57 (1977), 2–8. The scale of the 'purge' needs stressing: 100 attainders in Richard III's two year reign, as opposed to 140 in Edward IV's twenty-two year reign and 138 in Henry VII's twenty-four years: J.R. Lander, *Crown and Nobility 1450–1509* (London, 1976), pp. 307–8. For the plots see Ross, *Richard III*, pp. 123–4, 202–3.
6. D. Williams, 'The family of Henry VII', *History Today* 4 (1954), 77–84; S.B. Chrimes, *Henry VII* (London, 1972), pp. 3–15. Of course, the Cadwaladr of the

Tudor legend is a confection of a number of semi-legendary figures, first confused by Geoffrey of Monmouth.

7. On 4 February 1486 William Bret, draper of London was repaid £37 for six 'curas called harneys', twelve pairs of brigandines and twenty-four 'salletes' which Henry Tudor had bought in France: *Materials Henry VII*, I, p. 274.

8. C.L. Scofield, 'The early life of John de Vere, thirteenth earl of Oxford' *E.H.R.* 39 (1914), 228–45. K.B. McFarlane rightly queries his diehard Lancastrianism: *England in the Fifteenth Century*, p. 245 n. For Stanley's alleged role in his escape see Molinet, *Chroniques*, I, p. 434.

9. Goodman, *Wars of the Roses*, ch. 6.

10. Pollard, 'Tyranny of Richard III', provides a detailed analysis of the 'northern connection'.

11. Ross, *Richard III*, ch. 8. J.A.F. Thomson, 'John de la Pole, duke of Suffolk', *Speculum* 54 (1979), 528–42.

12. For possible disaffection among the old Neville affinity see *H.C.C.*, p. 572 (*Crowland*, p. 499). The king's return to Nottingham around 25 July 1484 marks the end of his last northern tour: R. Edwards, *The Itinerary of King Richard III 1483–1485* (Richard III Society, 1983), pp. 22–39.

13. On possible duplicity of Lisle, see Sutton and Hammond, *Coronation of Richard III*, p. 349.

14. M.J. Tucker, *The Life of Thomas Howard, Earl of Surrey and Second Duke of Norfolk 1443–1524* (London, 1964), chs. 1 & 2 surveys the rise of the Howards, and suggests (pp. 37–9) a role for the first duke in the murder of the princes in the Tower. A. Crawford, 'John Howard, Duke of Norfolk: a possible murderer of the Princes?', *The Ricardian* 5, no. 70 (1980), 230–4, mounts a powerful case for the defence.

15. M.A. Hicks, 'Dynastic change and northern society: the career of the fourth earl of Northumberland, 1470–1489, *Northern History* 14 (1978), 78–107.

16. M.J. Bennett, '"Good lords" and "King-makers": the Stanleys of Lathom in English politics, 1385–1485', *History Today* 31, no. 7 (1981), 12–17.

17. According to the sixteenth-century metrical history of the Stanleys, a feud with Richard of Gloucester had arisen from a dispute between their tenants. Richard assembled men in Preston, intent on burning down their mansion at Lathom, but retreated on encountering the Stanleys at Ribble Bridge. His banner was captured by Jack Morris of Wigan and remained as a trophy in Wigan church for forty years: Bodleian Library, Oxford, MS. Rawl. Poet. 143, fos. 18–18d. This encounter might have taken place in 1470: *C.C.R. 1468–1476*, p. 138.

5   The Road to Bosworth

Ross, *Richard III*, ch. 10 presents the European background to Henry Tudor's invasion. On the landing and march through Wales, see Chrimes, *Henry VII*, H.T. Evans, *Wales and the Wars of the Roses* (Oxford, 1915), E.W. Jones, *A Kinsman King. The Welsh March to Bosworth* (Aberystwyth, 1980). On the movements of King Richard, the Stanleys and other parties, Ross, *Richard III*, ch. 11 provides the soundest reconstruction. All have the problem of trying to derive a coherent sequence of movements from a few dated letters, Vergil's *Anglica Historia* and the ballads. Hutton, *Bosworth Field* is both fanciful and flawed. Kendall, *Richard III*, pp. 339–54, cuts too many corners.

1. Edwards, *Itinerary of Richard III*, pp. 6, 9; G.F. Farnham, *Leicestershire Medieval*

Village Notes, 6 vols. (Leicester, 1930–3), VI, pp. 159–77; *Records of York*, p. 177; *C.P.R. 1476–1485*, p. 471.

2. Tudor-Craig, *Richard III*, p. 62.
3. On the politics of the midlands in the Wars of the Roses, see W.H. Dunham, *Lord Hastings' Indentured Retainers, 1461–1483* (Connecticut Academy of Arts and Sciences, 1955); C. Rawcliffe, *The Staffords, Earls of Stafford and Dukes of Buckingham, 1394–1521* (Cambridge, 1978); C. Carpenter, 'The Beauchamp affinity: a study of bastard feudalism at work', *E.H.R.*, 95 (1980), 515–32; S. Wright, *The Derbyshire Gentry in the Fifteenth Century* (Derbyshire Record Society, 1983); I. Rowney, 'The Hastings affinity in Staffordshire and the honour of Tutbury', *B.I.H.R.* 57 (1984), 35–45.
4. Edwards, *Itinerary of Richard III*, pp. 36–7; *Harleian MS. 433*, II, pp. 228–30.
5. *Harleian MS. 433*, III, pp. 124–8. If the surviving Gloucestershire list is any guide, the commissioners named in December 1484 were largely those appointed in the previous May: *C.P.R. 1476–1485*, pp. 397–401.
6. *H.C.C.*, pp. 572–3 (*Crowland*, pp. 500–1); Vergil, *A.H.*, pp. 558, 561 (*English History*, pp. 212, 219); Molinet, *Chroniques*, I, p. 434; Evans, *Wales and Wars of Roses*, pp. 213–15.
7. Vergil, *A.H.*, p. 559 (*English History*, p. 215); 'Lady Bessy', lines following 525 and 661; Sutton and Hammond, *Coronation of Richard III*, pp. 327–8. For Skerne see *C.P.R. 1476–1485*, p. 375 and *Materials Henry VII*, I, p. 39. Skerne married Curteys' widow: B.L., Add. MS. 18,629.
8. Commines, *Memoirs*, II, p. 159; Molinet, *Chroniques*, I, p. 434; P.W. Hammond, 'The Scots at Bosworth', *The Ricardian* 4, no. 56 (1977), 22–3.
9. Evans, *Wales and Wars of Roses*, pp. 215–18; 'Lady Bessy', line 784.
10. Goodman, *Wars of Roses*, pp. 3–4.
11. 'Lady Bessy', lines 779, 821–8.
12. S.B. Chrimes, 'The landing place of Henry of Richmond, 1485', *The Welsh History Review* 2, no. 1 (1964), 173–80.
13. Evans, *Wales and Wars of Roses*, pp. 218–23.
14. Chrimes, 'Landing place', 177.
15. *Historical Manuscripts Commission. Twelfth Report (Manuscripts of the Duke of Rutland)* (H.M.S.O., 1888), I, pp. 7–8. *Paston Letters and Papers of the Fifteenth Century*, Part II, ed. N. Davis (Oxford, 1976), pp. 443–4. For William Allington, see *C.P.R. 1476–1485*, p. 488; *C.I.P.M. Henry VII*, I, pp. 13–14; P.R.O., PROB 11/8, fos. 17d–18.
16. Vergil, *A.H.*, p. 561 (*English History*, pp. 218–19); *Paston Letters*, II, p. 444.
17. P.R.O., E40/4790; *C.C.R. 1476–1485*, pp. 432, 431.
18. *Great Chronicle of London*, p. 237; *Records of York*, pp. 214–16.
19. Vergil, *A.H.*, pp. 560–1 (*English History*, pp. 217–18).
20. 'Bosworth Field', lines 345–418, provides itinerary. There is an interesting undated letter, quite possibly from 1485, in which Lord Stanley requests James Scarisbrick to meet him with 24 horsemen at Warrington to ride with him to London: Lancashire Record Office, DDSc/9/1.
21. *Materials Henry VII*, II, pp. 110–11; 'Bosworth Field', lines 460–1; *Materials Henry VII*, I, pp. 11, 202, 154, 9.
22. *H.C.C.*, pp. 573–4 (*Crowland*, pp. 501–2); *Records of York*, p. 216; Vergil, *A.H.*, p. 561 (*English History*, pp. 219–20).
23. Hutton, *Bosworth Field*, pp. 47–9.
24. *H.C.C.*, pp. 573–4 (*Crowland*, p. 502); 'Bosworth Field', lines 217–336; *Rotuli Parliamentorum*, VI, p. 276.

25. Hutton, *Bosworth Field*, p. 49, believed the earthworks to be the remains of the royal camp. J. Gairdner, 'The battle of Bosworth', *Archaeologia* 55 (1896), 159–78, more plausibly suggests (173–4) that it was Lord Stanley's encampment.
26. 'Bosworth Field', lines 401–16; 'Lady Bessy', lines 215–18 (these lines seem to be misplaced); *C.I.P.M. Henry VII*, I, p. 11; *Great Chronicle of London*, p. 237.
27. *Materials Henry VII*, I, pp. 201, 188.
28. Lindsay, *Historie*, p. 193; Vergil, *A.H.*, p. 562 (*English History*, p. 221). There were two knights named John Savage, father and son, one of whom was already in rebellion. Both Savage and Digby brought with them large numbers of kinsfolk: *Materials Henry VII*, I, p. 365–6; Leland, *Itinerary*, II, p. 18. On John Hardwick of Lindley, see Hutton, *Bosworth Field*, p. 65.

6 Ordeal by Battle

Given the problems of the evidence there are almost as many accounts of what happened on 22 August 1485 as there are historians. Readers of independent mind are encouraged to visit the battle-site and study the primary sources assembled in the Appendix. Hutton, *Bosworth* is the earliest reconstruction, and despite its flaws remains one of the most detailed accounts. R. Brooke, *Visits to Fields of Battle in England in the Fifteenth Century* (London, 1857), ch. 8 adds little. Gairdner, 'Battle of Bosworth' is the first professional account. Kendall, *Richard III*, pp. 354–69 is characteristically spirited but rather fanciful. More recently, A. Makinson, 'The road to Bosworth Field, August, 1485', *History Today* 13 (1963), 239–49 and D.T. Williams, *The Battle of Bosworth* (Leicester, 1975) offer succinct and sensible reconstructions. Ross, *Richard III*, ch. 11 is now the most reliable guide. Among other recent work, Goodman, *Wars of the Roses*, pp. 89–95 breaks most new ground.

1. The scene is evoked with laboured artifice in Reverend E. Trollope's address on the occasion of a visit to the battle-field by various learned societies in August 1862: Report, 'Excursion to Bosworth Field', *Transactions of the Leicestershire Architectural and Archaeological Society* 2 (1870), 112–50, esp. pp. 115–17.
2. *H.C.C.*, p. 574 (*Crowland*, p. 503). B.L., Additional MS. 12,060, fos. 19d–20; 'Bosworth Field', lines 179, 566. Goodman, *Wars of the Roses*, p. 95, brings out this point well.
3. Hall, *Lancaster and York*, 'Richard III', f. 33d.
4. Vergil, *A.H.*, pp. 562–3 (*English History*, p. 222), Nokes and Wheeler, 'Spanish account', 2; Molinet, *Chroniques*, I, pp. 434–5; Lindsay, *Historie*, p. 195.
5. The size of Richard III's army is a matter of some contention. Early estimates range from 10,000 in Vergil (*A.H.*, p. 563) to 70,000 in De Valera (Nokes and Wheeler, 'Spanish account', 2), but all sources agree that it was an immense army. On the presence of an illegitimate son, see Hutton, *Bosworth Field*, p. 322, and Seward, *Richard III*, p. 189.
6. Vergil, *A.H.*, p. 563 (*English History*, pp. 222–3).
7. The size of the Stanley army could also have been considerable. Though doubtless exaggerating, Commines (*Memoirs*, II, p. 160), Molinet (*Chroniques*, I, p. 434) and 'Lady Bessy' (lines 931–2) all provide figures in the range 20–26,000. Vergil (*A.H.*, p. 563) states that 3,000 were involved in the fighting, but only a proportion of the Stanleyites seem to have been committed. The fighting strength of Lord Strange in both 1483 and 1487 was allegedly of the order of 10,000: *Plumpton Correspondence*, pp. 44–5; Goodman, *Wars of the Roses*, pp. 104–5.

8. Vergil, *A.H.*, p. 563 (*English History*, pp. 223–4); 'Bosworth Field', lines 449–74. The only evidence supporting the notion that the two Stanley brothers positioned themselves at opposite sides of the battlefield is in the statement attributed to Henry Tudor that he had 'doubtful friends' on either side of the battlefield: Hall, *Lancaster and York*, 'Richard III', f. 32d. Vergil, *A.H. 1485–1537*, pp. 76–7 specifically states that Lord Stanley sent his brother to succour the pretender, while 'Bosworth Field', lines 567–8, says that he came at the king 'down at a back' or 'bank'. The role of Brackenbury is mysterious: though apparently a dedicated Ricardian he allowed Bourchier and Hungerford to desert to the rebels, and might well have sympathised with the Stanleys. Curiously, Lindsay (*Historie*, pp. 193–5) claims that 'Sir Edward' Brackenbury followed Lord Stanley's lead in actually betraying the king.

9. Hall, *Lancaster and York*, 'Richard III', fos. 30–32d.

10. E.g. Makinson, 'Road to Bosworth Field', 246–7.

11. Molinet, *Chroniques*, I, p. 435; 'Rose of England', lines 107–8.

12. Vergil, *A.H.*, p. 563 (*English History*, pp. 223–4); Hall, *Lancaster and York*, 'Richard III', f. 33; 'Bosworth Field', lines 449–74, 565–8; Nokes and Wheeler, 'Spanish account', 2; Lindsay, *Historie*, pp. 193–5, 198–9. It is impossible to accept that Stanley did not meet Henry Tudor until 24 August, the date from which according to sworn testimony (*Calendar of Papal Letters*, XIV, p. 18) he had known him well. If not simply an error or approximation (e.g. the nearest major feast day), this date might well have been the date of the first major council of the victors at which plans for the marriage had been set in train. When Lord Stanley was created earl of Derby two months later Henry VII referred to 'his distinguished services to us and indeed the great armed support recently accorded us in battle, both by himself and by all his kinsmen, not without great hazard to life and position': *Materials Henry VII*, I, p. 241.

13. *H.C.C.*, p. 574 (*Crowland*, p. 503); 'Bosworth Field', lines 497–544; 'Lady Bessy', lines 959–1010.

14. Molinet, *Chroniques*, I, p. 435; 'Bsoworth Field', lines 487–92. The excavation of gun shot on the site confirms the testimony of foreign reporters and the balladeers on this point. Vergil and his followers do not mention guns. Gairdner, 'Battle of Bosworth', 167–70.

15. For this custom among English archers, see Gillingham,, *Wars of the Roses*, p. 42.

16. The sixteenth-century translator (Vergil, *English History*, pp. 223–4) has not rendered Vergil's exact meaning on this point. Vergil, *A.H.*, p. 563 says that Oxford's men closed ranks, and that 'the others in the other part' organised themselves into a wedge. Perhaps what is meant is that the two wings drew in to form a triangle with Oxford's vanguard.

17. *H.C.C.*, p. 574 (*Crowland*, pp. 503–4); Vergil, *A.H.*, p. 564 (*English History*, p. 224).

18. For Clifton and Byron, where it is erroneously claimed that the former was slain, Beaumont, 'Bosworth Field: a Poem' in Nichols, *Leicestershire*, IV, p. 563; for Blount and Babington, Sutton and Hammond, *Coronation of Richard III*, p. 306; for Oxford and Ferrers, W.G. Hoskins, *The Midland Peasant. The Economic and Social History of a Leicestershire Village* (London, 1965), p. 24; for Oxford and Norfolk, Beaumont, 'Bosworth Field: a Poem' in Nichols, *Leicestershire*, IV, p. 561. Molinet, *Chroniques*, I, p. 435, states that Norfolk was brought a prisoner to Oxford who ordered his execution.

19. Almost all the sources agree that he was counselled to flee, though at various points in the engagement: Nokes and Wheeler, 'Spanish account', 2; Vergil, *A.H.*, p. 564 (*English History*, p. 225); 'Bosworth Field', lines 585–600. Molinet uniquely claims

that he actually sought flight: *Chroniques*, I, p. 435.

20. See the account in Kendall, *Richard III*, pp. 364–7, written, in the words of Ross, *Richard III*, p. 215n, as if he were 'perched on the crupper of the king's horse'.

21. Vergil, *A.H.*, p. 563 (*English History*, p. 224); Jones, *Kinsman King*, p. 11–12.

22. *H.C.C.*, p. 574 (*Crowland*, p. 504); *C.I.P.M. Henry VII*, I, p. 432; 'Bosworth Field', lines 625–8.

23. Molinet, *Chroniques*, I, p. 435; Hutton, *Bosworth*, p. 232. A Welsh tradition attributed the king's death to none other than Rhys ap Thomas: Jones, *Kinsman King*, pp. 13–14.

24. *H.C.C.*, p. 574 (*Crowland*, pp. 503–4), including emendation from Hanham, *Early Historians*, p. 100.

25. *H.C.C.*, p. 574 (*Crowland*, p. 504); *C.I.P.M. Henry VII*, I, pp. 22–3; Tudor-Craig, *Richard III*, p. 72. On the vast wealth of Sir William Stanley, see *Great Chronicle of London*, p. 258. The presence of rich booty in London market-stalls in the winter of 1485–6 is suggested by a curious tale. One Richard Anlaby bought a silver plate for £.6. The vendor assured him that it 'was won and taken in the last field'. It turned out to be the property of another Londoner who in his desire to win a bride had allowed himself to be tricked by a 'necromancer' into locking his valuables along with images of wax in a coffin: *Materials Henry VII*, I, pp.251–3.

26. The battlefield coronation is recorded by Fabian (*Great Chronicle of London*, p. 238) and Vergil (*A.H.*, p. 564; *English History*, p. 226), who attribute it variously to Sir William Stanley and his brother. More prosaically, 'Bosworth Field', lines 635–40, merely says that Lord Stanley handed Henry Tudor the crown. S. Anglo, 'The foundation of the Tudor dynasty: the coronation and marriage of Henry VII', *The Guildhall Miscellany*, 2, no 1 (1960), p. 3n. rightly warns that there is no sixteenth-century evidence for the thornbush legend, though, as Ross (*Richard III*, p. 225n) observes, the early adoption of this emblem by the Tudors still needs to be explained.

7 The Tudor Triumph

The sources for this important transitional period are alarmingly meagre. Polydore Vergil is the only real guide, although other chroniclers provide occasional insights. Much needs to be inferred from record materials, often retrospectively, as government departments did not get back into their stride until after Michaelmas. Needless to say, where the sources are lacking, little can be expected from modern historians. J.D. Mackie, *The Earlier Tudors 1485–1558* (Oxford, 1952), ch. 3, R.L. Storey, *The Reign of Henry VII* (London, 1968), ch. 3, Chrimes, *Henry VII*, and M.V.C. Alexander, *The First of the Tudors. A Study of Henry VII and his Reign* (London, 1981), ch. 2 provide the outline. Anglo, 'Foundation of Tudor dynasty' offers a full treatment of one theme. What is remarkable is the manner in which historians have glossed over many of the difficulties of this interlude.

1. Hutton, *Bosworth Field*, pp. 141–6.

2. Vergil, *A.H. 1485–1537*, pp. 2–5.

3. *Tudor Royal Proclamations*, I, p. 3.

4. C. Richmond, *John Hopton. A Fifteenth-Century Suffolk Gentleman* (Cambridge, 1981), pp. 226–7.

5. *H.C.C.*, p. 575 (*Crowland*, p. 504); D. Williams, 'The hastily drawn up will of William Catesby, esquire, 25 August 1485', *Transactions of the Leicestershire*

       Archaeological and Historical Society 51 (1975–6), 43–51.

6.   *C.C.R. 1476–1485*, p. 432; *The Chronicle of Calais in the Reigns of Henry VII and Henry VIII to the Year 1540*, ed. J.G. Nichols (Camden Society, old series 35, 1846), p. 1; *Crowland*, p. 504; B.L., Harleian MS. 2022, f. 26d; *C.I.P.M. Henry VII*, pp. 52, 432, 13–14; B.L., Add. Chs. 72144–6.

7.   *Rotuli Parliamentorum*, VI, p. 328.

8.   *Tudor Royal Proclamations*, I, pp. 3–4; on Percy, Molinet, *Chroniques*, I, 435 and Hicks, 'Dynastic change and northern society', esp. 89–96; on Fitzhugh, *C.P.R. 1485–1494*, pp. 16, 39.

9.   *Materials Henry VII*, I, pp. 548–9.

10.   *Materials Henry VII*, I, pp. 282–3.

11.   *Tudor Royal Proclamations*, I, p.4; Goodman, *Wars of Roses*, pp. 96–9.

12.   Anglo, 'Foundation of Tudor dynasty', 3–4.

13.   *Tudor Royal Proclamations*, I, pp. 4–5. Henry VII had sent out diplomatic agents to foreign powers by 15 September: A.F. Pollard, *The Reign of Henry VII from Contemporary Sources*, Vol. 1 Narrative Extracts (London, 1913), p. 18.

14.   *Materials Henry VII*, I, pp. 23, 6, 18–19, 34, 77–8, 7, 365–6, 40, 7–8, 77, 15.

15.   Anglo, 'Foundation of Tudor dynasty', esp. 4–10.

16.   *Rotuli Parliamentorum*, VI, pp. 275–8; *Crowland*, p. 511.

17.   Goodman, *Wars of the Roses*, pp. 104–5. The role of the Stanleys at Stoke was doubtless the subject of the (no longer extant) ballad circulating in Cheshire in the 1520s: Bodleian Library, Oxford, MS. Lat. misc. c. 66, f. 104.

18.   On Scrope of Masham, *C.P.R. 1485–1494*, p. 238. On Edward Frank, C.A.J. Armstrong, 'An Italian astrologer at the court of Henry VII', in E.F. Jacob (ed.), *Italian Renaissance Studies* (London, 1960), pp. 443–7. On Thomas Metcalfe, *C.P.R. 1485–1494*, p. 332. On Lady Lovell, *C.P.R. 1485–1494*, p. 304. On Widow Radcliffe, *The Register of Thomas Rotherham, Archbishop of York 1480–1500*, Vol. I, ed. E.E. Barker (Canterbury and York Society 69, 1976), p. 48. On Mistress Brackenbury, *Testamenta Eboracensia. A Selection of Wills from the Registry at York*, Vol. IV, ed. J. Raine (Surtees Society 53, 1869 for 1868), pp. 233–4.

19.   Alexander, *First of Tudors*, pp. 194–5.

8   1485 in English History

Rather surprisingly there is no full discussion of the place of 1485 as a turning-point in English history. Mackie, *Earlier Tudors*, ch. 1 and Storey, *Reign of Henry VII*, pp. 1–9 offer most food for thought. G.R. Elton, *England under the Tudors* (London, 1955) and most reputable works commencing in 1485 tend to view the whole late fifteenth and early sixteenth centuries as transitional. Myers, *England in Late Middle Ages* and J.R. Lander, *Government and Community. England 1450–1509* (London, 1980) demonstrate the value of tracing themes across the traditional divide.

1.   *H.C.C.*, p. 575 (*Crowland*, p. 505).

2.   Goodman, *Wars of the Roses*, pp. 1–5. George Neville's letter: *Calendar of State Papers. Venetian*, I, pp. 99–100.

3.   In general, see O. Halecki, *The Limits and Divisions of European History* (Baltimore, 1962); F. Bacon, *The History of the Reign of King Henry the Seventh*, ed. F.J. Levy (Indianapolis, 1972).

4.   D. Hume, *The History of England from the Invasion of Julius Caesar to the Revolution of 1688*, 10 vols. (London, 1803), IV, p. 42.

5. Medieval historians took the lead in overrunning the frontier: Myers, *England in the Late Middle Ages* and S.B. Chrimes, *Lancastrians, Yorkists and Henry VII* (London, 1964). Tudor historians like D. Loades, *Politics and the Nation 1450–1660* (London, 1974) and C.S.L. Davies, *Peace, Print and Protestantism 1450–1558* (London, 1977) made their forays, but C. Russell, *The Crisis of Parliaments 1509–1660* (Oxford, 1971) and G.R. Elton, *Reform and Reformation. England 1509–1558* (London, 1977) have conducted an orderly withdrawal from the fifteenth century. Lander, *Government and Community* and J.A.F. Thomson, *The Transformation of Medieval England 1370–1529* (London, 1983) now seem to be consolidating the medievalists' hold on the pre-Reformation era.
6. M. Levine, *Tudor Dynastic Problems 1460–1571* (London, 1973).
7. J.R. Green, *A Short History of the English People* (London, 1874), ch. 6 'The New Monarchy'; G.R. Elton, *The Tudor Revolution in Government* (Cambridge, 1953); P. Williams and G.L. Harriss, 'A revolution in Tudor history?', *Past and Present* 25 (1963), 3–58; P. Williams, *The Tudor Regime* (Oxford, 1979), Part I.
8. In general, see Lander, *Government and Community*, chs. 2 & 3; McFarlane, *Fifteenth-Century England*, p. 260; Storey, *Reign of Henry VII*, p. 5; M. Condon, 'Ruling elites in the reign of Henry VII' in Ross, *Patronage, Pedigree and Power*, pp. 109–42; C.A.T. Skeel, 'Wales under Henry VII' in R.W. Seton-Watson (ed.), *Tudor Studies presented to A. F. Pollard* (London, 1924), pp. 1–25, esp. 9–11; A. Allan, 'Yorkist propaganda: pedigree, prophecy and the "British History" in the reign of Edward IV' in Ross, *Patronage, Pedigree and Power*, pp. 171–92.
9. J. Hatcher, *Plague, Population and the English Economy 1348–1530* (London, 1977), p. 63; R. Davis, *English Overseas Trade 1500–1700* (London, 1973), pp. 11, 52.
10. In general, see Myers, *England in Late Middle Ages*, Part III, chs. 4 & 5. In the numismatic field, however, there was a sudden break: from the outset Henry VII's coins bore distinctively Renaissance motifs: C. Platt, *Medieval England. A Social History and Archaeology from the Conquest to A.D. 1600* (London, 1978), p. 205.
11. D.B. Quinn, *England and the Discovery of America, 1481–1620* (London, 1974), ch. 1.
12. R.S. Gottfried, 'Population, plague and the sweating sickness: demographic movements in late fifteenth-century England', *Journal of British Studies* 17 (1977), 12–37; Davis, *English Overseas Trade*, p. 52.
13. According to Rous (*Historia*, p. 213), Russell was an unwilling servant of the regime, and it is significant that he was relieved of the Great Seal both at the time of Buckingham's rebellion and Henry Tudor's invasion: *C.C.R. 1476–1485*, pp. 346–7, 432–3.
14. A. Goodman, 'Henry VII and Christian renewal' in K. Robbins (ed.), *Religion and Humanism* (Studies in Church History 17, 1981), pp. 115–25; W. Nelson, *John Skelton, Laureate* (New York, 1939), pp. 26–7.

INDEX

INDEX